Rainbow RISING

THE STORY OF RITCHIE BLACKMORE'S RAINBOW

Roy Davies

Helter Skelter Publishing

First edition published in 2002 by **Helter Skelter Publishing**
4 Denmark Street, London WC2H 8LL.

Copyright 2001 © Roy Davies. All rights reserved.

This book is sold subject to the condition that it shall not,
by way of trade or otherwise, be lent, resold, hired out or otherwise
circulated without the publisher's prior consent
in any form of binding or cover other than that in which
it is published and without a similar condition
including this condition being imposed on the subsequent purchase.

A CIP record for this book is available from the British Library.

ISBN 1-900924-31-5

Design by Chris Wilson @ CWDGA.
Printed in Great Britain by The Bath Press, Trowbridge.

Photos and images by courtesy of:
Michael Putland/Retna - front cover.
The Simon Robinson Collection - pages 20-21, 22,
24-25, 26, 27, 28, 32, 35, 40, 42, 47, 52, 56, 57, 58-59, 61, 74-75,
78, 101, 113, back cover/front flap (hardback).
Tonny Steenhagen - pages 36, 38-39, 44, 46, 60-61, 81, 105.
Theo Solberg - pages 82, 84-85.
Roy Davies - pages 87, 92, 99, back cover (p/b), back flap (h/b).
Frans Van Arkel - pages 96-97, 102-103, 108-109, 110-111.
Rob Fodder - pages 48, 104, 106, 107, 125, 126, 127.
Doogie White - pages 128-129.
Rob Flederus - pages 116-117.
Tour programmes on pages 131, 182-183, 184
kindly scanned by Jerry Bloom.

Every effort has been made to trace the copyright holders of the
illustrations in this book, but a number could not be traced.
The copyright holders concerned should contact the publishers directly.

Contents

	Foreword by Michael Heatley	4
	Introduction	6
Chapter 1	Pre-Purple Days	9
Chapter 2	Look To The Rainbow (1975-1976)	15
Chapter 3	The Rise And Fall (1977-1978)	49
Chapter 4	All Night Long (1979-1980)	71
Chapter 5	Difficult To Cure (1981-1984)	91
Chapter 6	Rainbow Revival (1994-1997)	119
Chapter 7	Renaissance Man (1997-2002)	133
Chapter 8	After The Rainbow	139
Appendices		165
	Rainbow UK/US Chart Placings	166
	Discography	167
	Details of Equipment	177
	Tour Programmes	182
	Gig List	185
	Songs Rainbow Performed Live	215
	Bootleg Discography	216
	Websites, Societies and Publications	248

FOREWORD

BY MICHAEL HEATLEY, CLASSIC ROCK MAGAZINE

IT WAS THE ROCK EVENT OF THE YEAR - if not the decade. Rainbow, the band formed by legendary guitarist Ritchie Blackmore, was set to play its first UK dates for fully 13 years. True, only a pair of late-1995 concerts had been scheduled, and both were at the middle-sized Hammersmith Odeon (now Apollo), but true fans had rejoiced at being able to see the Man In Black at closer quarters than barns like Wembley Arena would allow. As for the travelling, few of those die-hards hadn't already ventured further to see the most enigmatic and charismatic guitarist in rock music.

The concert had gone as planned - even better, if that were possible. A triumphant Blackmore walked off, leaving his instrument feeding back at the front of the stage, only for an audience member to grab the guitar, wrench out the lead and head towards the exit! It was such an audacious move that he got outside the venue before, apparently, being racked with guilt pangs and bringing it back. Whether the person who returned it to the stage was indeed the culprit or someone he'd entrusted the instrument to, they were rewarded with a pass to the post-gig party. A negligent roadie, we can assume, had his ears severely boxed in another location!

The story has an allegorical side, if you will. Because the following night's performance, guitar and musician having been reunited, would be the last time London would experience Ritchie Blackmore the 'axe hero'. Along with fiancée Candice Night, who was supplying the backing vocals at the Odeon, he had turned his attention to recreating Renaissance-era music played on a variety of (mainly acoustic) stringed instruments. This path, trodden to this day under the banner of Blackmore's Night, would be enough to test the loyalty of the fiercest fan, but it was a sign of his magnetism that many of Ritchie's following chose to accompany him on this diversion from his previous route.

And, to give him his due, he stuck with it. The third Blackmore's Night album, *'Fires*

Foreword

At Midnight', emerged late in 2001, when he confided to my Classic Rock colleague Pete Makowski that his decision to unplug had resulted in the business giving him the cold shoulder. "Promoters and management [said] 'Blackmore's going through one of his phases, we'll just let him get on with it.' And of course I'm still doing it." In the same month, his supposed 'nemesis', former Deep Purple colleague Ian Gillan, offered me the following - sincere, I'm certain - comment: "Ritchie's shown he's stuck to his new project and I'm very pleased he has. It's intriguing - and I see no reason why we shouldn't have a Scotch together at some time in the future."

Signposts pointing to a medieval musical future had been there to see in his previous albums, as far back as the debut's 'Temple Of The King' - but no-one had expected such a dramatic swing. Just like no-one had expected him to rejoin Deep Purple after spending the best part of a decade leading his own band and turning Rainbow into a brand name for classic hard rock. Musicians had come and gone as he wielded both axe and pruning shears, the excellence of the music his one and only concern, his individual guitar-work the constant factor in the story.

As the new millennium arrived, there were still no signs that Blackmore intended to plug in again, set the amplifiers to 11 and rock out in the fashion that had gained him worldwide renown. But one look at the relevant web sites confirmed that most of his fans, Blackmore's Night converts or not, still lived in hope of a return to balls-out Rainbow rock, preferably in the company of singer Ronnie James Dio, his right-hand man during the glory years.

One thing was certain, though - followers of Ritchie Blackmore had long since learned to expect the unexpected. Roy Davies is one of those followers, and, by combining his own researches and recollections with contributions from those Blackmore has worked with, he has told the story with no little wit and imagination. Now hang on to your Stratocaster, crank up the stereo and turn the page!

INTRODUCTION

SINCE THE ADVENT OF ROCK'N'ROLL in the fifties there have been many larger-than-life characters with which the public have identified and idolised. The explosion of the hard rock/heavy metal movement in the early seventies has - given its innate extroversion - thrown up more than most. But whereas many of these famous (or infamous) figures consciously seek the spotlight, one icon in particular stands apart from his peers, in being both highly venerated and charismatic yet singularly reticent and aloof. That man is guitarist Ritchie Blackmore.

Blackmore holds a unique place in the development of what came to be called heavy rock. After an apprenticeship served with several combos during the sixties' beat boom and as session guitarist with legendary producer Joe Meek, Ritchie became a founding member of Deep Purple. During the band's massive success in the early seventies, Ritchie became a seminal influence on what was then termed the 'underground rock' movement.

Since reuniting with his former Purple colleagues in 1984, and now several years into his second solo stint, he stands comparison with any rock guitar legend one could care to name. Yet despite a technical ability second to none, outside the hard rock sphere Blackmore has never been afforded the widespread acclaim his undoubted talents warrant. (It may not be unconnected to the fact that he was never part of The Yardbirds or John Mayall's Bluesbreakers, which is where most people look for geniuses of the electric guitar - Jimmy Page, Eric Clapton, etc).

The unfashionable nature of much of his musical direction and his reluctance to conform to media demands might also explain it. Yet with Deep Purple's *'In Rock'*, *'Fireball'*, *'Machine Head'* and *'Made In Japan'*, he helped invent the principles of intense guitar-led composition and dramatic performance that has spawned successive generations of heavy metal ever since. His contribution to and influence on rock music is incalculable.

However, Blackmore's tenure with Deep Purple does not tell the whole story. For eight years Ritchie also pursued his personal brand of rock with his own band

Rainbow, achieving a high degree of success in the process. While most may judge him primarily from his efforts with Purple, it was with Rainbow that, Blackmore pursued his own personal creative objectives, inspiring a whole new generation of fans often unfamiliar with his earlier career. It could be argued that, to appreciate the full breadth of Blackmore's artistry, one should pay closer attention to his years with Rainbow than with Deep Purple.

His aloofness and perfectionist tendencies alerted the media to the probability that the Blackmore psyche made good copy. They propagated the image of a difficult, volatile and perverse dictator - an image the man, by his own admission, has done little to refute. Once in the spotlight as the leader of his own group, his intolerance with subordinates led to a rapid turnover of musicians within Rainbow and a 'hire-em-fire-em' reputation that all too frequently overshadowed their musical worth.

Most that meet Ritchie find this reputation largely undeserved. The impression is of a intelligent, frank yet shy man of sensitivity and dry humour. So what was the real story behind the convoluted, often troubled but always fascinating history of Ritchie Blackmore? This book attempts some answers.

AUTHOR'S NOTE

THE FOLLOWING HISTORY has been put together from a multitude of sources over a four-year period. These include press articles, video and TV, interviews, promotional material, etc. Of particular value were the archives of the former Ritchie Blackmore Appreciation Society magazine Stargazer, its successor the Deep Purple Appreciation Society's Darker Than Blue, the more recent but equally excellent More Black Than Purple publication and the many information forums, fan clubs, websites and societies past and present worldwide.

My heartfelt thanks go out to all the guys (and girls) who, over the years, have taken on the daunting and demanding task of 'keeping the flame burning' for all us fans, and who have been unstinting in their assistance, advice and encouragement in assembling this history. Can I especially thank Michael Heatley, Jerry Bloom, Mark Welch, Simon Robinson, Nigel Young, Rob Fodder, Frans Van Arkel, Bob Richards, Diane Davies, Thierry Pierron and the staff at rockforever.com

Also the musicians who contributed to the book directly or indirectly, especially Don Airey, Graham Bonnet, Roger Glover, David Rosenthal, Joe Lynn Turner and Doogie White.

If I have forgotten anyone, my apologies. It's to you all that this history is dedicated.

Although Rainbow's central character is very obviously Ritchie Blackmore, some two dozen other musicians have also exerted influence to varying extents in the group's sound and style over the years. To ignore their contributions would be unforgivable. I have tried wherever possible to detail the background to the principal figures involved in Rainbow's development, not only to document their often interesting and varied careers pre-Rainbow, but also to plot their fortunes - in some cases, misfortunes - after leaving the group. This has involved tangential diversions into other band histories on occasion, but I feel this was justified in order to give the reader an overview of the contemporary hard-rock scene of which Rainbow formed such an integral part.

While every effort has been made to ensure the chronological and factual aspects of this account are correct, invariably errors and omissions do occur - I'm only human! Readers are invited to point out any such mistakes they may find. I have tried to maintain a dispassionate and unbiased perspective in an attempt to give a balanced point of view to every story, but there are certain grey areas surrounding some events where one has had to 'read between the lines' a little. The accounts in these cases are therefore purely based around my own editorial judgement and, unless stated, do not represent any opinions expressed by the persons and musicians concerned.

The reader may at times reach conclusions that disagree with mine and, given the subject matter, this is wholly understandable. The central figure to this account has without doubt stirred all our emotions (in both positive and negative senses!) for over three decades. All I can add is long may he continue to do so!

Roy Davies

Chapter 1

PRE-PURPLE DAYS

RICHARD HAROLD BLACKMORE was born in Weston-Super-Mare on 14th April 1945, though his family moved to Heston in Middlesex (in the western suburbs of London near Heathrow Airport and not far from the home of the young Jimmy Page) when he was just two years old. Attending Heston High School, Ritchie proved academically capable yet preferred physical activities and sports, being particularly gifted at the javelin. With adolescence came an interest in music. Impressed by the antics of Tommy Steele and the like on the TV pop programmes of the day, the 12 year-old Blackmore borrowed a guitar: "I would strum it, I couldn't play anything but it just looked right. I thought I must learn this instrument." He persuaded his parents to buy him a black Framus acoustic and, at his father's insistence, took classical lessons for a year: "That did me a lot of good because I learned about using a finger for each fret instead of just three and how to hold a plectrum properly."

Ritchie's other early influence was Big Jim Sullivan (at the time Marty Wilde's guitarist, and later the undisputed king of session guitarists in the sixties) who lived locally in Hounslow. Ritchie hustled Sullivan until the musician agreed to give him lessons, and Sullivan was suitably impressed: "He came round and played me solos from records note for note; I told him to play them his own way."

Ritchie held his tutor in awe: "He'd only been playing for two years but he was just about the best guitarist in England straight away. I thought I was learning pretty well until I saw him. I think he used to get fed up with me hanging around, but he taught me a lot." By the age of 13 Ritchie had joined his first group - though on tea-chest bass, not guitar! The 2I's coffee bar group specialised in Duane Eddy and Bert Weedon covers and also cashed in on the skiffle boom of the late fifties. Ritchie had also become friends with Mick Underwood who, although a couple of years younger, was the proud owner of a full drum kit. Ritchie upgraded to his first proper electric guitar - a Hohner Club 50 - and now formed a band with Underwood called The Dominators, this outfit lasting six months.

Ritchie left school at 15 and started work as a radio technician at Heathrow. Although he hated the job, he kept at it for two years to payroll his increasing involvement with music and the local concert scene. In early 1961 Blackmore moved on to the semi-professional circuit with Mike Dee and The Jaywalkers, with whom he recorded for the first time. Though 'My Blue Heaven' was rejected by Decca, the band found plenty of work, playing three or four times a week. Ritchie: "We played cover material, Shadows stuff, and did all the steps that went with it, suits and ties." Even at this early stage of his musical career, Blackmore's single-mindedness and total focus, leading to hours of rigorous practice, meant his formidable technical skill was becoming increasingly obvious.

Chapter 1

Now using a cherry red Gibson ES335 (*à la* Chuck Berry), he quickly built up a reputation around the west London gig circuit. Bassist Nick Simper, soon to be one of Johnny Kidd's Pirates, remembered seeing Ritchie play: "Everyone noticed Ritchie because he was so fast - amazingly so." The Jaywalkers had mutated into The Condors by the time Ritchie was spotted by Screaming Lord Sutch and asked to audition. "I passed the audition, and I think Pete Townshend also went, but strangely enough he failed."

May 1962, therefore, saw Blackmore step up another level in his professional career with Lord Sutch and The Savages. In these pre-Beatles days, the very visual, raucous shows presented by the likes of Sutch and Johnny Kidd was avidly consumed by rock-starved fans around Britain's provincial music circuit, and so a hectic six months of touring followed, though the stage costumes of animal skins and loincloths caused Ritchie some embarrassment. "I was as skinny as a rake. I used to hold the guitar so nobody could see the bones!" Drummer Carlo Little was hugely impressed with their newest recruit: "Ritchie was really great, used to do these amazing runs that left people gaping." Lord (David) Sutch: "He was very shy and bashful, but he was the best guitarist on the circuit even then. People would come from miles around to see him play his solos."

In October 1962, at Mick Underwood's suggestion, independent record producer Joe Meek contacted Ritchie with an offer to join instrumental group The Outlaws, currently lacking a six-stringer. "The drummer and bass player left to join Cyril Davies and The All Stars, and I was just left to try something else. So Joe Meek heard about this and asked me to join his band." With Underwood, bassist Chas Hodges (of Chas 'n' Dave fame!) and rhythm guitarist Kenny Lundgren the band also doubled as session band for the ebullient and eccentric Meek, who had hit pay-dirt in 1962 with The Tornados' smash hit 'Telstar' and whose astonishingly inventive experiments in lo-fi synthesised sound transformed an otherwise drab British pop scene in its fallow years between the emergence of Elvis and the arrival of The Beatles.

Recording at Meek's home-made studio above a shop in Holloway Road, London, Ritchie and The Outlaws appeared on hundreds of tracks backing other Meek artists over the next three years, including Tom Jones, Glenda Collins and future comic star Freddie Starr. The band themselves also released a series of singles. The Outlaws also supported Gene Vincent on two European tours, though the band's high-spirits and on-the-road antics got too much for Vincent and he dumped them. (These antics included clearing the American's dressing room of furniture and attaching stale beefburgers to the mike stands). There were bans from various venues for 'rowdiness'. The group also invented a way to while away the time travelling to and from concerts by attacking bus queues with flour bombs! Ritchie: "We had this habit of buying bags of flour, and we'd throw these things at people we saw on the way, preferably old women in wheelchairs. But it got out of hand, and we became very cocky and started throwing them at policemen, all sorts of people!"

Joe Meek then took bassist Heinz Burt from The Tornados and, with the addition of Blackmore and others, launched Heinz and the Wild Boys in May 1964. 'Just Like Eddie' proved a big hit, and a series of singles and an album followed. A summer season booked as support to veteran comic Arthur Askey was the cue for further misadventures. "There was this 12-piece orchestra, and when they went home at night, I'd add notes to the trumpeter's part. The next day there would be this couple of bars of awful trumpet solo, which didn't go down too well."

A solo Blackmore single, 'Getaway'/'Little Brown Jug' was recorded at the behest of record producer Derek Lawrence, backed by pianist Nicky Hopkins, drummer Mick Underwood, bassist Chas Hodges and Reg Price on saxophone. Early 1965 saw Ritchie on the move again with a return to The Savages, Ritchie recording with Sutch this time around. However Ritchie, along with Jim Evans and Avid Andersen, soon took the opportunity to relocate to Germany for a job as backing trio for Jerry Lee Lewis (which began Ritchie's lifelong love of Germany).

Drawn by Hamburg and the infamous Star Club, they formed the short-lived Three Musketeers in January 1966. "We dressed up as musketeers, coming on stage fencing as the drummer played two bass drums which was unheard of in those days, and only being a three piece, which was also unusual. The band was excellent, but far too advanced for the German public, because we used to play very fast instrumentals."

Earning some much-needed cash from sessions for Polydor in Germany, Ritchie returned once more to England to link up with Neil Christian, who was putting a band together to promote his recent hit single 'That's Nice'. He recruited The Musketeers for a six-month tour, before Ritchie spent a short sojourn in Italy with a band put together around singer Ricky Maiocchi, known as The Trip. His return to England coincided with the dramatic arrival on the scene of Jimi Hendrix. The effect on Ritchie (and indeed, the whole music world) was colossal. As a result, Ritchie soon acquired a Fender Stratocaster, one of Eric Clapton's cast-offs: "His roadie gave it to me because it had a bowed neck. It had a great sound for a wah-wah pedal, but the neck was bowed so it was difficult to play." More importantly perhaps, Hendrix's pioneering use of feedback and histrionics began to fertilise

Chapter 1

ideas in Ritchie's mind about how guitar-led rock could evolve.

David Sutch was soon in touch yet again, this time with a band idea called The Roman Empire. As visually-minded as ever, this time Sutch decked out his musicians in Roman soldier costumes. Ritchie toured with the band around the UK and Europe, followed up by a brief few weeks with Neil Christian again. But by this time things had moved on; the beat era had been superseded by R&B and vocal harmony groups, with the likes of The Hollies the latest 'in thing'.

With potential work drying up, the frustrated and almost penniless Ritchie decided to remain in Germany, living off his girlfriend's earnings. "I stayed there for about a year, practising about six or seven hours a day - there was nothing else to do." He had, by this time, had enough of the hired-gun lifestyle and wanted to make his own mark with his own band. Mandrake Root was the first attempt, though they didn't last long enough to play a single live gig. Around this time Ritchie ran across a group called The Maze at The Star Club, featuring a boyish bespectacled drummer called Ian Paice. Impressed by the lad's precocious talent, Ritchie told him of his ideas and offered to form a band there and then, though without other members and devoid of any long-term plan Ian understandably declined. Meantime Carlo Little and Nick Simper were backing The Flowerpot Men, whose ranks included organist Jon Lord. The trio discussed forming a band, with Blackmore mooted as guitarist. Although nothing came of it, his name was now 'in the frame' and would soon crop up again.

In early 1968 Chris Curtis, formerly of The Searchers, approached the tyro management team of John Coletta and Tony Edwards with a proposal to form a band around himself, called Roundabout. He persuaded Jon Lord to get involved and sent numerous telegrams to Ritchie in Germany, whom he had originally encountered five years previously. By the time Ritchie had travelled to the UK to join up with Lord, the mercurial and erratic Curtis had moved on to other things. Deciding to carry on and form a working band, the duo soon recruited Nick Simper, while a series of auditions eventually threw up Maze singer Rod Evans and drummer Ian Paice by March 1968. With Coletta and Edwards bankrolling the group, a live tour was booked under the Roundabout moniker for Denmark. After the first few gigs the band name had changed to Deep Purple (named for Ritchie's grandmother's favourite song). With a blend of Hendrix, Vanilla Fudge and classic arrangements, the debut album *'Shades Of Deep Purple'* was recorded over a weekend and threw up an immediate surprise US hit with a cover of Joe South's 'Hush'. A tour of the States followed and Purple's brand of power-pop for a while promised much. However, the initial impetus was soon lost; the lack of follow-up single success and the dysfunctional musical direction evident on the next two albums had the group thinking about changes.

Primarily, the main concern was Rod Evans' singing. Ritchie had heard Led Zeppelin's recent debut and thought the band needed a 'screamer' in the Robert Plant mould. Simper's more traditional bass work was also deemed unsuitable. Old friend Mick Underwood was playing with pop act Episode Six at the time and recommended Ritchie to take a look at their own singer. This led to the recruitment of Ian Gillan along with bassist and fellow Episode Six band member Roger Glover, who was recruited on the strength of the session recording the single 'Hallelujah'.

Roger: "Ian called me up and said 'I'm going to Jon's house, why don't you come along?' So I said 'okay', went down, and met Jon. Jon said 'What are you doing tonight, do you want to play bass for us on a session? We want to make a record' and I said 'sure'. Anyway, they were quite impressed, I made a suggestion about the middle eight of this song, which worked, and they seemed to like me." Thus, by mid-1969, what would become the classic Deep Purple line-up was in place.

The publicity surrounding Jon Lord's classical-rock crossover *'Concerto For Group and Orchestra'* in mid-1969 gave the band a welcome profile - and, it must be said, some critical notoriety - in the UK, albeit not in a rock context. Sessions continued for their forthcoming album, for which Ritchie had very defined ideas. "I was impressed with what Zeppelin did, and said I wanted to do that kind of stuff. The record was sort of a response to the one we did with the orchestra. I wanted to do a loud, hard-rock record. And I was thinking this had better make it because I was afraid that if it didn't, we were going to be stuck playing with orchestras for the rest of our lives. We'd purposefully made it so it hammered along every song. There was no lull - [there were] different tempos, but the energy level was high."

Undertaking a series of exhaustive tours in-between sessions throughout 1970, the growing swell of underground support was such that the release of the seminal *'In Rock'* in September 1970 marked the start of a spectacular period of success for Deep Purple throughout the early seventies.

Chapter 2

LOOK TO THE RAINBOW

(1975-1976)

AS 1970 SLOWLY DISSOLVED INTO 1971, the Deep Purple team were beginning to reap the considerable rewards of their hard work over the previous 18 months. After the disparate directions of the previous albums, *'In Rock'* had definite focus and a red-line intensity that few could emulate and captured the imagination of a whole slew of the rock milieu, selling in numbers beyond everyone's wildest dreams. The album became a blueprint for every aspiring hard-rock band in the years ahead. Aggression, virtuosity and frenetic improvisation became by-words for Purple's music from now on. With tracks like 'Flight of the Rat' and 'Speed King', guitar and organ ran rampant over driving percussion and soaring vocals, formulating the musical and compositional principles that still govern bands of the 'heavy metal' genre over 30 years later. Such is the power of music that the poignant 'Child in Time' even became a theme song for the Eastern European political movements in their mid-eighties struggle for democracy.

Further exhaustive and intensive touring on the back of this success had ensured the follow-up *'Fireball'* was similarly successful, while a series of unlikely hit singles had further heightened the group's profile.

But although everything seemed to be going so well, the first cracks within the band were starting to appear. Rock music as a business was still in its infancy, with no one too sure if it was to be a lasting part of youth culture or simply another transient musical fad. Management thus feverishly milked any commercial success of bands under their control, working on the principle that success could well be fleeting. The resulting intensive and punishing work schedules understandably contributed to the aggravation of both personal and professional relationships.

Deep Purple proved no exception, problems most obviously arising between Ian Gillan and Ritchie Blackmore. Singer and guitarist by now had completely polarised views of the band and its objectives, the remaining trio reduced to moderating the pair's bickering. Opinions had been particularly divided over the quality of *'Fireball'*. Roger Glover: "Compared to *'In Rock'*, *'Fireball'* is a contrived album; on the whole a bit of a damp squib. Ian seemed to go off the rails with attitude and drink problems. He and Ritchie were at complete loggerheads and Ian may have got to the point where he thought 'I'm the singer in this band; if Ritchie can behave like that, so can I.' So he became just as big an arsehole."

Ritchie was also critical of *'Fireball'*: "I didn't like it much. I got bitter and threw ideas to the group that I thought up on the spur of the moment. We made virtually everything up in the studio, we never had any time to sit back and think... the only time we got a chance to write was when someone was ill... quite often we arrive at the studios with no idea what we are going to do... there is no time to prepare anything anyway, but the fact is that it is the spontaneity of our music which lends it vitality and excitement."

With royalties beginning to ensure their immediate financial security, Blackmore started to look beyond what he considered might be the limited shelf-life of the band to a time where he could follow a more personally defined musical agenda. Late 1971, therefore, saw Blackmore concocting plans for a solo project. Although still committed to Purple, he aimed to utilise the brief periods of free time schedules permitted to work on this. During November 1971 Ian Gillan was taken ill, and so, with the luxury of a whole month off, Ritchie grasped the opportunity to gather together a group of musicians to thrash out a few rough ideas. Purple drummer Ian Paice and Thin Lizzy's Phil Lynott joined Ritchie at London's De Lane Lea studios during the month for the first of what became legendary as the 'Babyface' sessions. (Babyface was the proposed band name, probably inspired by Paice's choirboy looks!) Lynott had been invited at Ian's suggestion, the drummer having caught a recent gig and come away suitably impressed with the young singer-bassist. The call seriously displeased the Thin Lizzy camp, who saw Ritchie's interest in Phil as something that could disrupt their own plans, and even lead to the loss of their creative lynch-pin. Lizzy's manager Chris O'Donnell cynically dismissed the sessions as: "A few rehearsals which had Phil thinking he could live out his Rod Stewart/Faces fantasy."

Drummer Brian Downey recalled: "Ritchie came up to De Lane Lea while we were recording *'Shades Of A Blue Orphanage'* and he just plugged in his guitar and started jamming with us. We all completely freaked; Phil didn't want to leave Lizzy but he really wanted to work with Ritchie and he was in two minds." Blackmore recalled, some years later: "We actually made a couple of records. They still must be in the vaults. They were good but I think it may have been a bit near Hendrix. I was playing that way, and Phil was singing that way."

Over the years, the Babyface sessions have established themselves in Blackmore mythology, the line between fact and fiction blurring. It was rumoured in the seventies that the sessions resulted in at least two, maybe three finished tracks. During the early eighties Lynott stated that as many as five tracks were worked up, which he speculated still existed somewhere. Alas, the only known reels of master tape found archived thus far have proved to contain just three disappointingly rudimentary and incomplete backing tracks.

In December 1971, solo aspirations were put on hold while Deep Purple reconvened in Switzerland for the writing and recording of the next album. The sessions - and the events surrounding them - soon became legendary. Despite serious disruption (fire destroying the Montreux casino that had been the original recording venue, a frantic relocation to the empty Grand Hotel, etc.) Purple rose to the occasion with the multi-platinum *'Machine Head'*, a pivotal album which would define their sound and stage act for much of their future existence. Timeless classics like 'Smoke On The Water', 'Lazy' and 'Highway Star' would push the band to their commercial and creative peak, ensuring a place alongside Led Zeppelin and Black Sabbath in the British 'holy trinity' of bands that dominated hard-rock in the US and Europe through the seventies.

After the recording of *'Machine Head'*, Blackmore arranged more extra-curricular get-togethers for the following year when time allowed. Under the production guidance of long-time Purple associate Derek Lawrence, this time Free singer Paul Rodgers was also invited along. (The press got wind of this, and speculation about Rodgers joining Purple followed. Ironically he was approached to join soon after Gillan gave notice in 1972 but, unnerved by all the publicity, eventually turned the job down.) However, Blackmore's commitment to live work brought about by Deep Purple's further success during 1972 meant there were to be many disruptions and postponements over the coming months.

Although the quality and direction of *'Machine Head'* satisfied Ritchie's creative demands, his disenchantment came to a head with the efforts for the follow-up album *'Who Do They Think We Are?'*, commencing in mid-1972. Roger Glover: "Ritchie wanted the band to go his way, and of course the band didn't want that. I'd come up with loads of ideas and he'd just sit there and look at me. There was also a rift between Ian and Ritchie on a technical matter about Ian's singing. Ritchie didn't like the way Ian did certain things and Ian said 'I don't care what you think, I'm doing them my way anyhow.' This rocking the boat made *'Who Do They Think We Are?'* a very traumatic process, because Ritchie and Ian ended up not talking." The sessions proved the final straw for Gillan. With Ian's resignation late in the year (citing what he saw as impending musical stagnation) Blackmore also voiced his intention to leave the band and seize the opportunity to try something fresh, concentrating on a more permanent version of the Babyface project.

This was intended to involve - provisionally at least - both Paice and Lynott, although increasing success for his own band meant Lynott now opted to devote all his efforts to Thin Lizzy. Lucifer's Friend vocalist John Lawton (whom Ritchie knew from his time in Germany during the sixties) was another mooted to join, but negotiations broke down. Deep Purple management, meanwhile, were horrified to see the band fragmenting just as they were breaking into the lucrative American market (the band would sell 14 million units worldwide during the year). Pressure was brought to bear on remaining members Roger Glover and Jon Lord to continue under the Purple banner and bring in new musicians. Talks eventually led to Ian agreeing to remain on board if attempts to persuade Blackmore to stay were fruitful. "I wanted a new band." said Ritchie: "I didn't want to get a singer in and carry on where we'd left off. Ian Paice said it would be silly to abandon all our efforts."

To coax Ritchie back to the fold, it was proposed to yield to the guitarist what was effectively total creative control, allowing Purple to follow what musical direction he considered worthwhile. After the Babyface experiences, Ritchie was firmly convinced that a more commercial, bluesy approach (utilising musicians of a similar mould to Lynott and Rodgers) was worth pursuing. To this end, Trapeze vocalist/bassist Glenn Hughes had already been pencilled in as an ideal candidate early in 1973. This inevitably meant that current bassist Roger Glover was gradually eased out during the final months of the Gillan line-up in mid-1973.

The subsequent work with new members David Coverdale and Hughes sated Blackmore's desires with the highly successful 1974 album *'Burn'*, and led to some excellent live concerts on the supporting tour, although by the time it came to recording the line-up's second album his frustrations were beginning to resurface again. June 1974 saw the band reconvene at Gloucestershire's Clearwell Castle for the writing and rehearsal sessions that were destined to yield *'Stormbringer'*. It was during these sessions that Blackmore's dissatisfaction again came to the fore. Previously Purple's creative mechanism had been clearly defined - Ritchie was the catalyst for the basic musical riffs and ideas, the other members developing those deemed worthwhile into completed backings before lyrics and melody lines were layered over the top. Now Ritchie's ideas brought to the band were being rejected more often.

The two newcomers, initially unsure of their roles within the group, had been prepared to step back on *'Burn'* and let Ritchie dictate proceedings. But by the time of the Clearwell sessions, their self-confidence was high and they were understandably demanding more input of their own. Influences like the funky leanings of Hughes began to show through in the resulting demos. Ritchie's dislike of what he dismissed as 'shoe-shine music' would - as in earlier times - have resulted in the guitarist putting his point of view in no uncertain terms. Now, though, he was prepared to concede to the others, abdicating control in favour of a more suitable outlet for his ideas.

The growing disparity within Purple was never so apparent as with Ritchie's suggestion they cover a song that had appeared on a Quatermass LP entitled *'Black Sheep Of The Family'*. Recalled Ritchie: "I brought it to Purple and they rejected it because they hadn't written it. I couldn't believe they turned it down because they wouldn't get a writing credit, but that was the bottom line." The refusal to cover the song by Mick Underwood's current band was too much for the guitarist, who now resurrected his plans for solo work, deciding to record the song as a single.

Blackmore's plans were no secret to the music world; the intention to record an album outside of Purple at some time had been public knowledge since the Babyface days. Ritchie had previously approached David Coverdale to help write an LP outside the band, but in David's view this was a retrograde step ("I said 'It's like going back five years... you should go on, or do an instrumental album.'"). Ritchie, on his part, told the press: "I just want to prove a point to myself that I can do it on my own... I don't want to do a big solo thing." First, though, Blackmore had to find the appropriate musicians to assist.

On their 1972 autumn and winter tours, Deep Purple's support act was an American five-piece called Elf, fronted by the tiny but powerfully-charismatic singer Ronnie James Dio. Ritchie made a habit of checking out the bands booked as support to Purple, and it appears Elf (and Ronnie in particular) were taken note of. "The first time I did speak to Ritchie he walked over and said 'You know, you're a great singer...' and walked away. I thought 'Wow, that's amazing, what a compliment.'" Ritchie later explained: "Ronnie Dio was a very interesting singer because he has a range of about one and a half octaves, but he seemed to be able to utilise what he knew. He could go down instead of going up, so he was a very clever singer, but then I think he was a trumpeter before..."

Chapter 2

Born in Portsmouth, New Hampshire on July 10th 1940, Ronald Padovana had grown up in New York. After studying classical trumpet in his youth, he switched to the bass and, by the late fifties, had formed his first group at school. He modestly took the stage name Dio (meaning 'God') resulting from a childhood interest in the Mafia. "I was a real student of the subject, especially a guy called Johnny Dio from Florida. When you're a second-generation Italian growing up in America you don't have that many heroes, and I wanted to retain my identity via an organisation that didn't take any crap from anybody." 'Ronnie Dio' was born.

The band, with Ronnie on bass and vocals, Nick Pantas on guitar and Tom Rogers on drums were named The Vegas Kings, although, after the addition of Jack Musci on saxophone, they changed their name to Ronnie and The Ramblers. The line-up then became Ronnie and The Red Caps - under which name they recorded a single in 1958, 'Lover', on Reb Records. By 1961 Musci had left, Dick Bottoff had joined on guitar and the band had evolved into Ronnie and The Prophets. Backed by the band, Dio recorded several solo singles and an album, *'Dio At Dominos'*, over the next six years or so.

By the late sixties they were making a decent living playing the club and college circuit down the East Coast of America. Now billed as The Prophets, they had even opened for The Rolling Stones in 1967. By 1968 the band had evolved into The Electric Elves, shortening their name to The Elves soon after. The moniker was peculiarly apt as most of the band was less than five feet nine inches tall! Dio told of audience reaction to the group: "They didn't know what to make of us. Out we came, tiny people... there was plenty of laughter until we started and proceeded to bludgeon everyone to death with our level of power."

Elf circa 1972.
Left-right:
Steve Edwards,
Craig Gruber,
Gary Driscoll,
Ronnie Dio,
Mickey Lee Soule

The Elves' repertoire at this time consisted of mainly covers of contemporary hits of the day with a few of their own songs thrown in. They gained a reputation for taking freshly released material by major artists like The Who and The Beatles and immediately incorporating it into their own live set, usually before any live performances by the originators themselves! (A 25-minute segment of The Who's *'Tommy'* was performed live within weeks of its release, while Jethro Tull's 'Aqualung' was another later favourite.) By the end of the decade, three further singles had been released on various labels, including MCA. Following the death of guitarist Pantas in a car accident in early 1970 the name was once again changed, this time to simply Elf. By now Dio's impressive vocals, layered over a jazzy, heavy-boogie piano style, all driven along by Driscoll's powerful drumming, had given the band more of a unique identity. Now based in New York State, Elf were spotted by Roger Glover while they auditioned for Columbia Records in January 1972. "I first saw them with Ian Paice in New York," recalled Roger. "Paicey and I were blown away. They sounded so raw and exciting. It was hard to believe such an enormous sound could come from such tiny people... Ronnie had one of the best voices I had ever heard or worked with, before or since. The unusual addition of a piano, played by Mickey Lee Soule, made it very different and they had a solid writing partnership."

They impressed Glover so much that he and Paice offered to produce their forthcoming album. The line-up by this time comprised Dio (bass/vocals), Gary Driscoll (drums), Mickey Lee Soule (keyboards) with Ronnie's cousin Dave Feinstein and Doug Thaler (who went on to co-manage Mötley Crüe) on guitars and vocals. The tracks, mostly written by Dio and Feinstein, were recorded in Studio One, Atlanta during the April of 1972 and released only in the US by Epic, as *'Elf'*. By mid-1973 Feinstein had left (later resurfacing with power-metal act The Rods before a career in management), while Dio ditched the bass to concentrate on singing. The band line-up now was Dio, Soule and Driscoll with Craig Gruber (bass) and Steve Edwards on lead guitar. By the summer of that year Elf had signed to MGM in America and Purple Records in the UK, recording their second album at Manor Studios in England, again produced by Glover. Roger also sang backing vocals on one track. 'Carolina County Ball' was released by Deep Purple's Purple Records in

April 1974, in time for their UK debut as support on the May Purple tour. The album was released under the title 'L.A. '59' in the USA. While Elf were in the UK, Roger Glover persuaded Ronnie Dio to contribute vocal and writing skills to his 'Butterfly Ball' project, with Mickey Lee Soule also contributing keyboards.

Given Blackmore's liking of Plant/Rodgers-type vocalists and his familiarity with Elf, it was logical that he should approach Ronnie to sing on the proposed single, the session initially planned to be purely a one-off for a £1,000 fee. Once they were into rehearsals, Ritchie discovered he and Ronnie had a great deal in common musically, and this empathy became more obvious as they considered what they could put together as a B-side. In Dio's words, "We were on the road in Minnesota... Ritchie told me that we had to go into the studio in a couple of days to lay down a track, and asked me if I could write a lyric for him by the following day!"

The initial recording session was in a Tampa Bay studio on the evening of 12th December 1974 - a convenient free night in Purple's US tour schedule - involving Dio, Gary Driscoll and Electric Light Orchestra cellist Hugh McDowall. (ELO were also supporting Purple and McDowall had recently been giving Blackmore lessons) Playing back the recordings, Ritchie found he preferred the freshly composed flip-side - 'Sixteenth Century Greensleeves' - to the cover version. But perhaps more important to Ritchie had been the composition process itself.

With the guitarist being Deep Purple's catalyst for initial ideas, the other band members' input into anything he came up with invariably led to compromise. So often frustrated by this method of working, the way in which Dio openly embraced and translated his ideas into worthwhile results enthused Ritchie with renewed motivation: "The way he sang was perfect for what I wanted. I didn't have to tell him - he just sang it." Ronnie described his creative methods at the time: "I write mainly on bass, guitar or piano. I find melodies come quite easily from the bass, but it is my native instrument. Luckily for me, though, I don't need to write on any instrument because I can work in my head without any problems."

Thus did the writing partnership quickly develop. With Ronnie's co-operation, an album's worth of material was soon prepared, either written from scratch utilising ideas held back from earlier Purple sessions, often from as far back as 1972. (As Roger Glover related in 1973: "He started playing a riff, and we'd all joined in, said 'That's good, let's do that' and he said 'No, I'm not letting you do that, I'm saving that for my solo album' and of course the band got very annoyed.")

Meantime Glover had been out of Purple for over a year and was considering putting his own band together. He was aiming for a style similar to Little Feat and had provisionally called the group Footloose. Ronnie had earlier helped record a few demos and he was asked to join, although, to Roger's surprise, Dio turned down the offer as the gig with Ritchie had already been accepted. Roger: "Here was Ritchie thwarting me again - by stealing my protégé." (Ironically, in February 1976 the rest of Roger's band was 'stolen' by Ian Gillan to launch his solo career!). Tracks were recorded between 20th February and 14th March 1975 in the Musicland Studios in Munich, under the production guidance of Martin Birch. Ritchie was required for the upcoming Deep Purple tour commencing on 16th March in Yugoslavia, and so, without the time available to recruit other musicians, used Ronnie's colleagues from Elf. Recording was straightforward, the only snag encountered the accidental omission of three lines of verse from 'Man On The Silver Mountain', which had to be recorded later and spliced in. Other guest musicians included keyboard player Matthew Fisher of Procol Harum and a classically-trained singer called Soshana (also Blackmore's girlfriend at the time), although only the latter appeared to be on the final album mix of 'Still I'm Sad'. The single also appears to have been re-recorded at some later stage. Furthermore, Ronnie Dio changed his name during the recordings: "Ritchie said to me, 'What's your middle name?' I said, 'It's James.' Ritchie said, 'Usually when you make a name change, because of the numbers involved (Ritchie was interested in numerology), it works out for the best.' So I said, 'Sure. No problem.' It's got a ring to it. So I became Ronnie James Dio."

Ritchie was strongly rumoured at the time to have played on Elf's album, the excellent *'Trying To Burn The Sun'*, recorded at Kingsway Studios in London a few weeks prior to putting down his solo material. Although the guitarist's involvement has been since denied by both Glover and Dio ("I think Rog said, 'Should we ask Ritchie to play on it?'... But he didn't.") and more recently the man himself, the guitar work on songs like 'Liberty Road', 'Wonderworld' and 'Streetwalker' nevertheless contain certain very characteristic trademarks. Release of this album was held over until later in the year so as not to clash with the forthcoming Blackmore product. The results of these sessions finally convinced Ritchie to make his move and go it alone, and he announced his intentions to the Purple management. The other members of the band suspected something was afoot, such was Ritchie's obvious enthusiasm over his solo material compared to recent Purple efforts. His live performances on the tour also become more introspective, his solos less direct and more experimental, indicating that artistically his focus was elsewhere.

With the ability of hindsight, portions of his live work contained themes recently worked out with Elf and destined to be further developed over the coming years. (For instance, instrumental passages used in what became 'Man On The Silver Mountain' and 'Still I'm Sad' often turned up in the lengthy improvisations during Purple's 'You Fool No One'). He made his intentions known to the rest of the band on conclusion of their European tour in Paris on 7th April 1975. The official announcement to the press was made on 21st June. Deep Purple - perhaps unwisely, in retrospect - decided to carry on and short-listed several guitarists to replace Blackmore. Among them were Clem Clempson of Humble Pie (who was auditioned) along with Mick Ronson, Rory Gallagher and Jeff Beck (who were not). While Purple's self-destruction with eventual incumbent Tommy Bolin followed, all the members of Elf - minus the now obviously redundant Steve Edwards - joined Ritchie and Ronnie to become the first official incarnation of Rainbow. The moniker was taken from one of Ritchie's favoured haunts in Los Angeles, the infamous Rainbow Bar & Grill - a legendary magnet for musicians and groupies alike.

Ritchie now had the freedom to try and eclipse everything done previously with Purple and really attempt to blow the opposition away - and on his terms. Ronnie recalled their initial aspirations in a 1987 interview: "Ritchie's attitude was that the combination of the two of us was the one to really stamp some kind of signature on the band itself. That meant we were only answerable to each other. It was a fifty-fifty partnership." This, inevitably, meant the other musicians involved would become subordinate to the partnership: a policy that would go some way to explaining the bewilderingly rapid turnover of personnel that characterised the group throughout its existence.

The LP, titled *'Ritchie Blackmore's Rainbow'*, was released on the new Oyster label in August 1975. Ritchie had refused to have the album released on Purple Records, so the label was set up by Purple's managers - to whom Ritchie was still under contract - specifically for Rainbow. Oyster was distributed by EMI and, when Ritchie's contract expired, Polydor bought out the label. Ritchie told Creem magazine: "They're all Germans at Polydor and I have a weakness for them because they lost the war!"

Reaction to the album was varied, perplexing those who were expecting product much closer to the classic Deep Purple sound. It was an understandable premise, and this rather unfair comparison with former glories was something that would plague Blackmore throughout his subsequent career. Overall, if anything, the album owed more to the sound of Elf than to that of Purple, with Blackmore seemingly content to play down the solo aspect. ("I didn't want to make a solo guitar LP - that would have been boring. I think it's extremely difficult to sustain interest when you are concentrating on one specific instrument... We're going to have much more emphasis on melody. In other words, everything isn't going to be hung on a riff.")

He seemed more intent on establishing the record as a co-operative effort with Dio, though it was still perceived by many that the project was essentially Ritchie Blackmore plus backing musicians - the possessive nature of the album title didn't help (and even this was to cause conflict in later years). Ritchie viewed the album at the time as "A very subdued enterprise, the application of several ideas collected over a few years, with the aim of having fun." Ronnie gave the enterprise an immediately identifiable sound with an individualistic and powerful vocal performance while Blackmore showed a slightly more subtle, mellow side to his playing. Production by today's standards was muddy with Soule's keyboards buried in the mix for much of the time.

The acoustic-led 'Temple Of The King' and 'Catch The Rainbow' proved to be among the most promising moments. The latter (said to have been inspired by Hendrix's 'Little Wing') was Ronnie's personal favourite: "'Catch The Rainbow' is a classic number, probably the finest song Rainbow ever recorded." A glorious instrumental reworking of The Yardbirds' 'Still I'm Sad' - one of Blackmore's all-time favourites - was the only concession to the guitar freak-out many had expected. Although the arrangement proved so different to the original as to be hardly recognisable, Ritchie still earned the wrath of Radio 1's John Peel for adulterating such a classic!

Standing left-right: Craig Gruber, Gary Driscoll, Mickey Lee Soule, Ritchie Blackmore, Seated: Ronnie Dio

The lyrical meaning behind 'Man On The Silver Mountain' was explained by Dio in 1975: "It's a semi-religious song, that the man on the silver mountain is the kind of God figure that everyone is crying out to come down and save them, and give them money and chicks! Cures from diseases and all that! They basically cry out to him to come down and make them holy and full and rewarded." Ironically, the tune that had triggered the whole Rainbow project - 'Black Sheep Of the Family' - was one of the least successful tracks. Given the history behind 'Black Sheep', it was also surprising 'Man On The Silver Mountain' should be chosen as the promotional single, released in October 1975 across Europe backed with 'Snake Charmer', although Italy bravely plumped for 'Still I'm Sad'.

It was a very promising beginning, but the manifold technical shortcomings of the band members quickly become evident to Ritchie during recording, particularly after the individual virtuosity he had been used to - and took for granted - in Deep Purple. In July the first to go was Craig Gruber who, though he had contributed some highly adept bass to the album, didn't get on with the guitarist because of the way he considered Ritchie had hijacked Elf for his own ends. August 1975 saw a young unknown bassist recruited from a band called Harlot, having been recommended to Blackmore by his guitar technician Ian Ferguson.

Born in the Scottish highlands, Jimmy Bain had cut his teeth in several provincial amateur bands before emigrating to Vancouver with his parents. By his early twenties he was playing professionally in a band called Street Noise. Returning to London, Bain joined Harlot in early 1974, alongside drummer Ricky Munro, a colleague of Blackmore's in the short-lived Mandrake Root during the mid-sixties. Jimmy had recently turned down a job with The Babys (which at the time featured future AOR star John Waite and Journey's Jonathan Cain).

"I was living in London with a couple of roadies who were also Scottish... one of them worked with Ritchie. One day Ritchie phoned and told me he was forming a new band, and although I'd never met him before, we talked for two hours on the phone! Two days later he was watching me backstage at the Marquee in London... I walked in and there was Blackmore, Dio and their manager, and a couple of other people who'd flown in from L.A. to check me out.

"I wasn't that nervous, but the rest of the band were; they played terrible that

Chapter 2

night. Actually there was one point I got nervous. It was when I looked across over the crowd and saw these two expressionless eyes staring right at me. I thought 'Oh fuck!'... After that gig Ritchie offered me the job in Rainbow." Ronnie joked to journalists of Bain's appointment: "We heard there was this hot bass player in a band called Harlot who were playing at the Marquee. We thought he was rubbish, but he was all that was going!" Mickey Lee Soule and Gary Driscoll were next to exit, leaving during September - and, although they tried to resurrect Elf with new recruits, the band soon fell apart. Remarked Ritchie: "Driscoll had a habit of losing the tempo, then catching up!" Ronnie said of Soule at the time: "Mickey is a good rock'n'roll and boogie-woogie piano player, but he is lazy. He's not the type to go on stage with a synthesiser, a mellotron, an organ and a piano. He prefers to lie in the grass writing songs."

With the sacking of musicians he had worked with for many years, Dio explained at the time how his perception of the group differed from Ritchie's: "In my eyes, the guys I took with me from Elf were going to be the permanent line-up for Rainbow, but I think from the very beginning Ritchie had other ideas. Perhaps he knew I wouldn't leave without them so he decided to give the guys a chance. I like to think that Ritchie got rid of them simply because they weren't the right players and it has to be said that I did agree with him at the end of the day... it was only when I saw myself progressing and the rest of them standing still that I realised Elf was finished. It was sad - Elf was a very good band for its time - but time wasn't on our side. There were so many good bands around, we didn't get noticed." Blackmore confirmed the change in personnel was foreseen. "I knew a new line-up would unfold for the live gigs."

Word was put out that auditions were to be arranged in Los Angeles later that month with a view to recruiting a drummer. One of the dozen or so attending was a young man from the west of England named Cozy Powell. Ritchie had remembered being impressed by the drum sound on Jeff Beck's 1971 release 'Rough And Ready', and had made a mental note of Beck's drummer after seeing them play at the Roundhouse a few years earlier. In September Cozy received a phone call from Ritchie's guitar technician, requesting he fly to L.A. to try out. Auditions took place at the two Pirate Sound rehearsal studios, originally sound stages built by Columbia Pictures, now utilised by many name bands. Blackmore had booked both - much to the chagrin of Deep Purple who had intended to work up material for their forthcoming album at around the same time!

Jimmy Bain explained the audition procedure: "It was just Ritchie and me. To try them out he'd go into this super-fast song for about 20 minutes, it was like an endurance test." One of the last to be checked out, Cozy accepted an immediate invitation to join half an hour into his session. "Ritchie played a riff and the drummers just had to keep up!" was how Powell remembered the auditions in a late-nineties interview. "Ritchie could be difficult with drummers. Apparently one guy came along and set his kit up. He looked the part, got his suitcase out and changed into a black outfit, complete with gloves. Eventually he was ready and Ritchie said 'Get rid of him!'... the poor guy didn't play a note!" An official announcement of Powell's recruitment was made in early October.

Powell (first name Colin - the Cozy nickname came from famous jazz drummer Cozy Cole) was born in the sleepy Cotswolds town of Cirencester in 1947 and started playing drums in the school orchestra, thereafter playing along in his spare time to Sandy Nelson singles. "I had a half-decent sense of rhythm, but I didn't progress until I went to grammar school. A couple of other musicians there had started to put a group together and didn't have a drummer. Because of my riotous behaviour at school, I was told to play the cymbals - because I'd broken the drums!"

The semi-professional circuit was next (aged 15) with local semi-pro outfit The Sorcerers, who were heavily influenced by vocal harmony pop bands of the time, like The Hollies. The drummer with the Mancunian band, Bobby Elliott, became another early Powell idol. The late nights and usual on-the-road hi-jinks of band life began to impact on his schooling, and Powell left to take an office job for six months in order to finance the purchase of his first set of Premier drums. The Sorcerers ended up, like numerous other bands of the period, performing around the flourishing German club scene. "Every German city had its clubs... and we played in Frankfurt at the K52 and the Storeyville. It was really hard work, but it was good because it built up your stamina... You'd be drumming and playing for literally hours without a break. If you can learn to entertain GIs on leave in German clubs when they're pissed out of their brains at three in the morning, you can learn to entertain anybody!"

Fellow Sorcerer Peter Ball remembered Cozy as "a drummer who suited us down to the ground. We got better and better for his incredibly tight style and great time-keeping... Socially, anyone who knew him will vouch that he was a loon at all times." By the spring of 1968 the band had returned to England, becoming known around Birmingham and the burgeoning Midlands club circuit. Cozy was

Chapter 2

a familiar face locally, striking up long-standing friendships with fellow musicians like Robert Plant and John Bonham (both at the time unknowns in Listen), future Slade vocalist Noddy Holder, Fairport Convention bassist Dave Pegg and a young guitarist from Aston called Tony Iommi.

Cozy spent two months out playing with Casey Jones and The Engineers before rejoining The Sorcerers, who were about to undergo a name change to Youngblood and release a series of no-hope singles in late '68 and early '69. The group then linked up with the former Move bassist/singer Ace Kefford to form The Ace Kefford Stand, whose sound ended up as nothing so much as that of a second-rate Cream. While in the Stand, Powell began session work to earn a living, and by late 1969, Cozy, now lodging with former Sorcerers Dave and Dennis Ball, had had enough waiting around and the trio (adding vocalist Pete French) formed Big Bertha. Powell also worked briefly with US star Tony Joe White.

Indeed, up until now, Powell's talents had been applied to an eclectic range of musical directions but, inspired by John Bonham's powerhouse style, Cozy had started weight training to build up his own strength and stamina. Within a few weeks, prospects looked up when he landed the then highly prestigious drumming job with guitar icon Jeff Beck. Beck and Powell had met on several occasions in Germany and the guitarist was familiar with Cozy's now well-honed technique through his session activities. Cozy formally joined Beck's backing group in April 1970.

"The first album I did with Beck never got released. He and I went to Detroit and cut an instrumental album of old Motown hits... James Jamerson (Motown's in-house bassist who played on most of the label's hits) played bass, and the Motown brass section. They were the very last tracks cut in the old Motown studios... some of it was good, some of it was awful." Beck: "We got to Motown and we were like two kids in a candy store. Cozy said 'Just give me a minute to set my drums up.' And he moved the kit out of the studio, and this tape op came in and said 'You guys came for the Motown sound, right?' and I went 'Yeah' and he said, 'Well, it just went out the door.'

"Cozy wouldn't have it; he said 'I've come here to do what I do... on my kit.' If only I'd boxed his ears and said 'You play that kit.' It was stupid. For a start Motown had a drummer to die for - Benny Benjamin - and there's poor old Cozy thrashing his kit and poor James Jamerson not being able to cope with it... We must've been as weird to them as they were to us. It was costing a fortune, then we ran out of time and had to get out..."

The tours with Beck were an important learning process for the young drummer, playing for the first time in front of huge audiences, although naturally the guitarist remained the centre of attention: "Jeff was God in those days. Everywhere we went it was sold out and I've never seen that kind of adulation since... He could have had Farmer Giles on drums and Walter Gabriel [for non-UK readers, the latter is a central character in BBC Radio's popular countryside soap opera 'The Archers'!] on bass, and it wouldn't have mattered at all... it was Jeff they all wanted to see."

After the recording of two albums, *'Rough And Ready'* (October 1971) and *'Jeff Beck Group'* (July 1972), the band fell apart - as was normal with Beck's ventures in those days. Cozy: "Jeff was pretty difficult to work with because he couldn't make up his mind which style of music to pursue; one moment he was into Motown, then heavy rock, then a jazzy feel... It was like that all the time. We were all fired, but then he re-hired Max [Middleton: keyboards]. He asked Clive Chaman and me to rejoin when his relationship with Tim Bogert and Carmine Appice got shaky, but we said 'bollocks'. We were into other things."

Turning down a offer from Johnny Winter ("It was another Beck trip - Winter and me in search of other musicians. I didn't really want to go through all that again, so I said 'no'."), a brief return to session work followed before a couple of months in the summer of 1972 was spent with the band Spirit. By late 1972 he had joined up with the

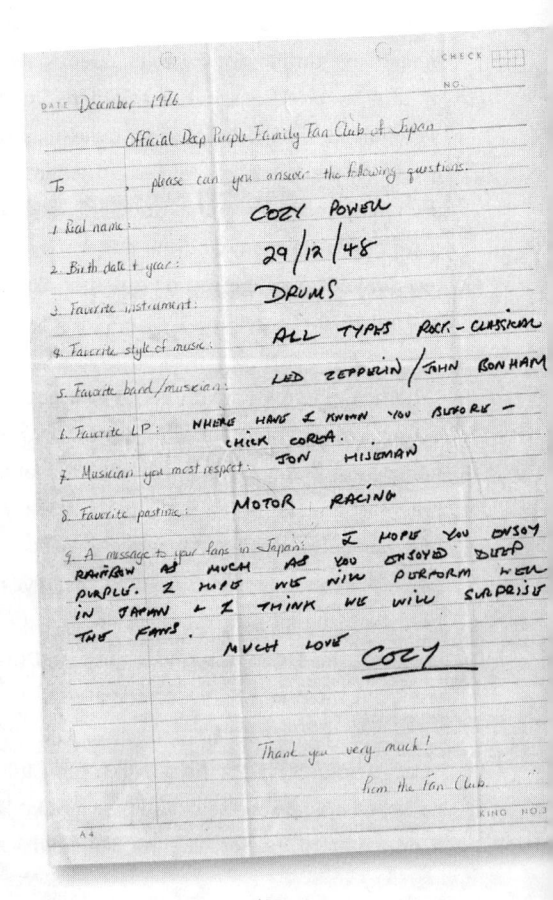

Chapter 2

Ball brothers again and, on recruiting singer Frank Aiello, formed Bedlam (although they were briefly called Beast). Dave Ball had been with Procol Harum for the previous year, after which he joined brother Dennis in Long John Baldry's backing group. One eponymous album was produced for Chrysalis Records and released in August 1973.

Again, while Bedlam tried to gain momentum, Powell busied himself with extra-curricular activities. Beck's studio producer had been impresario Mickie Most and Powell soon found himself drafted into many a session for artists signed to Most's RAK label, including such diverse acts as Julie Felix, Hot Chocolate, Donovan and Suzi Quatro. Cozy: "At the time, I was doing about 15 sessions a week in London. I had a fixer called David Katz who'd ring up and say, 'Do you want to do a film score today, or a pop band, or a folk singer?' It was good for a while, but then it all got a bit jaded because you got the old farts who'd been doing it for years and weren't very good. After a while I'd had enough."

Around this period Most managed to persuade Cozy to record an instrumental solo single. Featuring a repeated drum pattern coupled to a melody line based around Hendrix's 'Third Stone From The Sun', to everyone's amazement 'Dance With The Devil' became a smash and reached No. 3 in the UK singles chart during January of 1974. Most importantly perhaps, the track served to inspire a whole generation of youngsters to take up the drums. "The idea was all Mickie's... he gave us a rough drum riff. It took 20 minutes to record and I didn't think any more of it until a month later when I was asked to do Top Of The Pops, and it became this massive thing." Although Bedlam won decent reviews after a support slot on Black Sabbath's US tour, a lack of record-company commitment meant the band soon folded. To cash in on his chart success, the drummer convened Cozy Powell's Hammer in April 1974 (members of which included at various times guitarist Bernie Marsden, keyboardist Don Airey and Bedlam singer Frank Aiello). After releasing a couple more successful singles - 'The Man In Black' (reaching No.18) and 'Na Na Na' (No.10) - during the summer of 1974, the band found themselves touring on teenybopper bills supporting pop stars of the day such as Suzi Quatro.

Unable to shake off the image of a hit-orientated pop act and be taken seriously by the rock fraternity, Hammer broke up in early 1975. After this frustrating period Powell became very disillusioned: "I only cut 'Dance...' for a laugh. It all escalated until I felt I was losing credibility, that I'd got into a rut... I used to get embarrassed at having to appear on Top Of The Pops. I just couldn't see myself building up an audience of screaming little girls." Another band venture was proposed involving Humble Pie's bassist Greg Ridley and guitarist Clem Clempson in a power trio provisionally dubbed Strange Brew. Contractual problems scuttled the project before it started - although not before the promotional photos were distributed.

Powell had another passion in life besides drumming - the thrill of pure speed. Developing from his early fascination with fast cars and motorbikes, he was as at home behind the wheel of a car as behind a drum-kit and raced for Hitachi on the UK touring car circuit for a few months. Soon after along came the offer from Ritchie Blackmore: "He'd seen me at the Roundhouse with Beck. I didn't have enough money to follow the racing through properly and, although I was only in my twenties, I was a bit old. So I joined Rainbow - basically because I'd run out of money."

October saw the final piece of the jigsaw slot into place with the arrival of 22-year-old Californian keyboard player Tony Carey. Trained at the famous Juilliard School of Music, Carey had rebelled against a more traditional classical career in favour of contemporary rock'n'roll, playing bass in his youth before switching to keyboards. Prior to Rainbow Carey had worked with a variety of diverse acts, including Bobby Womack and Steely Dan. Most recently he had been a member of a country-rock quintet called Blessings, who sounded not unlike a poor man's Eagles, a band which also included Jeff Porcaro and David Hungate who went on to form the highly successful Toto a few years later. Originally recommended by Jimmy Bain (who was an acquaintance), the band met up with Carey and after a satisfactory try-out he was hired. Tony: "I played for about half an hour, then they brought in Cozy. I guess I kept up."

Rehearsals took place throughout the rest of October at Pirate Sound in advance of a short debut American tour. These sessions were particularly productive, with several new compositions worked out ready to be tried on the live tour. The initial shows, the first scheduled for 5th November in Pittsburgh, were cancelled to allow more rehearsal time and to enable the stage set to be finished. The spectacular visual centrepiece of the tour was to be an illuminated rainbow coupled to a computer-controlled lighting system. Standing over 29 feet tall, spanning 40 feet, containing 3,000 bulbs and costing £40,000, the rainbow had been an idea of Blackmore's following the headlining of the 1974 California Jam festival with Deep

---- Chapter 2 ----

Left-right:
Cozy Powell,
Tony Carey,
Jimmy Bain,
Dio,
Blackmore

Purple when a wooden version had adorned the main stage.

The fabrication of the rainbow was started by See Factor in New York in the summer of 1975 and was to be tested on the tour. It was made in four 15-foot sections to ease erection on stage and dismantling afterward. In Blackmore's view, "it created more electrical interference than I've ever worked with... the lights were generating more noise than I was!"

The first live performance by Rainbow was in Canada on 10th November 1975, with Argent as support. Ronnie recently remembered: "Our first gig was at the Montreal Forum, which holds 17-18,000 people, and we drew, like, 1,500 people. And that was probably difficult for Ritchie. It wasn't difficult for me. I hadn't played for that many people anyway most of the time except in Europe." The Philadelphia show on the 15th had to be interrupted because of sound interference problems caused by the rainbow's electronics. Modifications to both Blackmore's guitar and the rainbow initially cured this interference for the early stages of the world tour in 1976, although intermittent problems would continue throughout the rainbow's stage life.

Set-list running orders included as opener 'Temple Of The King', along with 'Sixteenth Century Greensleeves', 'Man On The Silver Mountain', 'Still I'm Sad', 'Catch the Rainbow', 'Self Portrait', and 'If You Don't Like Rock'n'Roll'. New numbers previously worked up in rehearsals included 'Stargazer', 'Light In The Black' and 'Do You Close Your Eyes'. At this early stage the set was changed frequently - witness the second show in New York - 'Do You Close Your Eyes' opened followed by 'Self Portrait', 'Catch The Rainbow', 'Man On The Silver Mountain', 'Stargazer', 'A Light In The Black' and an extended 'Still I'm Sad'.

Nearly two dozen shows were performed by the turn of the year; a few recordings survive from this tour, giving a fascinating insight into this embryonic stage of the group's live development as they experiment with song arrangements, solos and formats.

After the inaugural tour and a month off for Christmas, the next LP, *'Rainbow Rising'*, was recorded with Martin Birch at the Munich Musicland complex over a ten day period during February 1976. The material worked up during the previous autumn formed the bulk of the album. After further run-throughs in a disused club near Munich, recording was again fairly straightforward, although some drum tracks were later redone.

Ritchie was struck by the spontaneity of the sessions: "We didn't do much editing because Cozy insisted on recording everything straight through. A lot of times, a band will go through a longer song in sections, because you can throw in everything you want knowing you only have to play 180 bars. We only had one edit - quite astounding considering side two has two nine-minute songs on it." Such had been the band's focus that little in the way of extra material was recorded and no complete out-takes exist.

Jimmy Bain: "I liked the first album, but *'Rising'* was more of a band effort. *'Rising'* was a little short in terms of tracks. We always did the absolute minimum, never anything left over." The regime of the recording helped lend the tracks a raw and rugged feel. Cozy found to his surprise that Ritchie gave him complete freedom to come up with whatever percussion parts he considered appropriate to the basic riffs, and his contributions became a cornerstone of the overall Rainbow sound. "Ritchie just said 'Look, this is what I'm after - how do you feel it?' I would present him with the track as I felt it and we would build on it from there... most songs were done in two or three takes." Interestingly, the drums were set up in a corridor at the studios and a wooden alcove built around the kit to give the desired recording ambience.

Ritchie's dislike for the clinical ambience of recording studios (a result of his production-line sessions with producer Joe Meek) meant The Rolling Stones mobile studio was employed outside the Musicland facility with which to capture the best of the performances. Both Ritchie and Martin Birch were more comfortable using the mobile, having utilised it on numerous occasions in the past with Deep Purple. Birch later vividly described the sessions as "A bunch of hooligans getting together in the studio to make a good record."

Ritchie explained his vision of the LP to journalists: "A high-level energy affair, an aggressive thing, like with Deep Purple... our next LP will be based on a hypothetical meeting between Led Zeppelin and Deep Purple." It turned out to be no idle boast. The material was a definite progression from the earlier album, as the band was both essentially a new unit and more positive about their harder musical direction. Unleashed on the world in June, *'Rising'* was undoubtedly Rainbow's greatest critical and artistic triumph, and remains to this day a definitive example of the fusion between intense, forceful hard rock and neo-classical, sweeping symphonic influences. The dark, brooding, fantasy-art album cover (specially designed by Irish artist Ken Kelly, showing influences from Carlos Schwalbe to Frank Frazetta) gave a graphic indication of the musical style of the album contained therein.

Side one opened with 'Tarot Woman', a subtle Carey synthesiser introduction yielding to an ardent guitar riff that heralded a singularly uncompromising rocker. Dio explained the lyrical meaning: "It was originally called something else... the main character is told by this tarot woman that a chick is going to fuck him over; she tells him to beware a smile and a bright shiny face." As for the following track, Ritchie expanded on how the commercially-sounding Bad Company-like groove of 'Starstruck' was lyrically inspired by the exploits of one particularly infamous Blackmore-obsessed groupie: "'Starstruck' is all about this lump called Muriel who's been following me all around Europe for the last few years - a real lunatic. We play a concert in Paris and she'd be there and we'd fly to Lyon and she'd be at the airport waiting for our plane to arrive. One day I looked out my window and thought I saw the bushes move in the garden. I kept watching and sure enough she'd found my house, so I set my dogs on her!"

'Run With The Wolf' harked back to the earlier Elf sound, while 'Do You Close

Your Eyes' was a dense chromatic rocker as close to a love-song as this album would get. Side two was a stormer, comprising two epic eight-minute-plus tracks - 'Stargazer' using the extremely-prestigious Munich Philharmonic Orchestra complemented by the headlong adrenaline-fuelled charge that was 'Light In The Black' (originally titled 'Comin' Home'). Taken together, they formed what were arguably Blackmore's finest studio moments.

The origins of 'Stargazer' came from Blackmore bashing out the main theme on cello ("It doesn't really help my guitar-playing, but it puts another dimension into my songwriting"). Ronnie told of the lyrical meaning behind the tracks: "I'd had this idea for an epic song for a while... it was a matter of waiting for the right time to record it. The story tells of the trials and tribulations of a group of people who follow a wizard, and how they try to face up to his eventual death. I don't believe 'Light' works by itself, but when you juxtapose it with

'Stargazer' it does make some sense, as people struggle to find a light at the end of their despair."

The superb quality of the album was more attributable to the strength of the performances than the material. The group as a whole presented the work with such sledgehammer energy that can, still to this day, leave the listener drained. With Powell's explosive percussion and Bain's strident bass nailing everything to the floor, Blackmore's awesome guitar work is free to wreak havoc, topped by Carey's swirling embellishments and Dio's bell-like clarity and impassioned imagery. Birch's production sound on the original vinyl takes few prisoners either.

Two remixes were done in the eighties: one in New York which was used for most CD versions, and one in Los Angeles. The first CD version of the album issued in Japan in 1987 was derived from the L.A. master. As a result, the mix contains several clearly discernible differences to the original vinyl; the intro to 'Tarot Woman' is a mite longer, the outro to 'Run With The Wolf' fades out later and generally bass, keyboards and backing vocals are all much higher in the mix. The 1999 remastered CD reissue - originating from the New York masters - is more faithful to the original vinyl sound but arguably not as powerful.

This time around both the fans and critics were unanimous in their favourable response to the album. Cozy affirmed the album's lasting quality in 1997: "In retrospect, I think it's probably one of the best albums I've done. There are three or four tracks that were really outstanding and which summed up the music at the time, just when heavy rock was really coming into its own." Dio gave his view of the album some years later: "To be honest, I never realised what we had on our hands with that album but I well understood Ritchie's fears about it... because I came from nothing I was naturally more confident and I tried to convince him of that fact on numerous occasions."

The band commenced its inaugural world tour in Idaho on 6th June 1976, continuing across North America through the following month. Most of the 40 or so theatre dates were as headliners, but a few supporting gigs were slipped into the bigger arena venues as special guests of Jethro Tull and, on one occasion, Blue Öyster Cult. The amount of equipment required for the electronic rainbow meant the full stage set took some seven hours to set up, usually resulting in a 'one day on - one day off' schedule right through the tour.

There was an additional problem to be factored in - the climbing costs of touring, coupled with the fact that Rainbow were a new band seeking to establish themselves, meant they needed to ensure the shows were as fully subscribed as possible. To boost initially sluggish ticket sales, the decision was made to bring in Thin Lizzy, who at the time were riding high in the American charts with their deathless rock classic 'The Boys Are Back In Town' as support. In some East and West Coast cities they were even outselling the headliners.

It was a calculated risk on the part of the Rainbow organisation to have such a happening support band, as Lizzy guitarist Scott Gorham remembered: "We were in crushing form at the time and we really thought we could take Rainbow." To further this aim, Phil Lynott attempted a little psychology on Ritchie. Scott: "Phil and I were at the Rainbow Bar & Grill with Ritchie and John Bonham. Phil got it into his head he was going to wind Blackmore up about the tour. He was going 'Man, when we get on the road we're gonna kick your ass every night!' Bonzo thought it hilarious but Blackmore didn't really know quite how to take Phil's boasting."

The intimidation rebounded when, on the eve of the tour, Lynott fell victim to hepatitis. Lizzy's management reluctantly decided to withdraw from the tour although not before a further wind-up, this time at the expense of Rainbow manager Bruce Payne, with whom the Lizzy crew had already crossed swords over tour arrangements. Chris O'Donnell: "I told Bruce Payne if we didn't get everything we wanted on this tour we were coming off the tour. He said 'Oh yeah?', so I said to our crew 'Pack up, we're going home!' I didn't mention we'd have to pack up anyway as Phil was ill. The next thing I knew there was pandemonium. I'd called Bruce's bluff and he was crapping himself... I don't know how I kept a straight face!" Initially Rainbow covered the loss of support with some extended two-hour shows before Gentle Giant and then AOR-pomp second-raters Angel were brought in to flesh out the package. Some film footage shot at the Houston gig on 10th July was originally intended as a promo, although it is of very poor quality and was never used officially.

The set running order initially remained the same, but following the US dates 'Temple Of The King' and 'Light In The Black' were dropped altogether. To compensate, a version of Deep Purple's 'Mistreated' was included on Ritchie's instigation, although at first it was thought there might be problems with the singer agreeing to perform a Deep Purple song. Ronnie, though, proved to have no reservations: "Ritchie wrote the song and melody, Dave Coverdale just put baby-baby-baby on it! When he wanted us to do it he came up and said 'Eh, Ronnie, would you mind... if we played 'Mistreated'?' Ritchie was so meek about it as he didn't want to hurt my feelings."

Then Rainbow, at last, switched their efforts to the UK. The group debuted at the Bristol Hippodrome (with Stretch as support) on 31st August. Early arrivals outside reported overhearing a full version of Purple's 'Lazy' during the soundcheck. Ritchie realised that, as in the US, Rainbow needed to reach as many fans as possible in Britain: "They wanted us to do all these big gigs, Wembley Empire Pool and all this shit, but we don't want to go like a big band, we want to go in medium and do a few small-type places... They wanted us to do just London... I'd rather do ten gigs top to bottom."

A festival at Cardiff Castle on 10th September was pencilled in, the running order including Queen and Status Quo, but was ultimately pulled as the size of the venue did not allow the full rainbow stage set-up to be used.

They then got caught up in local politics prior to the Edinburgh concert. The Playhouse's electrical generators were sabotaged by a group of local residents angry at the recent high noise levels, and the show was delayed for an hour while repairs were completed.

Word of the band's gigs had by now travelled fast and several 'names' were in evidence at the two Hammersmith Odeon shows, including several members of Queen (long-time admirers of Blackmore's work), most of Colosseum, Ian

Hunter, Scott Gorham, DJ Alan Freeman, Dave Edmunds and old muckers Roger Glover, Ian Paice and Jon Lord. Ritchie courted further controversy at Birmingham - noting the heavy-handed attitude of two front-stage bouncers during his guitar-trashing he proceeded to throw the remnants into the crowd next to said heavies, pinning them against the stage in the crush. Blackmore then completed the lesson by pouring beer over the hapless pair.

With Deep Purple's recent disintegration, Led Zeppelin's self-imposed exile and Black Sabbath's pharmaceutically powered dive into mediocrity, a huge gap now existed in the heavy rock market and Rainbow had the perfect opportunity to fill it. Now enjoying the freedom total control gave him, Ritchie's renewed passion transferred to the live shows. His confident performances had the crowds treating the gigs like ritual service and even some sections of the previously apathetic rock press were now grudgingly searching for superlatives. Not only was the guitarist's reputation now elevated to iconic levels, but Ronnie James Dio also became lauded as an 'overnight sensation'. Proof of his ability was never more evident than with his interpretation of 'Mistreated', where his efforts often eclipsed the David Coverdale versions (the reader is invited to compare the *'On Stage'* version with the Whitesnake take on *'Live In The Heart Of The City'* and make his or her own mind up).

Cozy also basked in acclaim as a hard-hitting, ferocious yet skilful drummer, a superb exponent of double bass drum technique. Many a young rock drummer now aspired to become another Cozy Powell and red sparkle Ludwig kits began to proliferate among up-and-coming bands, no doubt to the satisfaction of a man whose lucrative endorsement deal was rumoured to be worth almost six figures a year. Jimmy Bain performed in a solidly workmanlike manner, serving to anchor the sound while instrumental mayhem often reigned around him. Tony Carey's exploits as a rhythm-section-oriented keyboardist complemented the live guitar work well. His solos showcased both nimble dexterity and virtuosity, although his occasional tendency to overplay could intrude during Ritchie's solo spots.

The shows started with a tape of Judy Garland singing 'Over The Rainbow', after which the band blasted into 'Kill The King'. This proved a storming rocker written around the time of the tour rehearsals (early lyrical versions were dubbed 'Got To Get Away') and yet to be committed to vinyl. Ronnie: "That song was written especially for the stage show. We felt we didn't have a song that was hard enough to open the show, so we put this song together. It's about a chess game - just the basic idea to checkmate the king or kill him. But you can read into it whatever you want." Jimmy Bain: "I was involved in the writing of that with Cozy, that was the first band thing we did. Had I still been in the band I'd have got (a writing) credit for it."

Ritchie explained the track from a musical perspective: "The riff was just a very fast one, which is my typical type of block chord in G - and it's just a very frantic up-front no-nonsense number." Thereafter, depending on Ritchie's mood, songs were improvised to varying degrees around their basic musical structure - much as had been done in Purple, although now with more emphasis on the lead guitar.

Blackmore's performances ran the whole gamut of technique and emotion. From heavy metallic chord riffing and Hendrix-like sonic bombast to quiet, delicately articulated runs and medieval doodling, Ritchie rarely failed to impress even the most cynical. 'Mistreated' was followed by 'Sixteenth Century Greensleeves', 'Catch The Rainbow', and 'Man On The Silver Mountain' leading into the epic 'Stargazer' and finishing with a lengthy 'Still I'm Sad', which provided a vehicle for keyboard and drum solos. Cozy's solo spot, first developed while with Jeff Beck, evolved over the years into a full- blown interpretation of the '1812 Overture', complete with drum riser, classical backing tapes (of the Minneapolis Symphony Orchestra), cannons and assorted pyrotechnics!

For 'Catch The Rainbow' Blackmore often reduced the mesmerised audience to a hush with subtle, introspective flights of the imagination extending the intro to the track for up to 10 minutes at a time. The lengthy solo during 'Mistreated' was at times simply inspirational, a prime example of a superb technician in complete command of his craft. 'Man On The Silver Mountain' often featured 'Blues', a simple blues refrain used as an effective change of mood first developed during his latter days with Purple, and often prefaced a guitar and keyboard question-and-answer segment.

What tends to be forgotten nowadays is that the band had a sense of humour. Blackmore allowed neither musician nor audience to take things too seriously. Depending on the guitarist's impulse, a few bars of assorted nursery rhymes, folk-song whimsy or classical pieces crept into the set (snippets of 'Starstruck', 'Lazy' and 'Smoke On The Water' also featured). 'Stargazer' lost a little in a live environment, principally due to the absence of orchestral accompaniment.

In those days before such technological advances as MIDI and digital samplers, the guitar was left to carry the riff unaided, the density of the studio cut being displaced by a much sparser sound, although Ritchie's sonic slide solo finale would often compensate for such shortcomings. A short, sharp ultra-heavy 'Do You Close Your Eyes' usually formed the encore, rounded off on a good night with some frenzied guitar destruction by Ritchie while the band churned away behind him. (Specially modified Fender Stratocaster seconds were sacrificed, glued back together and re-used the next night!) It was felt that with the sheer quality of concerts up to now that some ought to be taped with a view to a live album release at a future date.

Chapter 2

On the 13th September, Blackmore was an unusual guest for offbeat proto-punk art-rockers The Fabulous Poodles at the Speakeasy, along with Ian Hunter (although Ritchie only proceeded to get into an epic fight with a barman!) The Poodles, noting that neither of their special guests had offered to contribute to the cost of the sound gear as tradition demanded, dedicated a song called 'The Wrist' to the pair of them for some time afterwards! The 16th marked another Speakeasy appearance for Blackmore, this time with his old mentor Screaming Lord Sutch.

Rumours abounded at the time that Tony Carey had been sacked and then reinstated. Carey, nicknamed 'The Rash' by the rest of the band, had become the butt for many of Ritchie's pranks from early on in the tour. "Tony was a bit cocky," Cozy readily admitted, "and if you got like that with Ritchie that was it. We made his life a misery, to be honest!" These wind-ups were taken in good heart initially, although Blackmore, ably abetted by Cozy, frequently overstepped the mark. Others in the entourage could also be on the receiving end. During an overnight stop in Fresno, Jimmy's sense of humour was sorely tested when he awoke to find his hotel bed alight.

Jimmy remembered how the pranks sometimes backfired: "I remember Cozy scaled the side of this hotel in Germany and he had this fire extinguisher and he let it go. But he'd got the floors mixed up. He was supposed to be letting it off in Ian Broad's room, but he let it off in some German salesman's room. We were all woken up and ejected from the hotel!" Ronnie remained remote from these goings-on, principally because Ritchie knew the singer had a similar 'take-no-crap' attitude to himself: "He couldn't get away with it with me. If he'd had treated me that way, I'd have taken my talent somewhere else. I'm a person, and I need support and love."

Tony Carey on the other hand endured his bosses' practical jokes with gradually declining tolerance as the tour progressed. Carey was seen to leave the dressing room at the end of the Newcastle gig with a two-fingered farewell to the rest of the band. What happened next is unclear - a session player was rumoured to be ready to step in during October, but things did not work out and Carey continued, for the moment at least, as part of the band.

An extensive European foray followed in late September and October, supported by lascivious tyro boogie merchants AC/DC. Ironically, the young Australians had recently incurred Ritchie's displeasure ("...a new low in rock'n'roll"). Ritchie's request to get up and jam at their Marquee gig had been declined, apparently because AC/DC still held a grudge over a run-in with Deep Purple's roadies during the Sunbury Festival in early 1975. Favourable opinions were not unanimous regarding the concerts - the Swedish press amazingly slating the Stockholm show as "too noisy"!

The end of this leg of the tour was celebrated in typical Blackmore fashion. In Paris tour agent Eric Thomsen was stripped naked and strung up on a trapeze wire high over the stage during the concert!

The gig also saw Cozy and Ritchie swop instruments. Ritchie recounts that: "The audience were so boring - it was about the third number - I got on drums, Cozy got on guitar, and we started playing 'Peter Gunn'. The audience went crazy. They wouldn't clap because we were awful, and then we did 'Peter Gunn' and they thought we were wonderful! Only in France..."

Some Australian dates for November followed but several shows experienced crowd trouble - particularly at the Sydney show on the 16th when the band did not return for an encore. Ritchie's excuse was wickedly witty; owing to the recent local fuel shortage he couldn't obtain any petrol with which to cremate his guitar!

Deep into a solo spot in Adelaide, Tony Carey suffered several well-aimed jabs from the wings of the stage by an unknown assailant armed with a broom handle - Dio then promptly charged onto the stage riding said implement. The support for most of the tour was Australian group Buffalo, who before the tour had decided to split up once the support dates were completed. So unsurprisingly they were determined to enjoy themselves in their final days.

At Sydney's Holdern Pavilion, Ritchie's private dressing room was adjacent to one occupied by Buffalo. When the Buffalo entourage kicked into noisy party-mode,

Chapter 2

Blackmore launched a telephone directory over the partition and hit roadie 'Yogi' Harrison. The enraged Harrison pounded on Ritchie's dressing room door, which was tentatively opened by an unusually timid Blackmore. After a tirade of abuse, Ritchie meekly apologised and withdrew back into his room. It was only later that Harrison realised he had just abused one of the world's leading guitarists and got away with it!

Japan was next, the band's debut there being on 2nd December at the Tokyo Sports Centre, during which the band left the stage after the opening song in order to let the over-enthusiastic crowd calm down. The Kyoto show on the 10th witnessed the brief return to the set of 'Light In The Black'. More end-of-tour mischief ensued; at one show Carey's drawn-out intro to 'Stargazer' prompted the rest of the band to set up chairs at the other side of the stage and start to read newspapers.

The fun didn't end there - on 15th December their hotel was besieged by hordes of screaming teenage girls - though to everyone's disappointment they were looking for the Bay City Rollers, who were touring Japan at the same time. After nine highly successful concerts the band finally flew home on 17th December. Further to the German shows, Martin Birch had taped some of the Japanese dates with a view to releasing a live album exclusively in the Far East.

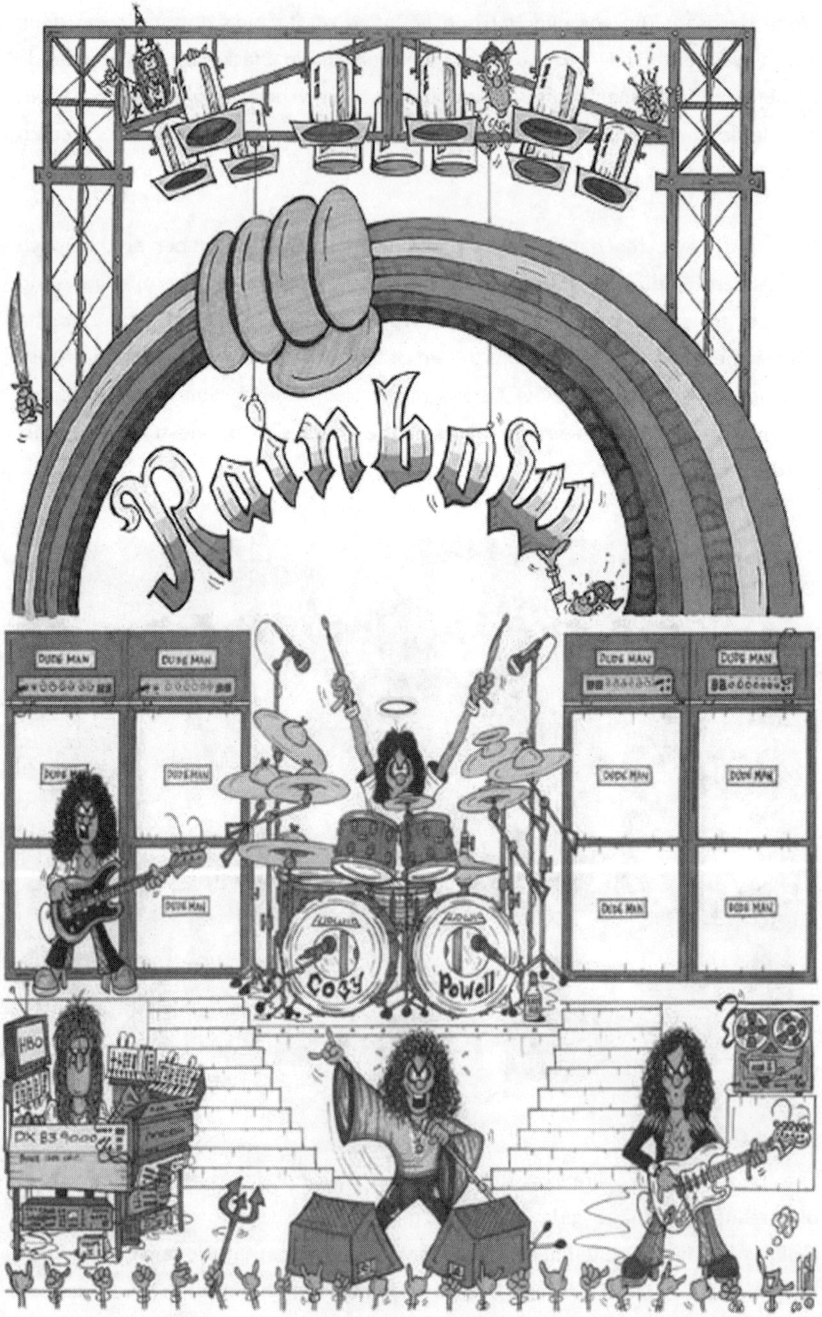
Rainbow
DUDE MAN
COZY
POWELL
HBO
DX 83 9000

Chapter 3

THE RISE AND FALL
(1977-1978)

OVER THE CHRISTMAS PERIOD, as Rainbow took a breather, Tony Carey and Jimmy Bain were informed they were no longer part of the band, although no official announcement was made. Bain got a call from Bruce Payne on 3rd January saying his services were no longer required, with no reason given for his dismissal. The astute Payne urged both musicians to hang around in case Ritchie changed his mind.

Blackmore was, apparently, unhappy with the bassist's ability: "Jimmy Bain was a great guy, fantastic person but his bass playing left a little bit to be desired." Jimmy confronted Blackmore about his sacking soon after: "When I got fired I was in shock. I went over to see him and he couldn't really give me a reason why he got rid of me. The decision had been made and I guess he thought he had to stick with it."

Both musicians had been under no illusion when they joined the group that they were regarded as hired hands and therefore 'on a wage'. The remaining trio had the main say in business and artistic matters and took a corresponding cut of the profits. With this in mind, their dismissal somewhere along the line came as no real surprise. Cozy elaborated: "I had to take an interest in the business side - they were looking to me to get things together, Ritchie just didn't really want to know."

Of Tony Carey's sacking, Blackmore said: "There were too many personality clashes with him, we just didn't get on. Musically he was very aggressive, but it carried over into his personality... There are certain sacrifices I'll make to have my music played properly but there's a point at which I have to take other factors into account." In February 1977, after the usual round of rumours, it was finally officially announced Bain had been axed for "not complementing the style and direction of the founder members." Insiders speculated Ritchie maybe also objected to being called 'Baldy' during an on-stage flare-up triggered by Jimmy's bass sounding out of tune! Bain voiced his frustrations: "Cozy used to say to me whenever I got uptight, cool it, you're only a sideman... It really got on my case he should say that - I was putting 100 per cent into Rainbow.

"One of the reasons I was asked to join was because I could write songs. The only people who ever got their songs recorded were Ritchie and Ronnie Dio although everyone else could write... I would have liked it to have lasted a bit longer than it did because I thought Rainbow was just on the verge of being

Chapter 3

one of the top five bands in the world...but I enjoyed every minute!"

Apart from the official press releases, Blackmore usually maintained a diplomatic silence about sackings. Rock hacks seeking an exclusive on the latest round of sackings could usually expect little more than a wry smile and a softly spoken "You know why!" Blackmore remarked years later with classic simplicity: "As soon as I discover that a musician in my band is not good enough he has to go, because I would expect to be kicked out of a band if I didn't play well." Although Craig Gruber was temporarily brought back into Rainbow (for all of four weeks!) he was soon replaced with former Uriah Heep and Tempest bassist Mark Clarke who, during the late sixties, had been a member of virtuoso drummer Jon Hiseman's jazz-rock band Colosseum.

Both Heep and Colosseum were contemporaries of Deep Purple during this time and Ritchie could not have been entirely ignorant of his existence or abilities. Clarke left Heep after only a few months to re-join Hiseman in June 1972, this time in a new endeavour called Tempest. Now playing rather more commercial straight-ahead rock, the band survived a couple of years but lacked real identity. Coincidentally, Clarke wrote a track for Tempest in 1974 called 'Stargazer'(!) that blatantly stole the riff to Deep Purple's 'Sail Away'. The virtuosity within the group was never in doubt, though, his fluid bubbling bass lines complementing guitarist Allan Holdsworth's technically flawless guitar-work. After guesting on Heep's Ken Hensley's solo album, Mark formed his own band under the moniker Natural Gas (which included several members of Badfinger and the ex-Humble Pie drummer Jerry Shirley).

He ran across Ritchie again when their respective bands shared rehearsal facilities in Los Angeles. Following the release of their decidedly average and poorly-received 1977 eponymous LP, Natural Gas appeared a commercial dead end. With Clarke about to put the band on ice, Ritchie offered him the chance to join Rainbow, remarking at the time: "I need somebody who can play things on bass as quickly as I play them on guitar." He considered Mark "...very good technically, and he's got a strong songwriting ability as well."

Munich's Musicland studio was again the hoped-for venue for recording the next album, which, to build on the vibe created so far, had been provisionally scheduled for a summer '77 release. However, this time the enterprise seemed ill-fated from the outset. Musicland was booked solid for several months ahead - at a time of severe taxation of high earners by Britain's Labour government, many bands were advised to record abroad - and it fell to Cozy to spend several time-consuming weeks trekking around a multitude of recording facilities throughout Europe, trying to find somewhere with a sound comparable to the German complex.

The controversial Château d'Herouville near Paris was eventually chosen, Cozy Powell claiming to have had the casting vote: "We liked the drum sound there." The Château had been previously patronised by David Bowie for his patchy *'Pin Ups'* LP, the Mahavishnu Orchestra for their valedictory 1976 set *'Inner Worlds'*, Pink Floyd for 1972's flaccid *'Obscured By Clouds'* and immortalised by Elton John's *'Honky Château'* release. While all this was going on, Dio filled in time with a session on backing vocals for David Coverdale's *'Northwinds'* album, appearing on the track 'Give Me Kindness'.

Left-right:
Tony Carey,
Blackmore,
Powell,
Dio,
Mark Clarke

Work on Rainbow's next opus commenced early in May, with Martin Birch again in the producer's chair. To record the necessary keyboard parts Tony Carey had been re-hired earlier in the year, albeit strictly on a session basis (he was never even listed on the album credits). This time, little in the way of material had been worked out in advance, so the creative process revisited the more spontaneous approach of in-the-studio, ad-hoc composition the guitarist had experienced with Deep Purple. Initially things went well but ideas and inspiration quickly faltered. Ensconced in a soigné French castle during the onset of glorious spring weather meant maintaining sufficient motivation to work was difficult. Ritchie told reporters: "We found after six weeks we'd done hardly anything - basically we're really lazy and if we can find a good excuse for not recording we do... I suppose the fact that we played football every day for ten days before we went into the studio didn't help to get things going."

The Gothic ambience of their surroundings seemed to invoke bad vibes. Ritchie: "At the studio we found that anything we did in the daytime always worked, but at night things would always go wrong. Some nasty stuff was at work. So we had to change our routine and work as fast as we could before the sun went down. If we recorded on channel 6 the playback would be on channel 13. The 24-track machine started working on its own." With a long-standing fascination for the occult, Ronnie and Ritchie attempted further investigation. A series of seances were arranged, with startling results.

Ronnie: "Ritchie was always the instigator, but he would never take part. Usually, it was myself and a roadie called 'The Ox'. The tape was always breaking while we were recording 'Gates Of Babylon', so we had a seance. Someone requested to speak to Chopin, who had owned the Château, and although there was nobody near it a piano in the room went 'boing!'... everyone fled!" Mindful of Blackmore's penchant for a wind-up, the duo crept back into the studio late one evening to check the tape machine out, only to find the tape mysteriously playing by itself.

At a subsequent seance, the 'spirit' whizzed the glass around the Ouija board so fast no-one could keep up! Dio: "Most seances will swear at you or use bad grammar, but this one said 'I am Baal, I create chaos. You will never leave here, don't even try.' We tried again later, and the spirit asked 'Where's Blackmore? Oh never mind, here he comes.' The door opened and in walked Ritchie! Even he turned ashen... I thought this was the last seance for me, as soon as it began. 'I am Baal, I create chaos.' I was fucking out of the room!"

Mark Clarke had his first taste of playing live with Rainbow through a handful of club gigs arranged in an effort to gel the band as a unit. "I only did a few gigs... One of them was in L.A., off-the-cuff. We also did a gig in Paris one night. We just showed up at this club and played. There was this other one... we played two songs and Ritchie smashed up the guitar and then just walked off and it wasn't even his own guitar... The guys in the band went 'What?' I could see Ritchie's roadie paying the guy out... that's how it was with Ritchie." (The guitarist in question is thought to be from Australian band Stampede, whose album Ritchie had been impressed with.)

Whether Ritchie came away wholly satisfied with the bassist's efforts is not known but concerns certainly arose during recording. Cozy recalled that, whenever they tried for a take, Clarke would often end up out of tune: "The red light used to go on and he'd go 'Stop, I'm out of tune.' He'd get this tuning key and go 'ding'... he was getting a little uptight, he'd bend the neck before the start of the take, just enough to put the bass out of tune. So he didn't last very long." Mark explained many years later: "I just remember being there for three months and it just wasn't working out, simple as that... There were no hostilities whatsoever... He [Ritchie] has very set ideas and that's fine - that's how he is."

Whatever incompatibilities there were they led to Clarke's departure in late May with just three backing tracks completed. Not surprisingly, given Carey's re-instatement, Jimmy Bain was the man approached to step in: "I knew they had a bit of difficulty replacing me. They gave me a call and I said 'I don't really think so.'" In the absence of an alternative, Blackmore went on to record all the bass parts for the album himself, overdubbing Clarke's efforts with the exception of what became 'Long Live Rock'n'Roll'.

The bassist's departure further delayed progress of the album, leading to more pressure on the band from an increasingly impatient record company. The lack of continuity thus far led to ideas being knocked into shape on a spasmodic basis while casting around for suitable personnel and arranging auditions. The lack of focus was never a good way to record an album, but as Ritchie admitted: "There was too much friction going down - but a lot of that was down to me."

As recording continued slowly through June and into July, Tony Carey was becoming increasingly isolated from the other members. Cozy: "At this time he was going into his room, spending six or seven hours sitting in his room with a pair of cans on, playing his keyboards... by that point he'd already worn out his welcome a little and started to get distant from the band." Ritchie and Cozy broke up the routine by amusing themselves with a series of practical jokes. After stoically tolerating falling roof beams, suddenly shattering windows and booby-trapped door knobs, Carey telephoned his father to cable him funds for an airline ticket and he fled the Château without warning, exiting the band for good.

Various unsuccessful legal proceedings to obtain outstanding payments due to him ensued (it was said that initial charges of attempted murder were quickly dropped!). Interviewed in the early eighties, Tony looked back on his time with Rainbow: "I was 21, everybody else was a hundred and twelve. I was definitely the kid. I caught a lot of flak for being the kid, in many different ways. It was a learning experience for me, it showed me how to play bigger things... it took me out of the garage band sort of network, as it were. A couple of the gentlemen that were in the band with me I still respect and admire today - a couple I don't."

Meanwhile, tapes for the proposed live album were edited and mixed by Martin Birch during March 1977. The double *'On Stage'* (proposed titles had included *'Chase The Rainbow'*) was released in July, and, at £6, was a pricey set for the time. The album conveniently filled the gap prior to the next studio effort, still far from completion. But to those present at the pulsating live concerts, *'On Stage'* quickly revealed itself to be very much a cut-and-paste job. Song introductions, solos and segments of improvisations were edited; sections of songs from other shows spliced in and the drum solo cut out completely.

The running order was altered to fit four sides of vinyl, the final album - incredibly, for a double set - clocking in at a derisory 64 minutes (Genesis' own double-live LP, *'Seconds Out'*, released a few months later, clocked in at a value-for-money 93 minutes). This meant the crowd-pleasing 'Stargazer' and encore 'Do You Close Your Eyes' were omitted. Precise sources of the performances were not listed, but on the whole were said to originate from the Japanese dates.

Further information remained sparse for many years, but recent careful analysis seems to suggest the first minute or so of 'Kill The King' is from Tokyo (the evening show performed on 16th December 1976) and the rest from Munich (29th September 1976). 'Man On The Silver Mountain' combines the early and late Tokyo shows of the 16th December, while 'Catch The Rainbow' is a largely unedited version from Hiroshima on the 14th. The edited 'Mistreated' came from the Cologne concert (25th September). '16th Century Greensleeves' appears unedited and featured the version aired at the evening Tokyo show, while most of 'Still I'm Sad' would appear to come from Munich.

Ignoring these edits, the album served to give a general representation of the excellent quality of performances on the tour. Especially memorable were the storming 'Kill The King', the lengthy guitar improvisation in the middle of 'Mistreated', and the prolonged keyboard and guitar interplay during the extended 'Blues' section of 'Man On The Silver Mountain'.

Polydor realised that the versions of familiar songs were simply too long for general radio play and issued a maxi-single unique to the UK featuring the live 'Kill The King', along with appropriate edits of 'Mistreated' and 'Man On The Silver Mountain'. Released later in the year and with minimal promotion, the single even managed to creep into the lower reaches of the British charts. In Germany a rare DJ-only promotional album of edited tracks was issued, interspersed with some eight minutes or so of an entertaining Blackmore and Dio 1976 Australian interview. The mid-eighties' compact disc version of *'On Stage'* is unique among the Rainbow back catalogue in that it was the first CD release to be re-mastered - resulting in a warm and formidably beefy sound.

In order to finish off the LP, the expected process of holding auditions for two new musicians and then rehearse the band for the scheduled British tour for September was postponed until later in 1977. It was said that tentative approaches to Jon Lord at around this time proved fruitless (he was still embroiled with other projects) and so the search continued for a keyboard player. Given Blackmore's standing within the business and his reputation for technical exactitude, there was no shortage of applicants, some with an impressive list of credits.

Among those considered were Matthew Fisher (ex of Procol Harum, and a former Lord Sutch 'Savage' with Ritchie), Eddie Jobson (Roxy Music/Curved Air) and Mark Stein (Vanilla Fudge/Tommy Bolin). Ritchie, however, bemoaned the lack of a player with a style he considered appropriate for the band: "The problem is finding someone who could play organ - it's really a rhythm instrument, but nobody seems to realise it." Surprisingly given the credentials of some of the candidates, a virtual unknown was hired. Canadian David Stone had become involved in recording work and played on the Ontario bar circuit soon after leaving school in 1969. He joined Symphonic Slam, a trio based loosely around an ELP/Atomic Rooster 'prog' style, formed by American guitarist Timo Laine. "Slam were my first major group, we cut an album [*'Symphonic Slam'*, A&M, 1976, recently reissued by Musea on CD] and were fairly popular in Canada... it was the first time I played to audiences of nine or ten thousand. Things went well for a while, but then business declined and we

Chapter 3

began to lose money. Timo went back to California."

On joining Rainbow, he commented: "Ritchie happened to hear us on the radio at the time he was looking for a keyboard player. He was taking shots in the dark at the time, trying to find the right guy, and he flew me down to L.A. to do an audition. He had a lot of people there but in the end he picked me because I was prepared to be as flexible as he required. The trouble is Ritchie wants a player as familiar with his music and antics as Jon Lord was."

The gruelling auditioning of some forty bass players saw 27 year-old Australian Bob Daisley complete the line-up in August. Originally part of early-seventies Antipodean progressive band Kahvas Jute (who yielded one now ultra-rare LP *'Wide Open'*), he came to the UK looking to form a band. Unlike Jimmy Bain, he boasted an extensive career pedigree. In 1971 he had replaced John Glascock in mercurial blues guitarist Stan Webb's Chicken Shack, before going on to work with Broken Glass, Mungo Jerry (where he played on three hit singles) and various others. He became a free agent again after the implosion of his latest employers, the erstwhile 'supergroup' Widowmaker. Their second LP (*'Too Late To Cry'* on Jet) had flopped as badly as their self-titled debut and had led to the band's swift termination. Daisley's patient toleration of the notoriously riotous Webb presumably made him an ideal choice for the increasingly erratic Blackmore.

Left-right:
Dio,
David Stone,
Bob Daisley,
Blackmore,
Powell

Ritchie remembered his recruitment: "Bob was the best bass player we could find and we looked for ages. There aren't a lot of people who want to play straight rock. When the good guys come along they're into this very hip jazz thing. To me there's no 'chance' involved with jazz - you've got so much there to deal with." Ritchie's penchant for bassists who used a pick also meant Daisley was preferred to the finger-style players proliferating at the time. Bob could also write and appeared to be an astute addition to the band.

A snatched week of rehearsals in September at The Who's Shepperton Studios (where they somehow conspired to blow up the dry-ice machine and damage the rainbow's computer) allowed the band to click, and the new line-up debuted with 40-odd dates around mainland Europe through the winter of 1977. As with the recording of the album, the tour was dogged with controversy. Not only was the initial show in Finland cancelled after the equipment was held up at Finnish customs but in Norway a riot ensued in Trondheim. Dio: "Our road crew and the band got into a fight with the audience! We were taken away from our hotel, deposited at the airport and told never to come back!"

Liverpool Empire, 5th Nov 1977. Ritchie appeared in one of the boxes playing guitar before demolishing his instrument and tossing it over the edge. Rainbow were banned from the venue.

The Vienna show saw Ritchie arrested and fined £5,000 for kicking and breaking the jaw of a bouncer he saw beating back fans from the front of the stage. Ritchie: "The security was made up of policemen... the guy went down, and within moments all exits were blocked. During the encore I ran off stage and jumped into a flight case that a roadie had ready for me... The crew told them I had run to the railway station, and my pursuers went there on motorcycles. My roadies rolled me outside and, just at the moment they were putting the case on to the truck, two policemen wanted to check the contents of the case... a few seconds later, I had won a nice stay overnight with full board. I was kept for a full four days. I felt like a prisoner of war!"

The only full concert footage of the early line-up was filmed at the very next gig in Munich on 20th October and broadcast by Germany's Rockpalast TV series. The show, arranged for the 19th, was put back a day. With Ritchie arriving late at the venue after being released from custody, Kingfish inflicted an extended support set

Chapter 3

on everyone, and the headliners finally appeared - to a reduced audience of a few hundred - at midnight. (Dio introduced 'Long Live Rock'n'Roll' as "a message we are trying to give to the world... except for Austria!") This video footage has been repeated several times on European television since and remains commonly available on bootleg video.

The performance is indicative of the standard of the shows during this time and, although it doesn't quite reach the peaks of some 1976 shows, is still well worth obtaining. (Watch for the moment in 'Do You Close Your Eyes' when Ritchie opts out of his usual mid-song guitar smash, but instead returns abruptly to the main riff, catching Ronnie napping who, in a panic, rushes back stage-left just in time to sing the next verse into Daisley's backing mike - only to realise he's totally lost in the sound mix!) British dates followed in November (Kingfish were again support) of which the second night at the Manchester Apollo saw arguably the finest Rainbow UK concert of any line-up.

With the further ground swell of support resulting from the most intensive tour schedule so far, the band now found themselves in a potentially tricky position. They had to try to balance the set's introspective moments with heavier material in order to satisfy both established fans and the newer head-banging faction. Compared to the last tour certain sections of the audience did appear restless during the quieter passages, although shrewd song structuring and judicious arrangements tended to ensure there was something for everyone. On the whole, this balancing act succeeded, though as a consequence it meant little on the new album could be slipped in without radically disturbing this balance.

Evidence from live recordings indicate that progression came from the improvisational variation based around the already established songs in preference to the introduction of completely new material. For example, the reprise of 'Night People' during 'Man On The Silver Mountain' where the structure and lyrics were ad-libbed from show to show. The set list thus remained identical to the previous tour apart from the inclusion of 'Long Live Rock'n'Roll' (though the middle portion unfortunately developed into a rather corny audience singalong) at the expense of the more demanding 'Stargazer'.

As for the new members, David Stone's expertise was difficult to judge, his efforts tending to be buried in the mix for much of the time. Apart from the usual 'Blues' segment, the occasional guitar-keyboard face-off at the start of 'Long Live Rock'n'Roll' and the established 'Still I'm Sad' intro/solo, he tended to be less demonstrative

Left-right: Daisley, Stone, Dio at Den Haag, 4th October 1978

than his predecessor Carey. Bob Daisley performed well enough, but added little extra to the overall sound and had no great on-stage presence. December was taken out from touring for one final album session at Herouville, with 'Rainbow Eyes' substantially re-done and 'Gates Of Babylon' the ultimate track to be recorded - certainly a case of saving the best until last. David Stone apparently contributed significantly to the latter track, but was never given a writing credit.

An extensive Japanese tour kicked off in early 1978 to a rapturous reception. The clamour for tickets meant an increased number of dates, though a lack of venues with adequate capacity meant promoters booked gymnasia and other such buildings for the concerts. The lack of proper safety facilities at many venues led to the tragic - but, with hindsight, unsurprising - death of a teenage girl crushed during the crowd's surge to the front for the encore at the Sapporo concert on 27th January. The death marred what had been a highly successful tour.

When *'Long Live Rock'n'Roll'* was finally released - almost a year late - in April 1978, it consolidated the band's position at the forefront of the heavy rock genre. With shorter, more commercial-sounding tracks and a cleaner, crisper sound, the standout was paradoxically 'Gates Of Babylon', a sprawling epic very much in the mould of 'Stargazer' (this time the featured classical musicians were the Bavarian String Ensemble). Ritchie told Guitar Player magazine it contained "...the best solo

Chapter 3

I've ever done, because it's the most intricate solo, yet at the same time it's not clinical. It wasn't just 24 bars of just playing E. They were strange chords, diminished-augmented - it was great."

A faithful version of live favourite 'Kill The King' was another highlight, while the Arthurian tale 'Lady Of The Lake' featured an unusual and innovative single-note guitar solo that fooled some into thinking it was actually played on keyboards. 'L.A. Connection' harked back slightly to the old Elf sound and was inspired, lyric-wise at least, by the sacking of Tony Carey. The title track's chorus owed a little to the Chuck Berry song 'School Day' and was certainly the most commercial song attempted so far, even cynics admitting the infuriatingly catchy hook had chart potential. Thus 'Long Live Rock'n'Roll'/'Sensitive To Light' was released as a single in March 1978 in advance of the album and did indeed give Rainbow a taste of UK chart action, getting into the mid-thirties.

The riffing rocker 'Sensitive To Light' borrowed heavily from Purple's 'Lady Double Dealer', while the ballad 'Rainbow Eyes' promised more than it delivered, revisiting the material of 'Catch The Rainbow' but failing to match its majesty. Many fans commented on the similarity to some of Hendrix's work, to which Ritchie admitted: "the inflection of playing fourths. Jimi used to play a lot of fourths." In hindsight the song was a surprising inclusion given Ritchie later stated several demos of ballads along similar lines had been written with Ronnie but rejected. "Because of the way I write lyrically, I find it difficult to do ballads" explained Ronnie, "I like to write more from real life and put into another situation." Ritchie said: "I started finding out he couldn't do a power ballad. He started going into a little girlie voice, and that used to bug me."

A track, 'Night People', had been reported earlier in the year but was not on the album. (According to Cozy: "All that really was a kind of a jam... Ritchie played chords, we all followed, and Ronnie came out with whatever came into his head... it never got finished.") A further outtake was rumoured to exist: 'Streetwalking' appeared on early studio reports but turned out to be a working title for what became the behemoth stomp of 'The Shed (Subtle)'.

The album was not as obviously groundbreaking as its predecessor. This was understandable given the status of its predecessor. Here the overtly deliberate approach meant the LP paled in comparison to the spontaneous intensity of *'Rising'*. The sporadic nature of the sessions didn't help either - this meant promising ideas evident on the LP remained underdeveloped without a creative continuum in which to mature - if they had then the album may well have matched the overall quality of the previous one. But most of the tracks on *'Long Live'* still sound surprisingly fresh many years later, having stood the passage of time somewhat better than some efforts on the first two releases.

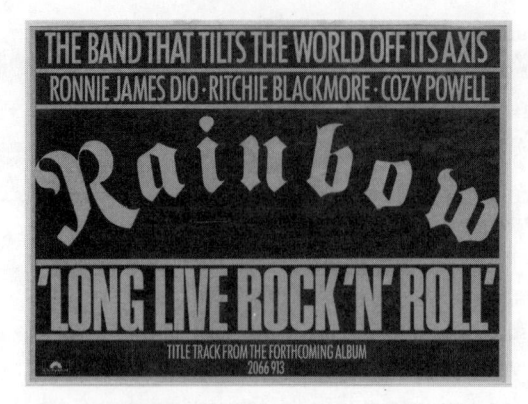

Ronnie Dio, though, was critical of the results: "It was an unhappy LP from my point of view. I saw Ritchie going through some changes that I realised were going to affect me for the worse as well as the others... I always find it kind of bitsy if I have to listen to it these days... there were some good songs but nothing that stands out." Yet, for all its faults, many followers have come to consider the album the obvious alternative to *'Rising'* as the definitive Rainbow album (Kelly Jones of The Stereophonics for one).

The 'No Thanks to Baal' note on the sleeve originated from the series of seances held during the sessions, while the original gatefold inner sleeve of a rather anonymous rock audience was in fact a suitably doctored photo taken during a Rush concert. 'L.A. Connection' gave further chart exposure with a Top 40 placing in September 1978.

The most extensive tour yet was planned to promote the new album, with over 40 dates booked in North America through the spring and summer of 1978. In order to gain optimum exposure and reach as wide an audience as possible, the plan was to occasionally play as support to a big-name band before then returning to headline the same cities later in the schedule. Ritchie explained the strategy at the time: "The other markets came first, Europe and all that. We took advantage of it rather than just playing around America as a small-time band. Now the only market left is America and we're the underdog. We're sharing the bill in some places. It's not like starting again, but its just something you do."

Chapter 3

Initially this was with REO Speedwagon, with openers No Dice, but coupling the rather laid-back soft-rock balladeers with the more intense Rainbow was bound to cause problems and as the tour wore on so relations between the bands and their entourages rapidly soured. Much to their chagrin, REO Speedwagon found themselves frequently upstaged by Rainbow, whose hour-long sets roused increasingly vocal audience reactions. In some cases, once Rainbow had finished their slot, supposedly sold-out venues ended up a third empty by the time REO appeared on stage.

Rainbow's musicians' natural tendency to improvise freely meant they often over-ran their allocated time. This prompted REO's manager to turn on the house lights before the end of the set one night, spoiling the atmosphere - the stage crew breaking up the ensuing backstage ruckus. Tales also did the rounds about Rainbow's crew mounting a 24-hour guard on their pyrotechnic set-up to prevent possible sabotage by the REO roadies. The 24th June show in Atlanta (now supporting the far more accommodating REO Speedwagon) was recorded by the BBC for syndicated transmission on American radio as the BBC Rock Hour, appearing on numerous bootlegs ever since. The broadcast and BBC transcription discs featured the complete hour-long set of 'Kill The King', 'Mistreated', 'Long Live Rock'n'Roll', 'Man On The Silver Mountain' and an epic 23-minute 'Still I'm Sad'.

It was on this US tour that Ritchie's reputation for irascibility - first established during Deep Purple days - was enhanced ten-fold. Interviewed by Sheila Prophet, the journalist's opinionated questioning annoyed Ritchie enough for the poor woman to suffer a particularly merciless Blackmore wind-up. This resulted in her penning the now infamous 'Bitchy Ritchie' article that subsequently appeared in the UK music press. Henceforth Ritchie was forever typecast as a 'moody bastard' (among other less flattering epithets) that reporters interviewed at their peril.

Following the final dates of the US tour in August 1978, the now-inevitable purge saw both Stone and Daisley depart in Blackmore's continuing search for musical perfection. Commented Dio: "David, though a great player, was just wrong for the band." The recruitment of Bob Daisley was partly to help on the creative side, so his dismissal before he had any real chance to contribute to the writing process seemed puzzling.

Rainbow was now at its peak of popularity as a band, featuring heavily in reader polls throughout the music press, both collectively and as individual musicians.

The group appeared on the verge of major global success. Yet this was against the backdrop of the recent British punk 'revolution' and in stark contradiction to the supposed obsolescence of the music Rainbow and bands of their ilk had been championing. Following that fated summer of 1977, such bands found themselves dismissed as irrelevant dinosaurs by British journalists who just months before had been singing their praises but who were now desperate to distance themselves from the old order and appear tuned-in to this happening 'new wave'.

The rest of Europe and America saw punk rather more pragmatically, as a natural progression from the attitude-heavy garage rock pioneered by American bands like the New York Dolls, MC5 and more recently The Ramones. In the UK, however, opportunistic impresarios seized on the style and transmogrified it into a lucrative subculture based around an anti-intellectual, anarchic stance with pretensions more towards music as a component of lifestyle. The mythical notion of British punk triumphantly sweeping away rock's so-called 'boring old farts' was initiated by the UK music press and unthinkingly parroted to the present day. The truth, for those with open minds, remains inescapable. The overnight annihilation of heavy and progressive rock never quite happened. For years after many promising young rock bands struggled with a record industry focused on finding the next Sex Pistols or Clash, many established rock combos (Zeppelin, The Stones, Queen, Pink Floyd and Rainbow) continued to flourish.

If evidence were needed that the rock establishment still had its fanbase, it was the now-diminished but unceasing media obsessions with a possible Deep Purple reformation. Originating with former Purple manager John Coletta, one story was whispered about to the press that plans were laid to do several shows in Spain, offering fans an all-in-one holiday package deal of flights and accommodation along with concert tickets. A TV link-up with most of Europe was also proposed. Another tale had it that a festival in Japan was being arranged, with all the Purple spin-off bands providing support.

Yet more gossip told how Purple were to be one of several bands reforming to play a festival on London's South Bank to mark the Queen's Silver Jubilee celebrations. Ritchie was reported to have agreed in principle to a reunion purely as a one-off for old time's sake, parallel to his involvement with Rainbow. However, once beyond the initial planning stages the whole affair became mired in legal disputes and profiteering. But this was only the initial movement of an accelerating Deep Purple-reunion bandwagon.

Chapter 3

As the seventies wore on, the record industry boomed. The decade up to 1979 had seen album sales hit record levels and, although punk somewhat predictably imploded, disco took up the commercial slack. The adolescent Western and Oriental audiences with an ever-increasing disposable income feverishly consumed the whole range of contemporary vinyl product. Within a rock context, the likes of Fleetwood Mac, Peter Frampton and The Eagles were prime movers of what was now termed 'corporate rock', purveying a brand of critically despised yet hugely popular softer melodic rock, particularly in the USA.

Keynesian economics informs us that boom is often followed by bust and so it proved with the record industry. The upheaval within the music business would be caused not by any sudden exciting artistic shift but by the mundane but far more fundamental effects of impending economic recession propelled by the oil shock of the late seventies. The knock-on effect on record sales first felt in 1978 had an impact upon many bands' validity and aims, Rainbow proving no exception. As the recession bit deeper a drastic reassessment was forced on many record labels' financial expenditure. *Chez* Rainbow, this period signalled the most fundamental shift in the group thus far and would have far-reaching effects.

Up until now, Ritchie had by and large financed the band out of his own pocket, drawing from his earnings when with Deep Purple and from the considerable royalties accrued since. Much of his business affairs were still handled by the same people within the Deep Purple organisation (although the Rainbow management had been taken on some years before by Purple's former US booking agent, Bruce Payne). But it was an arrangement that could not continue long-term, particularly after the death of Purple's accountant Bill Reid which left the money-related affairs of the ex-Purple members in varying degrees of chaos.

While the recent exhaustive tour had firmly established Rainbow in both Europe and Japan, support in North American was limited mainly to the East Coast cities. Other areas - particularly the midwest - remained unconquered. Ronnie Dio recently speculated on mid-western indifference: "We were more of an underground band here. Trends are different in America. The trend at the time was not for a band like us. But there are no trends in Europe. In Europe, they accept you for what you are. Especially because we were a classical kind of band and because Ritchie had a great reputation, they just jumped right on top of us over there.

"Over there, we were playing in front of 20,000 people at a pop. It was a real trendy time, and we perhaps didn't fit into the trend. It took a while for Rainbow to be recognised for how good it was. We never had a problem in New York. They were ready for it. But it was harder in the mid-west. New York was much more in tune with what was going on in Europe. I don't think it had anything to do with the material because all these years later, people yell out 'Play 'Stargazer!', 'Play 'Man On The Silver Mountain!'... It was just the climate of the times."

Although the band was based in the US (Ritchie had relocated to New York from California around this time), the guitarist had gone on record as stating he wasn't interested in continually flogging around North America for little or no return. But with the last world tour costing out at over £300,000, it was plain that, whatever Rainbow's artistic worth, the band had to tap the US market or die. The key to this midwest Eldorado around this time was with the emerging multitude of regional FM radio stations whose patronage could be highly influential in breaking a group into the big-time. Up to now, Rainbow's strident sound and extended format songs meant little of the material was deemed suitable by most major stations for airplay. Blackmore pondered this situation and decided to move towards a commercial style more palatable for radio.

He was also wearying of the band's current direction, commenting: "I was very angry at the time but I got to *'Long Live Rock'n'Roll'* and it had all gone and I suddenly thought where do I go from here?... I wanted to become a little more commercial. There's something about being played on the radio... something about that that maybe feeds the ego. I wanted to come across to the public and the fans at the same time. You don't want to lose the hard-core fans but you do want to capture the other side, the record-buying public."

To consolidate this proposed direction, some fresh ideas and a different perspective was needed. To this end, Ritchie surprised many in contacting ex Purple cohort and former writing partner Roger Glover with an offer to help write and produce the next Rainbow album. Although Glover had left Deep Purple back in mid-1973 he had maintained strong links with the Purple organisation as A&R and in-house producer for the Purple Records label. Always fascinated by the engineering side of the business, he moved into production full time, becoming involved with (and in some instances also recording with) such acts as Nazareth (yielding three Top 20 singles in 1973), Judas Priest, Status Quo and Rory Gallagher.

Chapter 3

In addition to these activities, Roger's first major solo work came about with *'Butterfly Ball'*, based on an award winning children's book of poems by William Plome, lavishly illustrated by Alan Aldridge. The production company British Lion (who had filmed Jon Lord's *'Concerto'*) proposed putting together a musical based on the book. Former Purple manager Tony Edwards was approached and suggested Roger as a candidate to compose the music. The venture inevitably snowballed; in addition to a final album, a 26-part TV cartoon series and full-length feature film were planned. Roger started work in June 1974, with help from fellow musicians and friends like Eddie Hardin, Ray Fenwick, Mo Foster and Les Binks.

The intention was to record with a wide range of singers and styles in order to convey each different animal character. Ronnie James Dio sang on three tracks in addition to co-writing two with Roger, while other contributors included Glenn Hughes, Tony Ashton and David Coverdale among others (and Judy Kuhl, the future Mrs Glover). The album was recorded at Kingsway Studios and released in December 1974.

One of the tracks featuring Ronnie was put out as a single and did very well: 'Love Is All', released in November 1974, became a No. 1 in Holland, Belgium and France. Unfortunately, though, the whole undertaking fell between two stools; rock fans saw it as aimed purely at a juvenile market, while the promotion of the project was insufficient to gain wide exposure with the more middle-of-the-road music public. Given the available finances, the project was very quickly down-sized to more realistic proportions; the film and series were cancelled, although a live concert performance of the album was arranged in a last-ditch attempt to raise flagging interest in financing the cartoon. An animated promo for 'Love Is All' was completed, apparently at astronomical expense. This cost notwithstanding, it was a shame the project was not followed through if the excellent quality of the animation was anything to go by. Meanwhile, three weeks of intensive rehearsals for the live concert quickly turned into a logistical nightmare.

The charity gala at the Royal Albert Hall went ahead on 16th October 1975 and saw the welcome return to live work of Ian Gillan, replacing the absent Dio who was now hard at work with Rainbow. Ronnie: "The live show deviated too much from the original concept. I wasn't too keen on the idea, so when Roger asked me to do the show I passed. I talked it over with him and he respected my opinion." A film of the concert was made and distributed later as a supporting feature in cinemas around the country. Unfortunately the often excellent performances featured in the concert footage were spoilt by the film company taking the liberty of interpolating some embarrassing footage of dancers lumbering around in animal costumes into the live Albert Hall action! The cartoon promo was also added. A concert video was released in the eighties but was soon deleted.

A return to writing and playing during early 1977 at Munich's Musicland yielded Roger's first solo album in April 1978 entitled *'Elements'*. The album had started out as a traditional rock album, but became based around four lengthy instrumental passages (vocals were kept to a minimum) representing each of the planet's elements of fire, earth, water and air. "It came from a poem I wrote... I don't know why I wrote it or where it came from... I'm not sure I understood what it meant, but I felt I had to interpret it through music."

Roger not only wrote the whole album (originally to be called *'Eyes Of Omega'*) but played most of the instrumentation, with help from Mickey Lee Soule, session drummer Simon Phillips and the Munich Philharmonic, also co-producing the finished article with Martin Birch. The material was weak and rather uninspiring in places. Although sounding what might be classified these days as 'Ambient' or 'New Age', *'Elements'* had at times little direction or purpose (Mike Oldfield has a lot to answer for!). No plans were laid to follow up with live dates, primarily because the LP sold so poorly. Then along came Ritchie Blackmore.

An offer to write again with Glover had been referred to by Blackmore during an interview as early as the summer of 1976, but nothing else seemed to have come of this. They had maintained links post-Purple, sharing the same manager in Bruce Payne. Ritchie's more recent approach was something of a surprise to Roger, given what had gone on between them with Purple. "I went to see them live in Chicago and talked to Ritchie. All the past was kind of forgotten. I didn't bring it up, and he didn't, and I felt good in a way that he was looking for me to help after what had happened in 1973." And so after some deliberation, Glover came back on board.

In 1996 he recalled how the offer was perceived as an admission that Ritchie had underestimated Roger's contribution to Purple and now belatedly realised his worth: "This was his way of saying he was wrong and my value, although he hadn't seen it at the time, he'd seen it since in the work I'd done. Also I'd kept my nose clean and hadn't spouted off to the press about what a bastard he was, and that I'd had some success, he had a respect for me that hitherto he hadn't. This was what I felt - whether this is true I don't know - but somehow it was a redemption."

Chapter 3

"I felt he'd be a barrier between me and Cozy, to stop us fighting and channel our energies more creatively," explained Ritchie, some years later. "Roger is very good with his patience, at helping people achieve something. His worst downfall is his ear for the mix - I don't think he knows what a good sound is!" Writing for the next album commenced immediately, and with the new commercialism in mind it was suggested to Dio that his 'sword and sorcery' lyricism would be inappropriate this time around. It was becoming increasingly obvious to Ronnie that, with Roger in the band, the close creative relationship he enjoyed with Ritchie was compromised.

"Roger became Ritchie's conduit, so he came to me and told me what Ritchie would like, that could I stop writing in such a fantasy-orientated way and write some love songs... The new direction was to write about more factual things, it was to be love-song orientated. Now I don't write that way, I won't write that way, but I tried to persevere in the band even though under those sorts of conditions I wasn't much of a contributor to what was going on."

Furthermore, other things were bugging the vocalist. Through the early days of the band both Dio and Powell were content to let Blackmore take the plaudits (and brickbats) but, more recently, they had both become dissatisfied with the popular perception that Rainbow was still essentially a Blackmore solo project. They felt that their collective contributions were not getting the recognition they deserved - either artistically or financially. Ritchie takes up the story: "I remember being in the studio and he came in with Cozy... he poked me in the back... 'We're not standing for this. You're on the cover of Circus magazine and it was meant to be the three of us... We're not going to be sidekicks.' I suddenly saw him in a whole different light. That was it, I knew we'd finished then because I couldn't talk to him. I saw him as this angry, bitter little man."

Dio openly admitted his unease: "I set out to be the best I could with the people I was working with. Ritchie took the credit but he also took the flak... that's what happens. My anger was the fact that Rainbow, through most of its days, has always been looked upon as Blackmore's Rainbow, and we were never told it was going to be that way. In 1976 we were assured that the band would be simply Rainbow, but it never happened. I was very disappointed with that, in fact everyone in the group was, especially Cozy."

These rumblings of discontent, allied with money arguments, resulted in inter-managerial niggles (Ronnie's personal manager, Wendy, was now also his partner) which did nothing to unite the band. Cozy commented on the erosion of relationships: "Obviously they were two very strong characters, and inevitably something was bound to give. I think Ronnie wanted his own band, to be the focus of attention, and inevitably there was bound to be a problem at some point... Ronnie was unhappy in Rainbow because he thought he was the star and wanted the limelight. Most guitarists and singers are like that."

Ronnie and Ritchie came to a mutual agreement that the vocalist would leave the band in order to put his energies into a solo career. Ronnie summed up the situation some 10 years later: "Ritchie decided our future lay in America and that's where the unhappiness and discontent stemmed from. Rainbow became a pop band and that wasn't what Ritchie and I had conceived of at the very beginning... Ritchie was desperately searching for some level of success in the States and total commerciality was the way to achieve it. It was a shame but he was wrong; Rainbow should have gone harder, heavier." In a 1982 interview, Ritchie reflected on their fruitful four-year relationship: "Ronnie was so good at producing lyrics and coming up with tunes... I could give him a vague melody and he'd know what I wanted... after he left, things went a bit sour. I was always close to Ronnie until he met up with Wendy, then it got strained after that. She was a nice enough woman, but we didn't really click."

Dio's departure was made public in January 1979. The exit of one half of the fundamental core of Rainbow - without doubt the most drastic change within the band to date - now served to firmly label Blackmore finally and definitively as a particularly capricious employer (the fact Dio left on good terms was conveniently ignored). Personnel turnover thereafter tended to grab the headlines, often at the expense of the band's music. Future articles in the press invariably centred on whom was in - or out of - the band. Ritchie did little to contradict this: "It's almost a vampire thing," he explained in 1980. "I feed on the blood of musicians passing through, and when the blood's dried up I get rid of them. I'm looking for the perfect line-up, like everyone's looking for the perfect woman."

The effort to radically change musical direction not only contributed to Dio's departure but would eventually result in Cozy Powell's resignation in 1980. David Coverdale had tried to coax Cozy away to Whitesnake in early 1979, but the drummer had declined, preferring to see how things panned out with Rainbow's fresh direction before considering his other options.

Chapter 4

ALL NIGHT LONG

(1979-1980)

SCEPTICS MAY GASP but, in the limbo following Ronnie's departure, the name at the top of Blackmore's short-list of likely replacements seems to have been - of all people - Ian Gillan. Ritchie turned up at the singer's house during a Christmas blizzard, but although warmly welcomed by his ex-protagonist, the guitarist ultimately failed in his efforts to persuade Ian to join Rainbow. Gillan countered the offer by asking Ritchie to join his own band instead (one can only speculate how long the partnership would have lasted had either accepted). As a goodwill gesture, a guest encore appearance with Gillan's band at the Marquee took place before Ritchie returned to the States (Glover was also at the gig but declined to play).

In December 1978, the band had at least managed to recruit ex-Cozy Powell's Hammer and session journeyman Don Airey on keyboards. Hailing from Sunderland and a graduate of the Manchester College of Music, Don turned professional in 1972, learning his craft on the cabaret and cruise circuit before joining Hammer in 1974. When Hammer folded, Don played on numerous sessions before, in May 1975, joining his guitarist brother Keith as a member of Jon Hiseman's revamped outfit, Colosseum II. They cut three albums of rather anodyne jazz-rock of the *'Return To Forever'* stamp between mid-1975 and December 1978, and also co-operated with the Lloyd Webber brothers to compose 'Variations', the Paganini-derived theme to the UK's long-running TV arts programme The South Bank Show.

Developing the earlier band's sound into a much more accessible and mature style, they promised much. However, Colosseum II was a prime example of a band in the wrong place at the wrong time. The late seventies were certainly not conducive to souped-up jazz-rock (however powerful or technically inventive) and the band was always going to struggle. Don had also recently contributed to Gary Moore's 1978 solo *'Back On The Streets'* and Black Sabbath's *'Never Say Die'*. "Cozy phoned and asked me to come over to New York and audition," Don recalls. "I went to Ritchie's house, played a couple of bits of Bach to him, and then we messed around with a piece that eventually became 'Difficult To Cure'. After that, Cozy, Ritchie and I sat in a rehearsal room for three weeks in December 1978, working on the music that would become *'Down To Earth'*. Then, to my relief, just before Christmas and the day my wife phoned to say she was pregnant with our first child, they offered me the gig."

The search for a singer continued while material for the next album was written and demoed by the band, once more comfortably settled into a French château (this time Le Château Pelly-de-Cornfeld) and utilising the Maison Rouge mobile

Chapter 4

studio for recording. Rainbow announced their arrival with a bang, Blackmore's roadie Ian Broad crashing the band's Jaguar into the main entrance and nonchalantly asking the stunned receptionist for a room. The usual pranks were soon under way, Don initially being the target. "When we were recording in the Château I was in this bedroom that was called The Chapel. It was a very spooky room and there were all kinds of noises going on. I went in there one night and as I pulled the curtains there was a ghostly, hooded figure behind the curtains - I just ran out thinking I'd seen something awful. In fact it was just Cozy! But he was dressed as a monk; it was pretty frightening. I wouldn't go back in there and I was hearing all kinds of things. It was just the band playing tricks on me, and eventually Ritchie came over and said 'I've got a tape I want you to learn.' He played all these sound effects I'd been hearing. I never felt such a fool in my life because they really had me going! There was a great atmosphere in the band, it was like a kind of family."

For recording, Cozy christened his new Yamaha custom drum kit. Roger commented on the renewed partnership with Ritchie: "He's the kind of guitarist who can only play what he writes. Unless you give him a song that is totally finished, he has to have the freedom to write his own parts. It makes things a little more difficult at times..." Roger also explained his modus operandi as Rainbow's freshly-installed producer: "Every producer has his own style. There are some that completely dominate and don't let the group have any say whatsoever and others that let the band do exactly what they want. I fall somewhere between the two. I listen to everyone but, basically, I have the final say... I also like to see Ritchie just open up and let loose. Sometimes when he's tuning up he plays the most brilliant things - then, when it comes to a solo, they're not there."

Fifty or so singers had sent in tapes and, with time pressing, the more promising half-dozen or so candidates were flown out to try out over the next few weeks while the band worked on the backing tracks. Ritchie: "We were auditioning other singers, and it was costing two thousand dollars a day for the mobile. So we were in a castle spending a fortune, and we didn't have a singer. We'd come down to breakfast at one in the afternoon and there'd always be a new guy sitting at the breakfast table." Among those unsuccessful in their efforts were Geordie (and future AC/DC) vocalist Brian Johnson, Ralph Thomson, former Lone Star frontman Kenny Driscoll (who had also worked with Gary Moore) and Eazy Street's Maltese singer Marc Storace (later of Krokus). Don also remembers another candidate. "There was one terrifying man who was from the North East and he'd been in the

SAS. A very nice man, but he just assumed he'd got the gig. He was walking around going 'I'm really gonna enjoy this' and of course he never even got to sing because it was obvious he wasn't cut out for it."

Trapeze vocalist Pete Goalby auditioned (although initially he took some persuading) early in the year, and even got as far as recording a few vocals for the album in Geneva. He finished 'Since You Been Gone', although his efforts were reportedly later erased and, by February, he had been fired. Ritchie: "We found the singer we had recruited for the job couldn't sing above a top A... so we sent him away... A good lead singer is hard to find - and they're very difficult to replace. I do have to relate to a vocalist. I think the problem is I expect them to have a range of five and a half octaves... I want to be able to write a song with all these octaves available."

Around this time former Sensational Alex Harvey Band's Chris Glen was rumoured to have tried out for the bassist job. Ritchie had also been chasing sometime Jethro Tull member John Glascock but he turned down Blackmore's overtures. Jeff Beck's former bassist (and Cozy's band mate) Clive Chaman was tried out briefly before Jack Green (ex of The Pretty Things and, briefly, T Rex) was found. He was employed on a probationary basis at the start of the album sessions, but did not appear to fit in well. Ritchie: "The rest of the band all hated him! He was in Rainbow a week and I've been friends with him ever since." This friendship led to a rare Blackmore session for Green's solo album 'Humanesque' (RCA), released in the spring of 1980.

With the lack of any other obvious replacements and with time pressing, Roger took over bass duties in time for recording. Although this was agreed at the time to be a purely temporary arrangement, in the eventual scheme of things it soon assumed permanence. "Don heard him play and said 'Roger plays really well...'" Ritchie explained, "I went 'He's all right', then all of a sudden he's on bass... But it wasn't something that was worked out." Roger revelled in his return to playing in a band once more: "I joined after a jam in my home in England... it was me, Cozy, Don Airey and Ritchie. It was such a great jam that I naturally fell back into bass-playing again. Cozy and I got along really well, as bass and drums should, and so I started again. It took me two weeks to hit form."

Chapter 4

Most of the backing tracks were well underway by the time the search for a vocalist finally ended in April. With the more usual avenues now exhausted, a near-desperate clutching at straws commenced. Don recently related how fate took a hand: "How we found Graham was amazing. It was just Cozy playing 'guess-the-single'. He had all these tapes and he just went 'what's this?' You'd have a millisecond of it, get a bit more, but one night we heard The Marbles' 'Only One Woman'. What happened to that guy? Wonder where he is? That's how we found him." Further investigation revealed the lead singer to be one Graham Bonnet, a fellow who, serendipitously, Roger had been involved with on the session scene.

Graham was surprised at the interest, having never even heard of Rainbow before. "I got a call from Roger Glover saying would I like to audition for Rainbow. I said 'who?' I was more into the R&B thing and pop stuff. So this was an opportunity to do something a bit different." With hindsight, the enquiry had some ominous signs. In Blackmore's words: "Roger spoke about him to his producer and got all these positive replies, but he could sense a catch... he could sense there was something missing. But he flew in to join us and started singing and he did great. He did 'Mistreated' really well."

Left-right:
Blackmore,
Powell,
Graham Bonnet,
Don Airey,
Roger Glover.

Born in 1947 in Skegness, on the barren Lincolnshire coast, Graham Bonnet had started singing at an early age: "I modelled myself on Helen Shapiro - when she was 15 I was 11, she had a deep voice for a girl... and I used to sing in the same way. I sang all her stuff until my voice broke. I used to have a two-octaves range - now I have three and a half." Bonnet's first musical forays were with local groups the Blue Sect and a jazz collective called The Skyliners. By the late sixties Bonnet had teamed up with cousin Trevor Gordon to form The Marbles (Bonnet on vocals/guitar, Gordon on keyboards/vocals). A residency at London's Revolution Club followed, where Bee Gee Barry Gibb spotted them.

Gibb invited the duo to meet impresario Robert Stigwood and they were duly signed to Polydor, the first single becoming a instant hit - 'Only One Woman' in October 1968, written by Barry Gibb and backed on the record by The Bee Gees themselves (this was the track Ritchie had remembered). Their second single, 'The Walls Fall Down', was also moderately successful. An eponymous album featured several of the Gibb brothers' compositions. (Collectors should seek out for a copy as a lucrative investment!)

Other, less successful singles followed: 'Whisper In The Night' (a Roy Wood song) on RCA, 1973's 'Trying To Say Goodbye' (by Neil Sedaka) for RCA, and 1974's 'Back Row In The Stalls' on DJM. Graham had joined Southern Comfort in 1972 as touring bassist, but the gig was short-lived. This was followed by a brief dalliance with acting in the shape of a leading role in an obscure low-budget film 'Three For All'.

Bonnet turned down an offer to join the Electric Light Orchestra in 1975, and returned to recording with several (now rare) singles and a self-titled solo album on Ringo Starr's Ring O Records label in September 1977. A poppy, almost disco-flavoured effort, it did nothing in Europe but, like the singles, was successful in Australia where it went gold. Personnel included Mickey Moody on guitar and the brilliantly maverick ex-King Crimson drummer Mike Giles. Follow-up *'No Bad Habits'* had rockier pretensions in comparison to the first and was again an Antipodean success. It also boasted a tenuous Blackmore connection in the shape of former Outlaws drummer Mick Underwood, who performed on the record.

Once in the Rainbow camp, Bonnet was immediately put to work. Roger Glover had already written lyrics for some tracks, and described them - with tongue firmly in cheek - in the following way: "I thought the hard-rock quality was lacking, and it lacked sex - as sex is the most potent form of excitement, I tried to introduce tit into the music!" This left Bonnet to work out and record the melody lines. Graham: "One tune would be written probably four different ways with four sets of lyrics and we would pick the best parts and put it all together... which is why it took so bloody long!

"I was basically told what to do... although I did write with Roger I was never credited... Do you remember 'All Night Long'? Roger wrote all the lyrics, but the tune was partially mine. I was a fool and didn't say 'Wait a minute... I wrote that.' The same happened with Don Airey - he wrote a lot of the arrangements and was never given credit for it."

Things did not run smoothly recording-wise either: "I just didn't get it together vocally. I felt down and strange. It was the place - it was like a haunted house... and I said to Roger 'I can't do it, mate' - the vocals were all wrong, so I guess I don't like castles. I remember Roger put me in this Château in the dining room or whatever it was and we tried to do vocals in this room... it just didn't work. It wasn't right and we didn't know what we were doing. We had no songs as such, just grasping at straws, and it really needed to be done 'in the office' so to speak instead of the middle of the countryside..."

Bonnet and Glover therefore hopped on a Jumbo and relocated to the more conventional surroundings of Kingdom Sound Studios on Long Island to record all the vocals. It was a move that won the singer's immediate and enthusiastic approval. "I can't explain it, I just love to be in a proper work area and [the Château] just didn't feel right to me. But as soon as we went into a studio then it started to happen."

Blackmore, in retrospect, saw these initial problems with the singer as indicative of more serious difficulties Rainbow would encounter in the future: "We started recording with him and Graham's going 'I can't sing... I have to be in a studio.' We're going 'But we're in a castle in the middle of France, it's fantastic!' That was the first thing with him. Then it got out of control - 'I'm not feeling too well today.' We're going, 'We'll do it tomorrow.' Then the next day came, then the next and the next, and it went on and on."

The first single was deemed vitally important to establish the band's new direction and was intended to heighten their profile with a greater cross-section of the record-buying public. The song, chosen some months before, was a cover. 'Since You Been Gone' had been written by former Argent guitarist Russ Ballard and been previously recorded by South African all-girl group Clout (who had a big UK hit with 'Substitute'). The song had also been covered by US band Head East. Ritchie explained: "I first heard that at my manager's house, and he asked me what I thought of the song. I said it was a hit, and wanted to do it, and he was quite surprised. I did 'Since You Been Gone' because I thought it was an extremely good melody, and I listen to it now and feel quite proud of it."

Roger agreed with Ritchie, though Cozy harboured serious doubts, complaining that its overly commercial nature was the antithesis of what he had always considered Rainbow to be about. (Such was Cozy's objections that, during recording, he refused to run through the drum part more than twice.) But the choice of tune was vindicated when, during the late summer, the release became a massive smash in most markets except, ironically, the supposedly sovereign American FM radio-driven market.

The old axiom of 'being in the right place at the right time' was underlined by the timing of both single and album, which appeared as the rock world was going through a significant evolution. From the US, the revolutionary guitar technique of Eddie Van Halen had brought the 'axe-hero' to the fore again, while in Britain the vacuum left by punk meant a new generation of metal bands was fast approaching, made up of musicians raised in the traditions of heavy rock but possessing a fresh approach.

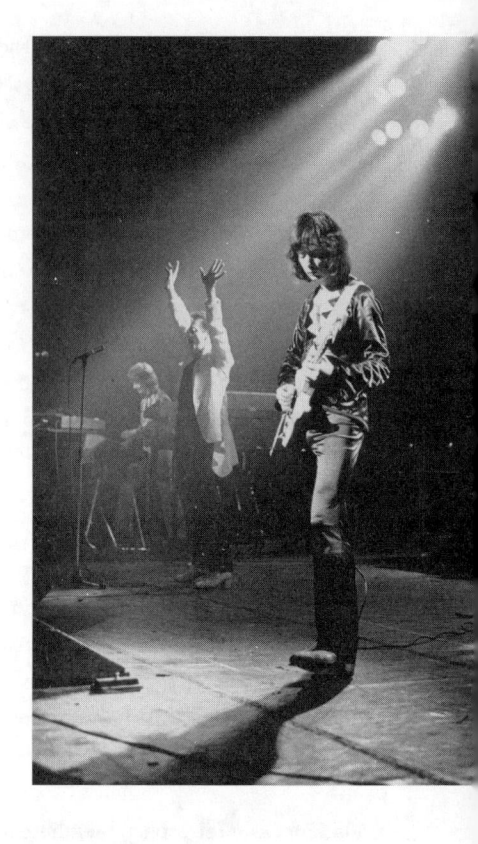

In the years around the turn of the decade this upheaval gained serious momentum, and for a few brief months even found favour as the 'hippest' musical genre with the media who, with their love of pigeonholing music, dubbed it the 'New Wave of British Heavy Metal'. A whole clutch of young musicians weaned on Purple, Zeppelin and the like took the hard-rock sound formulated a decade before and ditched its more sophisticated or indulgent aspects in favour of a more direct, upfront cutting edge. This time attitude and dynamic energy were as vital as technical proficiency.

Although Rainbow were, in reality, established well before the arrival of this new wave, such distinctions were immaterial to the immediate generation of teenage fans suddenly turned on to hard rock. Blackmore's reinvention of Rainbow meant the Bonnet-fronted line-up were perceived not as a leftover from the seventies but a credible and integral part of the current scene - up there alongside the young guns of Iron Maiden, Diamond Head, Saxon *et al*. The band's change in direction had mirrored the evolving rock scene perfectly. Rainbow was now in the ideal position to exploit this success.

Despite Ian Gillan's oft-quoted criticism of Blackmore's supposed musical insularity - "His favourite groups are Neil Diamond and Abba, I don't think he's even heard of the Chili Peppers!" - Ritchie usually appeared better versed than most with developments within the contemporary music scene. In mid-1980 he played Iron Maiden's first LP to Martin Birch, suggesting he might be the perfect producer for them. The result was a fruitful 10-year partnership between band and producer which led to huge global success.

The new direction thus paid off immediately with the single and was further reinforced by the release of the album in August 1979. *'Down To Earth'* ultimately become the band's most commercially successful album, propelling the band to the zenith of their popularity. Blending elements from the critically reviled but highly successful AOR wave in the US (pioneered by Boston, preserved in aspic by Journey and Foreigner) with the British riff-driven approach, Rainbow were among the vanguard of UK bands peddling an accessible brand of melodic rock within the rapidly expanding 'NWOBHM'. It showed the new hard rock had the ability to produce undeniably commercial material with chart potential, yet still be comfortably defined as 'heavy'.

First listen to *'Down To Earth'* showed the post-punk lessons were well heeded. Tracks were stripped-down and direct, honed towards a focused four-minute blast of high energy. The previous bias towards Blackmore's lead guitar was supplanted by a more rounded presentation. The song was the overriding factor now. What solos remained, while still impressive, were concise and firmly within the song structure. As with *'Rising'*, the impression was of a whole new band and another fresh start. 'Eyes Of The World' proved the only concession towards a more traditional 'sweeping epic' direction.

As a rhythm unit, Glover and Powell meshed as though they had played together for years while Graham Bonnet's voice, although not to everyone's taste, provided the band with the required power and - just as importantly - an immediate and unique identity. Compositionally, the songs seemed consistent but conservative, relying on tried and tested ingredients. In hindsight this was understandable, given the band were feeling their way in both a compositional and personnel sense.

Lyrically, the absence of Dio's mysticism also took some getting used to. Glover's and Bonnet's efforts sometimes failed to avoid the more obvious lyrical clichés of the times. Interestingly, the lyrical content of 'All Night Long' appeared to be inspired by Blackmore: "I'll often think of a theme, like 'All Night Long', which is about seeing a girl off the side of the stage when you're playing live, and she looks nice, so you want to get to know her, and that song was loosely based around that. I had some lyrics for that which I gave to Roger and which he changed around a lot, but I don't usually come up with lyrics at all - I concentrate on construction and I always have a vague melody in my mind."

Although he now admits to cringing at the lyrics, at the time Roger dismissed unfavourable comments over their mildly chauvinistic content. "I had a lot of criticism for 'All Night Long', but I don't think I should have to defend the things I write... a lot of my stuff is a bit tongue in cheek!" These minor quibbles notwithstanding, taken on its own merits there was enough good moments on the album to suggest the new line-up - given time - had a promising future.

The overhauled Rainbow sound was greeted with something approaching abject horror by the more ardent Dio-era (and older Purple) fans, who saw it more as a cynical sell-out to commercialism and the FM-driven lure of the Yankee dollar. From this point on, the Rainbow fan-base would be polarised into distinct factions.

It was the success of the NWOBHM, of bands like Rainbow and of albums like 'Down To Earth' that suddenly woke record companies to the fact that, with little effort past some half-decent promotion, hard rock music, when handled correctly, could be a licence to print money. And so the first half of the eighties saw the commercial golden era for the metal genre. Between 1980 and 1986, up to a quarter of the UK album and singles charts at any one time featured what could be classed as AOR, hard rock or metal acts.

Although the lasting worth of much of what came out could be questioned (particularly the L.A. 'glam' wave that reached its nadir with the likes of Poison), the mass appeal both sides of the Atlantic was undeniable. Over the next few years, the world would witness a glittering shoal of awesomely popular stadium-rock acts

Chapter 4

who carved their own niche within the mainstream market.

As major FM players then, the 1979 Rainbow American tour kicked off in mid-September in a similar fashion to the previous year, this time with a series of dates supporting Blue Öyster Cult. The shortened support set was based around cuts from the new LP, including 'Eyes Of The World', 'All Night Long', 'Love's No Friend' and 'Lost In Hollywood'. Modified (read shorter!) versions of 'Man On The Silver Mountain', 'Long Live Rock'n'Roll', 'Catch The Rainbow' and 'Kill The King' were retained.

The band returned again to various venues during November as headliners, Ronnie Montrose's Gamma providing the support. Bonnet viewed the tour with some trepidation: "I was scared shitless that I wasn't going to be accepted by the audiences who had hair down to their bums - this short-haired yobbo coming up with the Hawaiian shirt on... 'surf's up!'" It was soon evident that, despite the power of his voice on record, this nervousness manifested itself during the live shows. Rainbow's on-stage intensity and sheer bludgeoning volume was not the type of music to do any favours for a vocalist lacking in self-belief. Bonnet sounded uneasy - particularly with the band's older material - with his efforts often sounding throaty and forced.

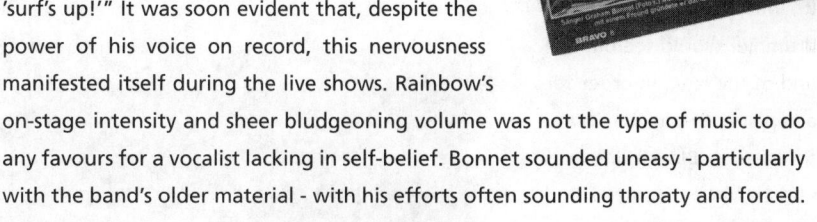

His very different stage presence and singing style to that of Ronnie Dio hardly helped. His tongue-in-cheek flippancy and lightheartedness grated on those used to the earnest intensity of the pocket-rocket Dio. The on-stage unease transferred to Ritchie who more often retired into his shell, failing to attempt the personal highs of previous tours. His live work, such a feature of earlier campaigns, became less improvisational and more restrained this time around. The band's stage presentation was transformed as a result, the group emerging as more of a collective than individual musicians.

Although many of the shows were still enjoyable, this was the thin end of the wedge for the fans who remembered and had revelled in the red-line intensity of 1976. 'Eyes Of The World' proved an impressive opener, while 'Love's No Friend' tended to inspire Blackmore to some of his best work. The lengthy 'Lost In Hollywood' took over from 'Still I'm Sad' as a vehicle for band solos. 'Since You Been Gone' somehow failed to work well and remained largely underdeveloped as a live performance, though 'All Night Long' fared a touch better.

Don Airey proved an asset to the band and, in a live context, contributed more than his predecessors to the overall sound - perhaps because he ensured his keyboards were well up in the mix! Roger Glover undertook bass duties in the same typically undemonstrative but proficient way as with Purple, complementing Cozy's usual impressive efforts as the pair provided the crucial rock-solid foundation to what were sometimes erratic live performances.

The German tour pencilled in for December was cancelled in order to promote the album further in the US. But by now Powell's growing disaffection with the way the things were going musically was reaching boiling point, and finally set the seal on his future with the group. "The whole idea of Rainbow when I joined was not to be a pop band," said Cozy a few years later, "We started to get lighter and lighter... Ritchie and I fell out over a number of points, and I thought it best to leave - it was a mutual decision and he and I are still good friends."

It was agreed that the drummer would see out the end of the tour, in order for a replacement to be found at leisure. Blackmore was said to have contacted Bad Company's Simon Kirke soon after but, if these rumours were true, nothing came of it. Meantime Cozy's Ariola solo release *'Over The Top'* involved a star-studded cast of Jack Bruce, Gary Moore, Clem Clempson, Max Middleton and the now-ubiquitous Don Airey. It was a measure of Cozy's (and indirectly Rainbow's) popularity that the LP proved a very healthy seller in the Far East. Unusually for an instrumental album (and by a drummer, to boot!) it went gold in Japan. Even in the ever-cynical UK it reached a creditable 34 in the LP charts by January 1980.

January 1980 saw Rainbow visit Scandinavia, supported by Reeperbahn and, on the 19th, the band booked into the Sweet Silence studio in Copenhagen to record a B-side. Inspired by his Long Island residence, the superb 'Weiss Heim' ('White Home') was heavily influenced by Bach's Prelude No. 1 from 'Das Wohltemperierte Klavier', with some emotive and poignant guitar work. The instrumental proved a prime example of Roger Glover's ability to draw the best from Blackmore who had been toying lazily with the basic tune over a two-year period, wondering how to proceed.

The live running order now included - at Ritchie's instigation - a version of Carole King's sixties classic 'Will You Love Me Tomorrow'. First recorded by the Shirelles, it was also a legacy of Bonnet's earlier pop repertoire that he had covered for his 1977 album. Roger had collapsed on stage at the end of the gig in Cologne, suffering from a bad bout of flu, while the Munich show saw a backstage confrontation between Ritchie and former Purple singer David Coverdale that culminated in a much-publicised brawl. Given the recent history between the two, this was hardly surprising.

Many of the musicians involved with both Coverdale's Whitesnake and Rainbow had been in numerous groups and sessions together, and were on friendly terms. The respective camps became embroiled in some initially good-natured rivalry as to who could sell tickets quickest, shift the most albums, enter the charts higher, etc. This was enthusiastically seized on and fuelled by the music press (a common practice to fill column inches that saw its nadir in the risible 'Britpop war' of 1995 between Oasis and Blur). Whitesnake apparatchiks sought to fan the flames and goad Blackmore. (Badges spotted at Whitesnake concerts of the time bore the acronym K.R.A.P. - 'Keep Rainbow Away Please!')

During some recent press interviews David had been uncomplimentary - on occasion scathing - about both Blackmore personally and Rainbow as a group, for little apparent reason other than as a further wind-up. His unexpected appearance back stage as the guest of the Munich concert promoter (a fact quickly - and gleefully - passed on to Ritchie by Cozy) so enraged Blackmore that the situation quickly degenerated.

Graham Bonnet had by now assumed the mantle left by Tony Carey as patsy for Blackmore's practical jokes - as demonstrated by the disappearance of a suitcase full of Bonnet's beloved Hawaiian beach shirts and their cremation in a mystical ceremony! The guitarist was also alleged to be behind the super-gluing of all the hotel room locks on several occasions.

In anticipation of the imminent UK tour February 1980, the follow-up single 'All Night Long' was released on the first of the month, matching both the earlier single's commercial edge and chart success. UK dates sold out in a trice and the tour opened in Newcastle on 19th February. By the time the tour got to the UK, the already fragile relationship between guitarist and singer had steadily deteriorated. Ritchie: "We told him 'Graham, your hair is too short, you look like a cabaret singer, so can you grow your hair?' By the time we did Newcastle City Hall, it was actually getting down to the back of his collar. We had a watch on him... and sure enough, he jumped out of the window, ran off and had a haircut. So it came to show time and we went on stage and I was looking at the back of his head with this military-style cut. I was that close to taking my guitar off and just going 'whack' across the back of his head."

Bonnet: "I remember that day my hair to me was like a bloody mess; it was all over the place. If you've got short hair you have short hair. Now people shave their heads and that's kind of cool now, but back then to have short hair wasn't the thing, it wasn't the uniform of a so-called rock singer. Before the gig I went and got my hair cut, didn't say anything to anyone. I came on stage that night. I remember the look of shock on his face, jaw dropping to the floor."

The Wembley Arena concert on the 29th ended in controversy with Blackmore being accused of inciting the crowd to riot after refusing to play an encore. Fire extinguishers and chairs (among other movable objects) were hurled on

Chapter 4

stage and £10,000 worth of damage was caused. Reasons for the band's non-appearance varied, from the support band going down a little too well for Ritchie's liking to Ian Gillan failing to turn up after promising to guest on the encore.

Ritchie later tried to explain: "There's something about the London audience. I feel like slapping them around... it's got to be the venue. The regulars turn up, the 'high society' is there, there's certain holes in the audience where they're not responding... All I felt was rejection - it was like playing in a mausoleum - so I decided not to do an encore." Ritchie's refusal to play the obligatory encore was something he felt strongly about: "I played concerts during which I felt uncomfortable - because we were tired, because we didn't play well, because the sound was bad, because nothing worked.

"During these shows I often refused to play encores. I love to play encores if the feeling is right, but I refuse if the gig is rotten; for me, it's important to be 100% honest." Although the UK performances had met with a decidedly mixed reaction, mid-May saw a six-date tour of Japan where the fans - always among the most loyal - took to the new line-up with little reservation. (The visit even prompted the somewhat bizarre spectacle of Graham Bonnet lookalike competitions.) This was followed by a short spell back in Copenhagen during late May, preparing material for the next album. During mid-1980 Don Airey guested on former UFO/Scorpions guitarist Michael Schenker's debut album, recorded in London with Roger Glover producing.

Glover, Blackmore and Powell; taken during the 1980 European Tour

In the meantime Paul Loasby, the man responsible for the day-to-day arrangements of the recent UK tour on behalf of promoter Harvey Goldsmith, was about to leave the Goldsmith organisation in order to set up his own company. He planned to develop an idea he had for a day-long summer festival dedicated specifically to bands from within the heavy rock and metal genre. He approached Bruce Payne with a proposal for Rainbow to headline the inaugural event.

This was agreed to in principle and the venue chosen was the bleak Castle Donington motor-racing circuit in the featureless countryside of southern Derbyshire. It could hold up to 100,000 fans, was near to the industrial Midlands (where much of the HM fan-base was situated) and had easy access to transport links. Once concerns from the local council and residents had been resolved arrangements were quickly implemented for the event to take place on Saturday 16th August 1980. The rest of the bill was quickly confirmed as a nicely balanced mix of British and International metal and melodic rock: US act Touch - also managed by Rainbow's Bruce Payne - Riot, Saxon, Canada's April Wine, The Scorpions and local Brummie heroes Judas Priest, then just about the hottest ticket in UK metal on the strength of their seminal *'British Steel'* LP.

Prior to the festival a state-of-the-art quadraphonic sound system was brought in and fully tested, performing impressively during rehearsals. Parallel to a Judas Priest sound-check just days before the event, a test for the council of Cozy's pyrotechnics resulted in an explosion heard some three miles away that blew out all the P.A., causing £18,000 worth of damage. Cozy played the incident down: "They (Priest) weren't too pleased - there was a lot of swearing going on!"

Ritchie and the band prepared with three small warm-up dates in Scandinavia between 8th and 10th August. The Malmo show on the 9th was a short hour-long affair. Performed in the open air, it started raining as they went off stage for Airey's solo spot so they didn't bother to come back on! Blackmore promised some surprises for those attending the festival (eventually a official crowd of over 35,000) and fans arriving at the site early enough to catch the sound-check heard a live work-out of 'Weiss Heim' that, regrettably, never made the set.

Arrangements were made to hoist Ritchie up on guide wires into the lighting rig during the middle of the show, but the hoist machine broke down and plans were abandoned. On the day itself, Blackmore prepared with some quiet meditation in a candle-lit tent specially set up in the back-stage area. Cozy Powell remembered: "Being my last show, it was a bitter-sweet festival for me and I was determined to go out with a bang. There was a lot of tension in the air when we took to the stage and, on the night, it was every man for himself."

The event (for once) caught the attention of the more mainstream media and was taped for national radio and TV, Rainbow's performance being broadcast as a BBC half-hour TV special. The time-slot restraints meant some savage and none too subtle editing which robbed all sense of spontaneity from the performance, Ritchie's guitar-trashing in particular appearing very contrived. 'All Night Long', 'Catch The Rainbow', 'Eyes Of The World', 'Will You Love Me Tomorrow', and 'Long Live Rock'n'Roll' were aired along with the guitar sacrifice.

The music weeklies ran true to form in totally misunderstanding the concept behind the event. They had a field day gleefully slating everything and everyone concerned. When Rainbow's UK publicist Jennie Halsall read Melody Maker's scathing review over the telephone to Bruce Payne she was, scandalously, sacked on the spot (she gamely responded: "But I lasted longer than most band members!").

A souvenir album was released in October featuring contributions from each band on the bill (excluding Priest, who had their own live LP out at the time - despite the fact that *'Unleashed in the East'* was, by that time, nearly a year old). The two tracks from Rainbow - 'All Night Long' and 'Stargazer' - seemed strange choices considering the former featured a lengthy irrelevant 'sing-a-long-a-Graham' section while the latter highlighted Bonnet's struggle with the older material. In the meantime, on 20th August Ritchie had encored with flavour-of-the-month, neo-metal glam-rockers Girl at the Marquee for the standard 'Born To Be Wild'.

By the time of the festival Cozy's replacement had already been recruited. American Bob Rondinelli, a 25 year-old former drum tutor from Long Island, ex of New York covers band Samantha, was another heavy-duty stylist from the Carmine Appice school and had recently been strongly linked with Kiss, whose drummer, Peter Criss, had just quit. "I knew I was on the short list, even though I couldn't sing, but as soon as Ritchie offered me the gig I had no hesitation in accepting."

Bob Rondinelli

Ritchie was pleased with Powell's replacement: "He's got a lot of animal instinct, he hits the drums really hard, and he knows why he's hitting them hard. He's got a helluva lot of technique... I saw him playing on someone else's kit which kept falling apart, and I could tell straight away that he was a great drummer." Rondinelli flew over to take up an observer's role at

Donington, and took up his new job with immediate effect.

Thus the last member of what many considered the definitive Rainbow line-up had now departed, and for some long-standing fans it marked the close of the band's most productive era. Cozy became ultimately one of the longest-serving members of Rainbow for several reasons. He was one of the few musicians able to empathise with Blackmore on a musical level, which went a long way to earn Ritchie's grudgingly-given respect. This enabled him to voice his opinions with relative candour. Most importantly, perhaps, Cozy provided Ritchie with a strong musical foil to push him that bit harder. Besides his formidable drumming talents, Cozy had an innate ability to focus band ideas, to be able in an instant to judge the worth of creative efforts and keep things on track.

Ritchie: "Cozy was a very strong character, when we disagreed we really disagreed, this man was fire." Cozy summed up in a nineties interview: "I never had a problem with Ritchie... he can be difficult, but I'm difficult as well, so we bounced off each other... I just felt that a couple of singles were selling out... I didn't think they were right for Rainbow. By then the band had veered off at a tangent... it all started to get a bit thin. A bit like a love affair, we'd grown tired of each other." Whatever the musicians' or fans' view on the merits of each line-up, most were agreed things were never quite the same again.

In mid-1980, comments to the press from several independent sources seemed to suggest that some of the Purple Mark II line-up had agreed, in principle, to a fresh proposal to reform and all that needed to be decided was the timing. The departure of such a central figure as Cozy appeared to have prompted Blackmore to reconsider recapturing former glories. Ritchie was reportedly dissolving Rainbow in readiness to reform Deep Purple with Gillan, Glover and anyone else they could co-opt to make up the numbers - Don Airey, for one, was seriously considered. But events elsewhere conspired to leave this plan dead in the water.

A series of live dates advertised as Deep Purple, during the July and August of 1980 around the US, had sent the rumour mill into overdrive. However, all was not as it seemed and one of rock's better hype stories took shape. This 'Purple' proved to be none other than former singer Rod Evans fronting a band made up of unknown session musicians (and not very good ones at that!). A management company with a reputation for just this type of dubious exploitation was behind the sting. In the light of the resulting furore, the other former members soon twigged that any sort of compromised line-up in the future would draw the same criticism and be unacceptable to the fans.

Legal arrangements now required a minimum of four bona fide ex-members in order to be able to officially call the undertaking Deep Purple. With a reported offer of £4 million for a proposed line-up of Coverdale, Lord, Paice, Glover and Blackmore, it must have tempted all concerned. But, with Coverdale, Lord and Paice happily ensconced within Whitesnake at the time, the idea was dropped.

Indeed Blackmore was himself busy with his own ends - ideas for the next Rainbow album were being tossed around at Sweet Silence Studios, Copenhagen over a six-week period in mid-1980. Engineered by Flemming Rasmussen, at least six backing tracks were taped. Studio progress reports listed 'Gypsy', 'Nightwinds', 'Smoke' and 'Doom' but these were probably working titles for said backing tracks, re-named for the final album. Meantime Bonnet spent time away recording a solo album in America - a contractual obligation arranged before his involvement with Rainbow.

But, out of the blue, soon after the group reconvened for more recording early in September, he quit the band. Graham explained: "It was very unproductive for the next album and nothing was happening in rehearsals. Everybody was bored with each other, Cozy had left the band, Bobby Rondinelli came in playing drums and rehearsals were basically 'Well I don't think I want to be here, shall we go to the pub or something?' There was one song that was written for us by Russ Ballard, 'I Surrender' - the only song there was, a whole song as such. So Ritchie would come to rehearsals and play his bass pedals, do his thing and look around and say 'Have you got any ideas?'

"Don and I played something to him one day. He said 'No - I don't like that.' 'Okay, so what shall we do - is the pub open? Go for a walk. I'm hungry; anything but...' It was very unproductive. So it was an unhappy time too because Cozy wasn't there. We were all kind of friends and it seemed to break up the family a little bit. I started to record 'I Surrender', put down some backing vocals, and I thought 'I'm not enjoying this any more, this is not fun.' I went back to Los Angeles, and they called me up and said 'Why have you gone back home?' I said 'I don't want to do it any more.'

"That's when they said that if I sang the songs I liked on the album, the tracks I liked to sing, they'd get another guy to sing the other ones, whatever they may be. I told them that wasn't really going to work - you don't have two singers in a band, it's like having two guitar players. I don't think that will work, I don't want to do that. Because I had in my mind that maybe I could do something by myself at this point, that was it. I left. I wasn't fired, I left."

Press speculation was that the departure between Bonnet and the Rainbow organisation regarding his image was the main reason for his exit. With his clean-cut, 'James Dean-like' persona, Bonnet was antithetical to the jeans-and-leather, shaggy-maned metal image. This should not have mattered that much, but, with the emergence of the promotional video as an increasingly powerful commercial tool, management quickly recognised the significance of strong, direct and market-targeted visuals and these previously trivial issues began to loom large. (Indeed, even Ritchie felt the need to keep pace - the thinning Blackmore thatch was, allegedly, discreetly supplemented with a hairpiece.)

But the real dissatisfaction with Bonnet was his idiosyncratic personality and lack of songwriting input. For this album it was not expected that Roger Glover would be handling both lyric-writing and production. Although Ritchie later told of Bonnet's inflexibility - "There was no giving on the part of the singer" - Cozy Powell suggested that tales of a total absence of input during his time in the band were not strictly true. 'In fact, he wrote most of 'All Night Long'... they aren't the most inspired lyrics, but it was a hit!"

Ritchie: "Graham was a nice enough guy, just completely lost. In Denmark we asked him how he was and he'd go 'I feel a bit strange, I don't know why.' Colin Hart said 'Have you eaten?' and he replied 'That's it - I'm hungry!'" Roger perhaps best summarised feelings towards Bonnet at this time: "God gave you a great voice, but took away everything else!"

With a solo record to promote and the chance of a promising career courtesy of his now higher profile, perhaps Bonnet saw this as a better option than remaining with the band and putting up with what he saw as all the associated pressure and hassle. One can only speculate on how much more success the line-up could have achieved over the next couple of years with what was, even to their harshest critics, undoubtedly a commercially rewarding formula. In Bonnet's estimation: "If Rainbow had worked at it a bit more they could have been as big as Zeppelin. But Ritchie throws his talent away on stage, and after Cozy left it took a real dive."

Chapter 5

DIFFICULT TO CURE

(1981-1984)

WITH THE SUDDEN ABSENCE of a singer, Rainbow took a short break in the autumn of 1980 as press talk and rumours of possible Bonnet replacements began. One name that briefly cropped up as a possible frontman was 20 year-old Bruce Dickinson, then vocalist with emerging British metal quartet Samson. "There were these rumours I was going to join Rainbow. I got this strange phone call once in the middle of the night from Ritchie's roadie saying 'Are you available?' I'm like, 'Of course I'm available, Ritchie's my favourite fucking guitarist!' But I never heard any more." (Bruce, of course, went on to join Iron Maiden the following year.)

A replacement for Bonnet was confirmed in late September 1980 with the recruitment of 29-year-old Fandango vocalist Joe Lynn Turner. Hailing from Hackensack, New Jersey, Joe had started out in the early seventies with a Hendrix and Deep Purple covers band called Ezra. After leaving college with a degree in education, he went fully professional with Fandango in 1976. "We were good writers, but we didn't know whether to be The Eagles, Kool & The Gang or Bad Company," Joe remembered. "A lot of potential, a lot of talent, but no direction."

Nonetheless the group built up a healthy following on the East Coast circuit, supporting the likes of The Allman Brothers and The Marshall Tucker Band. Between 1977 and 1980 they released four albums of competent soft rock on RCA: *'Fandango'*, *'One Night Stand'*, *'Last Kiss'* and *'Cadillac'*. The latter is easily the pick of the bunch, including their most familiar track 'Blame It On The Night' which has been covered by the likes of Ted Nugent and Rage.

Joe Lynn Turner

Blackmore phoned Turner and, the singer recalls, "told me that he'd heard about me in Fandango and was a fan... He told me he was looking for a new singer and invited me over to a place in Long Island. They played me some of the *'Difficult To Cure'* stuff that was being worked on and asked me to throw some melodies and lyrics over it. Next thing I knew, I was asked to stack some vocals on 'I Surrender'. I then realised they were recording my vocals and wiping Graham Bonnet's... Ritchie then came over with a six pack, cracked open

Chapter 5

a couple of bottles and offered me the job."

In 1998 Joe described what he saw as the reasons behind his recruitment: "Mostly he wanted versatility, that I could offer freshness as well, a different style and slant to the music. He liked the soul in my voice... he liked a real clean, pointed voice." Ritchie agreed: "He had a very melodic voice so he would actually sing la la la and it wasn't aaaaargh!... if you don't have melody you don't have anything, and Joe Lynn Turner had a lot of melody; he could be in different moods but there was something about him I really liked. He was kind of innocent, in a way."

As the band reconvened in Copenhagen in November to finish the album, Joe's demonstrative, ebullient and excitable character (along with his talent for mimicry) was interpreted as cockiness by some in the crew who, upholding the finest Rainbow traditions (and no doubt prompted by a certain guitarist!), decided to 'initiate' their newest recruit. Joe answered a knock on his hotel room door and in walked Ritchie and several 'guests' who calmly proceeded to throw everything in the room out of the window! The window only swivelled open 45 degrees so, according to Joe: "They had a tough time with the TV!"

Next morning a worried Turner, apprehensive about the inevitable confrontation with the hotel manager, was consoled when the manager dismissed the damage as 'not too bad' - apparently Bob Marley and his entourage had recently left far worse behind them. Ritchie also had a dispute with the manager over hotel noise keeping him awake, to such an extent that the guitarist relocated his amp and Stratocaster to his room one night to demonstrate what real noise was!

Several demos laid down by the Bonnet line-up ended up being finished off by Turner. Ritchie recounted how the struggle with a previously-written backing (that became 'No Release') was quickly resolved by Turner: "I'd written the music to it and I said 'It's just a blues...' It's up to the singer what he does. I could go into what Graham said but I won't. Then Joe came along and went 'Oh, yeah, I'll sing that' and came up with his own tune. It was great, it worked straight away. I still don't like the tune particularly - it's all right, but he did a great job on a bit of a throwaway song." (Interestingly, given Ritchie's remarks, Joe gets no writing credit for this track on the album.)

For the first time since Rainbow's formation, songwriting was on a more democratic footing for, in addition to Turner and Glover, Don Airey was credited on three of the seven originals. Joe found, much to his surprise, Ritchie was open to many creative suggestions: "Ritchie loved 'The Song'. He was a real song man, and this may surprise people. He was not just a guitar guy. Working with him was very collaborative... he would allow room and growth. Working with him was productive too, because it was always important to him to get the best song possible... he couldn't care less if he played a long solo. A lyric or message would really move him and you would not think that about him being a guitarist, but it's true. He is very fair and would actually leave a lot up to me... sometimes he'd give me bits and pieces of music and I'd end up putting it all together."

The album, entitled *'Difficult To Cure'*, was released during February 1981 and highlighted the further evolution in style initiated by *'Down To Earth'*. This was due in no small part to Joe's greater melodic sensibility and his smoother, more soulful delivery compared to either of his predecessors. With so much written with Bonnet's voice in mind, Joe's vocal efforts occasionally sat uncomfortably with the backings. And so the last vestiges of the earlier era were ditched in favour of a crisp, punchy, keyboards-favouring mix.

Allied to a slick production sound, it was freely admitted by Blackmore at the time to be a deliberate (some might say desperate) attempt to crack the American market. Ironically, Roger had serious misgivings over this final sound: "I went through terrible nervous breakdowns wondering if it sounded right, and just before it came out, I was shitting bricks. I didn't think it was good enough. I couldn't put my finger on it but there was something I didn't like, a certain clarity that wasn't there. About a week before it was due out I was calling up our manager and saying 'Can I re-mix it? I really think I can do better' and he's going 'No, it'll cost too much money.'"

Blackmore's love of classical music brought forth 'Difficult To Cure', a storming version of 'Ode To Joy', the choral finale from Beethoven's Ninth Symphony. Ritchie: "I remember watching a football match during the seventies between Germany and Holland, where they had 90,000 people singing this tune, which sent shivers down my spine. Ever since that day, I've loved that particular melody, although I don't especially like Beethoven."

The instrumental included a furious guitar solo that ranks among Ritchie's best studio moments of his entire Rainbow career. (The manic laughter at the end of the track was sampled from the Laurel and Hardy thirties film classic 'Way Out West'.)

Chapter 5

Don Airey remembers that "'Difficult To Cure' took forever. Bobby Rondinelli had real problems playing a shuffle, so eventually we scrapped what we had. I laid down a backing track with a Minimoog hitched up to a Sequential Circuits sequencer, and we built it back up from there. The drums went on last and are fairly impressive, I have to say."

The track proved to be a very popular addition to the live set, snippets having been featured in the occasional Dio-era show and fuller versions aired on the *'Down To Earth'* tour prior to release of the studio recording. Indeed, rocking-up the classics suddenly became the done thing; German guitarist Uli Jon Roth also featured a version of 'Ode To Joy' on his early-eighties tours.

The frantically-paced 'Spotlight Kid' was, according to Joe, lyrically inspired by Blackmore himself and became the set opener for future tours. It included another blisteringly fluid guitar solo and a virtuoso Airey organ romp. The energetic 'Can't Happen Here' highlighted an environmentally-conscious lyricism, while 'I Surrender' was another Russ Ballard song chosen for inclusion early on in the sessions. Highlighting Turner's formidable ability on power ballads, the track preceded the release of the album and reaffirmed Rainbow's singles success with the band's highest UK chart placing at No. 3.

Unsurprisingly, given the circumstances around the recording, the album sometimes sounds diffuse. The aforementioned highlights notwithstanding, it had more than its share of filler; a cover of Brian Moran's 'Magic' proved a bland pop throwaway and the self-penned 'Freedom Fighter' was a good idea weak on execution. 'Mid Town Tunnel Vision' was built around a well-worn traditional blues riff and featured a jaw-dropping (though rather brief and understated) guitar solo, while to some the backing riff in the aforementioned funky 'No Release' showed a strong similarity to Jeff Beck's 'Plynth'.

'Maybe Next Time' was an attractive instrumental in the 'Weiss Heim' mould and, according to Don Airey, happened very quickly: "Ritchie's first take was one of the most beautiful pieces of guitar playing I ever heard - though, to my amazement, he scrapped it, and put a composite together of other takes." Interestingly, some of the album's promotional material tantalisingly mentions a track called 'Schwarz Heim' which could have been a follow-up to the earlier instrumental, though is more probably an early working title for one of the 1981-83 instrumentals or backings.

Seven weeks of dates were arranged for North America, starting in Canada in February (with Pat Travers co-headlining) before the European leg in June. 'Jealous Lover', a track that could arguably be defined as the first true Turner/Blackmore composition, was recorded (Eric Clapton looking on with interest) during April at the Orpheum Theatre in Minneapolis. Joe: "We needed to record a B-side but we kept putting it off until we finally got a mobile unit... It was Ritchie's birthday and he'd had his acoustic stolen, so there was a bit of a moody going on. Ritchie and I made up the arrangement in a little room in the theatre, and he showed the music to the rest of the band while I sat frantically putting my thoughts together lyrically... We did it to an audience of one - tour manager Colin Hart."

Rotterdam Ahoy, 13th June 1982

The track was lyrically based around an argument Joe had with his girlfriend the previous night. Although originally used as the B-side to 'Can't Happen Here', a 'Jealous Lover' four-track EP saw the tune picking up extensive airplay on US radio, who saw it as somewhat less politically sensitive than the original A-side. The band's Boston show on 7th May was officially recorded for the US-syndicated King Biscuit Flower Hour radio show (and bootlegged in 1983 as the *'Electrified'* set). Some excellent concerts were reported and the European tour (including more than a dozen British dates with Aussie boogie-rockers Rose Tattoo, starting 10th July) was again eagerly anticipated.

The Rotterdam Ahoy Arena gig on 13th June also appeared as a bootleg recording some time later, originating from soundboard tapes done for the band. A basic video was apparently shot of the Essen gig and was aired in 1982 by the short-lived UK fan-club at one of their bashes. The next single was 'Can't Happen Here.' It quickly became another hit in the UK, spurred on by the extensive tour schedule. With the more accessible sound further broadening their appeal, concerts were again well-attended.

Although Joe Lynn Turner proved a marked improvement on stage after the erratic Bonnet, it was soon obvious many of the original die-hard fans would never relate to Turner as they had to Dio, despite the former's undoubted vocal and writing

Chapter 5

talents. Joe: "If I hadn't had Blackmore by my side then it would have been a absolute nightmare. He defended me because he believed in me."

New singers always have the toughest time integrating into a new band. As frontman/woman, they carry the show, or at least share its burden with a star instrumentalist. In the UK the reception was particularly chilly - several hoots of derision and catcalls for the return of Dio might have fazed a less self-confident performer, but Turner brazened it out. His dark good looks helped too, and ensured that audiences featured a few more women - something uncommon at Rainbow concerts just a few years earlier.

Some of Joe's schizophrenic stage antics did draw some raised eyebrows, not least from Blackmore himself. One minute he'd appear the very epitome of a powerful and dynamic macho rocker, the next he would find him hamming up it up with a simpering butchness. Joe himself admitted: "I got a bit carried away with being the front man in Rainbow. You can get away with the preening in the States but it does not work in the UK. I was probably too cabaret, I was never going to be the typical heavy metal frontman... but I know that all that leaping around and stuff was too much." Ritchie agreed: "We took him on stage in Europe and he got crucified. Backstage I pulled him by the throat and told him 'You've got to stop all the pansying. You're not Judy Garland!'"

Turner coped with most of the older material confidently enough, particularly impressing on the type of soaring power-ballads that really suited his voice - witness the live versions of 'Love's No Friend' where, on a good night, he was superb. Rondinelli was visually impressive, and his bare-handed drum solo proved an interesting take on a hackneyed theme and almost up to the high standards set by his illustrious predecessor. Musically, 1981's tour was superior to its predecessor, with Blackmore appearing more confident and stretching himself - and the band - a lot more often.

To the surprise and delight of the die-hards, the old Purple chestnut 'Smoke On The Water' was even dusted down and added as a crowd-pleasing encore this time around. "We had been fooling around with the song in rehearsal," Joe commented, "and Bobby and I said 'It's great - let's do it' but Ritchie kept saying 'No, I left all that behind long ago.' Then one night he started the riff, and we looked at each other and went 'Right!'"

In addition, snippets of Hendrix standards 'Fire' and 'Hey Joe' were also resurrected occasionally as encores or inserted into medleys. The set list of the time typically ran: 'Spotlight Kid'/'Love's No Friend'/'I Surrender'/'Man On The Silver Mountain'/'Catch The Rainbow'/'Can't Happen Here'/'Lost In Hollywood'/'Difficult To Cure'/'Long Live Rock'n'Roll'/'All Night Long'/'Since You Been Gone'/'Smoke On The Water'. In Britain the band fell victim to technical gremlins - particularly in Edinburgh, where poor sound marred the gig, and Leeds. "All I could see was pillars and the sound system," Ritchie recalled of the latter. "I went 'This is fucking awful' and then the guitar amp blew and I walked off stage in a huff. Suddenly Bobby's drum skin went and he walked off as well, leaving Don and Roger playing and Joe singing away." The London jinx struck again with the second concert at the Hammersmith Odeon being another night to forget. To balance these out, the performance on the first night at Hammersmith and the two at London's Rainbow Theatre were considered the best shows of the European leg.

The whole tour proved to be far more relaxed all round, with Ritchie's humour and pranks well to the fore: during Pat Travers' set in Philadelphia, a football was periodically thrown across the stage! At another show, Blackmore's sense of fun extended to Rainbow's set. At an appropriate moment in Joe's solo spot the band sneaked off stage unnoticed and left JLT to furiously ad-lib for several minutes. Ritchie: "I would signal to the drummer and we would stop... we took it down to a whisper and left him there. He wasn't the kind of guy to laugh it off. He wanted to use it as his big opportunity!"

A gig in France saw similar pranks: "Joe did this bit where he got the audience to participate while we backed off a bit, and then came back in... I said to the drummer and bass player 'Come on, we're leaving.' So we came off stage and Joe didn't know he was on his own. We got down into the orchestra pit and Joe couldn't see us and we started throwing vegetables at him. So he started swearing at the audience 'You bastards, you French bastards' and picking up

Chapter 5

the tomatoes and throwing them back. Finally Joe realised it was us - but it was too late, the audience was in uproar."

Don Airey had special memories of what turned out to be his final gig with the band: "It was in Hawaii and Ritchie's stack blew up. If ever that happened, I used to take over and do a bit of a keyboard interlude. On this occasion, I did a keyboard solo lasting twenty-five minutes! After nearly half an hour, there was no sign of anybody and they'd all gone. Ritchie just went 'Ah, I can't be bothered' and they all went back to the hotel. I was left on my own. Nobody came on to stop me. I was getting desperate; I was playing 'Hawaii Five-O' and 'Hawaiian Love Chant' and eventually it just came to a stop. It wasn't very pleasant. When I got back to the hotel, nobody seemed to care very much."

The tour finally ended in late August 1981. Airey then dropped a bombshell by walking out of the band, citing boredom as his main reason for leaving. "I thought the band was getting too transatlantic, and after three years it was just time to move on or be moved on. Bashing our way through old Rainbow and even old Purple material wasn't doing any of us justice, and certainly wasn't doing what is left of my brain any good at all." Don went on to a three-year stint with Ozzy's band - bashing his way through old Black Sabbath material!

Roger Glover receives a parking ticket, Rainbow Theatre 1981

A *'Best Of Rainbow'* double compilation released in Japan during February 1981 sold well enough for Polydor to release a similar package in Europe, ready for the traditionally high-volume sales period before Christmas. Reprising some of the band's best studio moments up to and including 'Difficult To Cure', the double proved a very healthy seller, but inevitably for the more dedicated fan the enterprise suffered from poor sleeve design, an absence of extensive sleeve notes and an unimaginative choice of readily available tracks. Polydor then blithely exported the European compilation for sale in Japan!

99

Prior to commencing the latest round of recording in late November, new blood was introduced in the form of 21 year-old David Rosenthal, who had played in cover bands in his native New Jersey when only 13, before attending the Berkeley College of Music. Ritchie described his recruitment: "I had a lot of people come to the auditions... while most of them had the rock'n'roll thing off they couldn't play any classically orientated piece on their own. I was given a tape by a friend... it was a piece by Liszt performed at the Boston University of Music. I said this guy is far too good for us, he'll probably be a musical snob, but after I'd auditioned everybody I could find, I invited him down and he played in such a brilliant way that I asked him to join."

There was also speculation as to the future of another old hand, and soon Roger Glover followed Airey by lowering his lifeboat. Apparently the bassist was unhappy with the heavy touring schedule and Jack Green was rumoured to be ready to step in. (Roger was reported as saying he had quit Rainbow no less than three times for various reasons, only for Bruce Payne to persuade him back a few days later.) But Glover did, at least, stay around for one more album.

A rented house in the wilds of Vermont was the location for writing sessions where four or five promising ideas were developed. Joe: "Ritchie would play bass pedals and chords for hours. There was always brilliant stuff, but I had to go through two-hour-long tapes to find cool riffs and piece together parts that would make a great song... I would go to bed with my headphones on and listen to all these pieces of music. I might hear one part I liked maybe in the beginning of the tape and then, 40 minutes later, hear the perfect part to go with it. Then I'd put them in a key and play it."

Recording took place at Le Studio, Montreal, through December 1981. The studio came highly recommended to Roger by Nazareth, and had just been vacated by The Police after recording *'Ghost In The Machine'*. The facility included excellent accommodation and overlooked a picturesque frozen lake. The sessions almost came to an abrupt and tragic end, when, as Joe recently recalled: "Roger and I decided that it would be a great night to take a walk on the frozen lake. After getting halfway across we started to hear the crack-crack of the ice below us. Luckily we laid down, and started crawling back to the shore!"

To everyone's delight the creative process was, for once, surprisingly easy and productive, with minimal disagreement among the main songwriting triumvirate.

Chapter 5

As Joe recalled, the methods employed were of his choosing: "Arguments do go back and forth during the process, absolutely. I do have one personal rule and that is 'If you don't have an alternative idea, don't go saying I don't like this or that.' If you have a complaint, fine, but have a solution or idea to go with it. If someone says they do not like something and has no alternative the wheels just stop turning and the whole creative process can shut down. On the other hand, you cannot be so philosophically attached to some part of a song that, when someone makes a suggestion, you can't be flexible with it."

The recording was completed within just five weeks with the usual humorous *divertissements*. During sessions, Ritchie and David Rosenthal had a disagreement about an improvised fugue in 'Miss Mistreated'. At dinner a few days later, Ritchie reminded David of this and asked one of the entourage to put the patio lights on. There, neatly placed on the patio, covered in snow were the entire contents of David's room - bed, lamp, tables, even his shoes! The keyboard-player was not the only one to fall prey to Blackmore's pranks. As Joe crawled into his bed after one particularly heavy drinking session late one night he thought it felt 'slimy' yet smelt quite nice - Ritchie had helpfully 'shampooed' the bed!

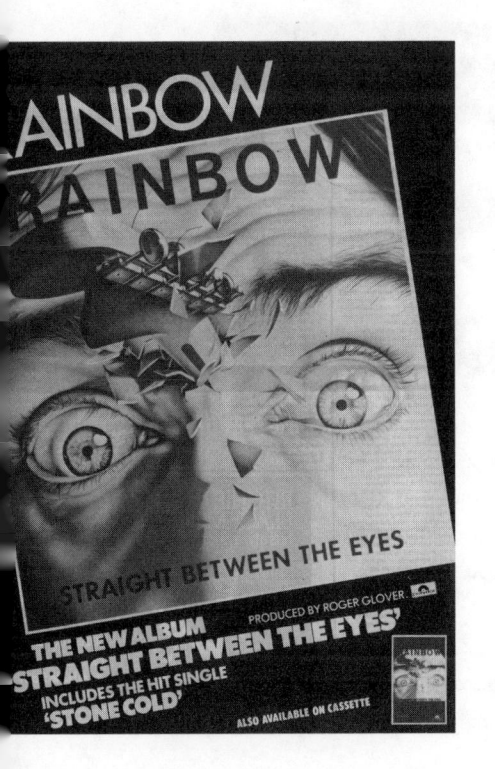

'Straight Between The Eyes' was released in June 1982. The album title originated from the way Jeff Beck had first described Jimi Hendrix's playing to Ritchie back in the sixties and the sleeve featured a Jeff Cummins illustration. Turner helped to integrate the vocals and music, although the AOR direction took another giant step towards an expansive, lighter, stadium-rock sound. Nevertheless, Joe would ardently defend the increasingly commercial sound: "For some reason, that seems to be a dirty word with everyone. But all of the bands I know, Led Zeppelin included, are commercial - who are they kidding? We're tired of not reaching the American public, tired of not reaching people who like a decent song."

The simplistic metallic stomp of 'Power' (distantly related to 'Do You Close Your Eyes?') appealed to the metal-heads, while the melodic identity Turner gave the band was exemplified by the catchy 'Miss Mistreated' and 'Tearing Out My Heart'. 'Death Alley Driver' was the obligatory up-tempo, take-no-prisoners opener this time; lyrically it was motivated by "dealers, those who abuse drugs or anyone who is on the way to killing themselves or others and not seeing the stop sign" and was instrumentally reminiscent of Purple's 'Highway Star'. The promo video featured a biker chased by a car containing the Grim Reaper (played in the video, at Joe's suggestion, by Blackmore himself).

The attractive ballad 'Stone Cold' was part inspired by the blizzards during recording and by a chance comment by Roger to Joe about an ex-girlfriend leaving him 'stone cold'. Released prior to the album, the single was destined to become their last Top 40 entry in the UK, yet only made a slight dent on the US charts even after heavy rotation on rock radio stations. ('Death Alley Driver' was intended as the follow up in the US but was dropped after the disappointing showing of 'Stone Cold'.) The loose funk of 'Tite Squeeze' showed the band could 'get down and groove' with the best (eat your heart out, Glenn Hughes) and was one of Glover's personal favourites. "A natural song to do... the tracks that sound fresh are the ones you accept mistakes and all, because they happen to feel good."

Album closer 'Eyes Of Fire' seemed a little out of place within the context of the album. Almost harking back in feel to the raga-tinged neo-classical epics

Chapter 5

of the Dio era, it lacked a sufficiently strong theme to work completely, though it did feature the Montreal Symphony Orchestra arranged by David Rosenthal. This time Joe's lyrical inspiration was a girl he met in a bar in Montreal named Erica (with the eponymous 'eyes of fire').

The tour promoting the album in the late spring and summer of 1982 played to crowds of 10,000-plus in the major US and Canadian cities, although smaller 1,500 seat venues had to be booked outside these areas. The biggest crowd (over 15,000) was for the headlining of a festival at Allentown Fairgrounds in mid-June. Support on this tour included at various times The Scorpions, Riot, UFO, Saxon, The Rods, Iron Maiden, 38 Special and Krokus. Turner's lead vocals were effectively complemented with off-stage backing from singers Dee Beale and Lin Robinson.

The stage show boasted a lighting rig featuring two movable spotlight 'eyes' (as on the album cover) to somewhat dubious and often frankly tacky effect. New tracks performed live included 'Miss Mistreated', 'Power', 'Death Alley Driver' and 'Stone Cold', all of which had some attractively roughed-up edges added to the otherwise studio-faithful versions. Highlight of the show for many, however, was the lengthy improvised version of 'Tearing Out My Heart' that featured an excellent Turner performance and culminated in a archetypal Blackmore 'You Fool No One'-type guitar blitz.

Rotterdam Ahoy, 16th November 1982

The only non JLT-era tracks usually featured were a singalong 'All Night Long',

'Smoke On The Water' and 'Long Live Rock'n'Roll'. The takes of 'Catch The Rainbow' rarely lasted longer than five minutes - yet such was the strength of the composition that these still impressed, Joe's slightly revised lyrics complemented superbly by the backing singers. Rosenthal showed little evidence of nerves or inexperience and slotted in seamlessly on stage. As the tour progressed he supported Ritchie's guitar work very effectively. "I'm called on to make the guitar sound bigger while not drawing attention to myself," David explained in an interview. "A lot of times you don't hear me in the mix, but if you mute what I do, the guitar would suddenly sound smaller. I know how to make my voicings intertwine with what the guitarist does."

Again, friendly rivalry between headliners and support led to some good-natured attempts at one-upmanship. Krokus cheekily attempted to upstage Ritchie one night with guitarist Fernando Von Arb demolishing his guitar with a huge axe at the end of their set. In response, Ritchie paused suddenly just before his guitar trashing, shrugged his shoulders and simply lobbed the undamaged guitar into the bemused audience! He then carefully and concisely ripped each string in turn from a second guitar!

The essence of the live shows on this tour was captured by film footage released on video as *'Live Between The Eyes'*. Featuring around 75 minutes of the San Antonio concert on 18th August, at the time it was the first official record of the band in this increasingly popular format. The band fortunately avoided the often stilted nature of live performance on tape or film; the well-shot, well-edited performance retained an organic quality and Blackmore, in particular, comes across well.

Roger Glover did several radio interviews to promote the album and tour, during one of which Joe called up on air and reminded him of a rehearsal the following day! A short rest followed before the obligatory half-dozen Japanese dates in Japan during October while all-female British metallers Girlschool accompanied Rainbow through

Chapter 5

Scandinavia and Germany the following month. During this time, a misjudged guitar demolition in Frankfurt earned Ritchie a painful black eye and badly bruised nose. (Also around this time he was spotted sporting a lapel badge: 'Everyone's entitled to my opinion!')

During a stop at a Spanish hotel on the European leg, UFO bassist Pete Way caught sight of Ritchie in his monogrammed pyjamas, to which Way remarked wistfully: "A legend was shattered that night." The tour finished later that month, for the first time with no UK dates scheduled. Blackmore, it was said, considered the band to be "over-exposed" in its homeland.

Though the tour had been a success and the line-up (for once) appeared settled, soon after it was over Rosenthal, Rondinelli and Turner were abruptly given notice of dismissal. This was less to do with personal or musical differences than renewed rumours in the wind of something bigger and better for Blackmore. There had recently been further approaches to both Glover and Blackmore by ex-manager John Coletta regarding a Deep Purple reformation.

The initial deal offered the vocalist's post to David Coverdale, who turned it down - wisely as it turned out, given the phenomenal success of the next few Whitesnake albums. This time though, Ian Gillan was agreeable, having just put his own band on hold while he recuperated from vocal chord surgery. Shows were even pencilled in for the vast untapped markets of Eastern Europe, which were just opening up to the west and proving to be particularly avid consumers of Purple's brand of heavy rock.

But, once again, the project stalled, one source alleging that this time it was Ritchie who had pulled out in favour of one last concerted effort to conquer America with Rainbow. It also was said that he had sought assurance that the deal would be no more than a short-term get-together, whereas the others wanted a more permanent arrangement. (Blackmore: "Ian said 'hurry up and make up your mind or I'm off to join Black Sabbath!'") Another version of events cited a blazing row between Gillan and Blackmore over the division of publishing royalties, culminating with the allegedly inebriated Gillan throwing a beer over Ritchie and walking out. Whatever the reason, the redundant Rainbow musicians were all swiftly reinstated early in 1983. Rondinelli would not remain for very much longer however, ultimately dropped because of (according to Bruce Payne) "inconsistency". This accusation was instigated not by Blackmore but, allegedly, Joe Lynn Turner - a sign of his increasing status within the group. The search for Rondinelli's replacement initially led to 29-year old Tico Torres, drummer with New Jersey pop-rockers Frankie And The Knockouts. Tired of constant touring, he turned the job down, as he did an offer from Ozzy Osbourne soon after. Little matter, however, as he was shortly to hit the big time with Bon Jovi.

For several months leading up to 1983, Roger Glover had been hard at work writing and recording tracks in preparation for a solo album. The recording involved both David Rosenthal and Aldo Nova's former drummer Chuck Bürgi. A friend of Joe Lynn Turner since 1975, Bürgi was yet another musician from the vibrant New Jersey/New York scene who had first recorded with jazz-rock guitarist Danny Toan. He had toured with Al DiMeola on his 'Elegant Gypsy' tour before replacing Phil Collins in Brand X for 1978's *'Masques'*. A year on, he joined Hall and Oates for two LPs.

His extensive session history included work with Michael Bolton, Bon Jovi and Diana Ross, while cutting two albums as a member of cult AOR band Balance during the early eighties. Originally recommended to Roger by Joe, Chuck's jazz-influenced chops were proficient enough for him to slot neatly into the new Rainbow line-up. Although Ritchie disliked 'jazzy bassists', drummers of a similar bent were deemed okay: "He's a slight jazzer, but I like that jazz inflection because when I'm doing a little bit of syncopation he catches it every time."

Initial ideas for the new album were worked up through the early part of 1983, culminating with rehearsals during March.

Chapter 5

Vermont was again the location for further pre-production in May where 'Street Of Dreams', a track first conceived some three years earlier, was finally finished. A residency at the Sweet Silence Studios during May and June followed. Originally Le Studio, Montreal was to be used again but was booked solid, the band returning to the Copenhagen facility as Ritchie particularly liked the studio's guitar sound. The engineer for the project was again Flemming Rasmussen, soon to win renown by becoming resident producer for Metallica.

Recording was punctuated with a round of recreational activities, including a Thin Lizzy concert and a soccer match against the Iron Maiden crew (Rainbow going down valiantly 5-4). Other faces showed up: Blackmore, Glover and drummer Ian Paice were spotted deep in conversation in a Copenhagen night-club, leading to press speculation that Paice was either about to join Rainbow or the Deep Purple reunion was back on. Uncharacteristically, the writers in the band came to the studio with a lot of prepared material, though much was quickly discarded and several new songs composed on the spot.

Above and opposite:
Bristol Hippodrome,
11th September 1983

With Roger busy on what would become his solo *'Mask'* album, most compositions were credited to Blackmore and Turner. Roger: "I think the emergence of Joe as a writer within the group was the biggest difference on this album. In fact I did no writing whatsoever, I concentrated on production - not that I don't like writing, it's just the way it turned out." Despite (or maybe because of) Glover's lack of input, a somewhat rockier collection of tracks ensued with September's *'Bent Out Of Shape'* (the title came from an American slang expression for alcoholic over-indulgence).

The laid-back Toto-like vibe of 'Street Of Dreams' was decreed by Polydor to be the first single but it failed to get much chart action; this was perhaps partly because the promo featured a hypnosis scene, giving rise to fears it could lead to viewers being accidentally 'hypnotised' - the video actually came close to being banned by the networks. A surprising but ultimately inspired cover was an instrumental interpretation of Howard Blake's popular soundtrack from the animated Christmas film 'The Snowman', showcasing some hauntingly mournful guitar work and beautifully atmospheric keyboards.

The excellent 'Can't Let You Go' featured a over-the-top Gothic organ intro while the fast and frantic 'Firedance' and the catchy 'Stranded' (the latter's chorus refrain owing much to Marc Bolan's 'Children Of The Revolution') proved to be among the best material recorded by the Turner fronted line-ups. The telegraphed 'Drinking With The Devil' and 'Make Your Move', however, were less successful. Rainbow began the tour in the UK in September 1983, with ex-Runaway Lita Ford as support. Behind the scenes, things had been rocky for Blackmore right up to the tour's start: "I got injured in a game of football which developed into a muscle spasm which set off all my other muscles and in the end I couldn't play. I was tingling all along my arm. This was just before the European tour and I didn't think I was going to make

Bristol Hippodrome, 11th September 1983

it. Every time I put on a guitar strap I pinched a nerve and couldn't move my fingers properly without pain. I had a masseur on the road with me all the time and it was touch and go whether I was going to make the dates. It turned out I had an arthritic joint in the back of my neck. So I went to a physiotherapist and started doing exercises and everything's been okay."

Several concert recordings were made during this leg of the tour for a possible live album in the near future. Recordings of the Cardiff show at St. David's Hall on 14th September were syndicated by RKO and aired on US radio. Some British concerts were also reportedly professionally filmed for later use. Ritchie's offer to patch things up with David Coverdale was amicably accepted by the singer and he agreed to encore with Rainbow on one of the UK dates, although voice problems brought on during the recording of the 'Slide It In' opus prevented him from appearing at the Sobell Centre concert as arranged. Blackmore also took time out to guest with old friend and pub-rocker Jackie Lynton.

The live set was based largely around the LP. A typical running order was: 'Spotlight Kid'/'Miss Mistreated'/'Fool For The Night'/'I Surrender'/'Can't Let You Go'/'Catch The Rainbow'/'Drinking With The Devil'/'Difficult To Cure'/ 'Power'/'Blues-Stargazer-Stranded' medley/'Death Alley Driver'/'Firedance'/'All Night Long'/'Since You Been Gone - Long Live Rock'n'Roll - Smoke On The Water - Kill The King' medley.

The single released in October on the back of the tour, 'Can't Let You Go' fared little better than its predecessor. The American leg of the tour in late '83 (The Scorpions supporting) revived interest there again, helped along by a Grammy nomination for the Blackmore instrumental 'Anybody There?'. Stylistically another close relation to 'Weiss Heim', Ritchie's piece was pipped by a track by Sting.

Elgar's 'Pomp And Circumstance March No.1 in D' now preceded the show, the only nod to earlier eras usually being the perfunctory run-through of 'Catch The Rainbow', a sing-along 'All Night Long' and short, teasing snatches of other previous classics dependent on the guitarist's whim. 'Firedance' highlighted some great driving drum work from Bürgi, who proved a busy, flexible stylist capable of following Ritchie's improvisations when required, although occasionally guilty of overplaying.

Shows were consistent and enjoyable but, for the long-standing fans that remembered the mid-to-late seventies, the nights where Blackmore's performance was truly inspirational were rare. Clearly the guitarist's mind was elsewhere.

Ritchie had always been aware of how the omnipresence of Deep Purple tended to overshadow his efforts with Rainbow - which was something all the 'ex-members' had to tolerate with their respective endeavours. Blackmore had long given up trying to shake off being pigeon-holed as simply 'former Deep Purple guitarist...' and endured the continuing mania for nostalgia with weary resignation. Recently, though, he had started to see things in a new light: "I used to come off stage and ponder that there were so many Purple fans around." Maybe they were not such bad times after all?

Rainbow now looked like a busted flush in comparison. "I enjoyed the band's softer phase... 'Stone Cold', 'Street Of Dreams', stuff like that I really liked, but it died a death in Britain - which hurt a lot... and every time I wanted to play a real hard-rock song, Joe couldn't quite manage it... so in the end I got frustrated and that's when the first really serious thought of a Purple reformation entered my head... and the money was so ridiculous I said I'd do it!"

Joe Lynn Turner also knew the end was near, although not surprisingly he had a rather different perspective as to the reasons: "Originally I had wanted to do a solo thing within the framework of Rainbow because of the usual crap; I had a lot of

Chapter 5

stuff that wasn't right, blah blah... Ritchie was cool about it but even then Bruce Payne wasn't pulling his finger out... so every spare moment I had was spent chasing up record companies to see if there was any interest. I think Ritchie really didn't like the idea of that because I was getting too involved in my own thing, so the seeds of splitting the band and putting Purple back together were sown... We were talking on the way back to New York from Japan after our last tour and came to an agreement that it would be best for me to do my own thing and for him to put Purple back together."

Much later, in an interview from 2000, Turner expanded on the theme: "The band was supposed to have been put on ice, not to break up... What happened was - and I only found this out recently - that Bruce Payne manipulated the split. I remember him approaching me on the last tour, telling me Deep Purple were getting back together and that I would be doing a solo album for Elektra, and then Rainbow would reconvene. But it never happened, because Payne told Ritchie I didn't want to do Rainbow any more and that I was gonna go off and do this solo album. Ritchie was terribly disappointed and, because he's this generally uncommunicative guy, he never approached me and asked if it was true."

Some feelers - initiated by Ian Gillan - were put out involving the members of the Purple Mark II line-up and preliminary meetings took place in America early in 1984. This time contractual and managerial issues were agreed. With a short Rainbow tour of Japan already booked, the last few concert commitments remained to be honoured. Ritchie marked the event of Rainbow's final date in Tokyo on 14th March by taking the opportunity to fulfil a long-held ambition when a full orchestral backing was used for a scintillating rendition of 'Difficult To Cure'.

The guitarist later enthused: "I really liked the way it turned out. David Rosenthal wrote an extra piece and we did that with an orchestra, and that was very integrated, and that worked." In addition to being taped for another possible live album, the concert was filmed and released in Japan on video in July 1984. The Deep Purple reformation was finally officially announced that April, albeit to a general sense of cynicism from the music world. Exit Rainbow.

As a final coda to the Rainbow era, both Glover and Blackmore suggested the 1983 live Japanese recordings be worked up for release. Their ever-intransigent record label, Polydor, insisted instead on a more general compilation, resulting in what became the double album *'Finyl Vinyl'*. With rare studio tracks and various live performances, the collection was collated by Roger Glover and mixed in White Plains, New York, during early 1986. (Roger came up with the eventual title, though Ritchie was quoted as saying the proposed title at one stage was 'Are We Having Fun Yet?') Glover remarked of the project: "I could have wished for better recordings in some instances - still, they reveal that dangerous quality in musicians found only at live gigs, not always playing safe. So here they are, warts and all."

'Since You Been Gone' originated from Donington, 'Man On The Silver Mountain' and 'Long Live Rock'n'Roll' from the BBC's 1978 Atlanta recording, while several JLT-era tracks from the 1981-83 tours were featured. The bulk came from the 1982 San Antonio video soundtrack and the final 1984 concert at the Tokyo Budokan; the overall sound quality was a little disappointing and rather thin in parts. The original guitar solo in the live version of 'Man On The Silver Mountain' was thought unsatisfactory, so Ritchie promptly recorded a new solo to be dubbed in.

A version of 'Stargazer' was also mooted for inclusion but parts of the recording were considered substandard. Rumour had it that Ritchie had even seriously suggested getting the original musicians together again to overdub it in the studio. The B-sides 'Bad Girl', 'Jealous Lover' and 'Weiss Heim' were also included, the album mistakenly crediting Bob Rondinelli on the latter instead of Cozy Powell.

Pick of the live tracks was 'Difficult To Cure' from Tokyo, showcasing both a great guitar prelude and the grandiose orchestral contribution (though this too featured guitar overdubs). 'Street Of Dreams' was a cassette-only inclusion, while the great version of 'Tearing Out My Heart' was omitted from the CD to keep the release to a single disc. These were reinstated for the 1999 CD re-mastering, making the release a short double, although the sound is better.

The simultaneous Polygram video release, *'Final Cut'*, collected together most of the promo videos and concert footage from the band's mid-to-late career, although disappointingly it did not feature any Dio-era footage due to 'insurmountable' contractual problems. In November 1990, however, a rather more suitable

Chapter 5

tribute to the band appeared with the appearance of a live album culled from the 1976 German tour. Entitled *'Live In Germany'* and released on the Connoisseur label, the release was co-ordinated by long-standing Deep Purple and Blackmore aficionado Simon Robinson.

The original intention had been to include one or two of the better tracks on the label's planned *'Blackmore Rock Anthology'* compilation. However, the quality of the concerts was so high that the archived tapes became a project in their own right, the best performances cherry-picked from the master tapes available of the four shows recorded during the German leg of the tour.

This time, the absence of extensive editing and the preservation of the correct running order gave a more faithful indication of the rampant power and technical capability of the line-up. The 100-minute show caught the band in a slightly looser, more relaxed mood than the Japanese dates, with 'Man On The Silver Mountain' ending with a great jam, Dio improvising lyrics on the spot. The vocal-guitar question-response section at the end of 'Mistreated' conveyed a fabulous live atmospheric vibe.

A seventies' version of 'Stargazer' was caught officially on record for the first time, featuring an imaginative keyboard intro and positively manic guitar climax. Stripped of the visual impact of the guitar destruction, the latter portion of 'Do You Close Your Eyes' has little happening aurally and so sounds overlong. Blackmore's work in 'Catch The Rainbow', on the other hand, was nothing short of breathtaking. The dynamic range of the performance and the seemingly casual way the band kick in to take things to the very edge while still maintaining control frankly puts the majority of bands (particularly those in the synthetic-sounding nineties) to shame. One can only speculate on Rainbow's fortunes if this version (or something similar) of their live show had been released at the time, in preference to the compromised *'On Stage'*.

So, in hindsight, what legacy had Rainbow left? With sales figures of over 14 million units worldwide and a score of gold discs to their credit, the band was undoubtedly commercially successful. Their considerable live reputation from the early days on meant Rainbow also became a prime concert draw. Their resultant standing as one of the most popular rock acts of the late seventies and early eighties is an undeniable achievement, even to the sternest critic. But, to Ritchie Blackmore at least, artistically Rainbow never seemed to quite live up to his own demanding expectations.

Few would argue that Blackmore drove and was largely responsible for Rainbow's huge success (and, even from his own point of view, its eventual failure). Even though the 'Ritchie Blackmore's Rainbow' moniker was belatedly dropped in favour of a more collective nomenclature, there was never any doubt as to who was the head honcho. So why, with such personal control, did the band - by his own admittance - ultimately fail to attain his own objectives?

Blackmore: "I was always looking for that nirvana, something you can't touch - it's not tangible. Maybe the problem is I'm not happy with my own musical abilities... I'm seeking it out in others." The instinctive guitarist found it hard to channel his natural talent, and the resultant frustration was a major factor in his intolerance with band members he felt couldn't relate to what he was attempting to do. "I was always looking for those people I knew were out there that were great musicians who never had exposure, and I was always looking for the perfect member of the band - which I never really found, because there wasn't a perfect member."

Roger Glover: "He's one of the most difficult people I've ever had to work with - but that's balanced by the fact that he's also one of the most gifted people I've ever had to work with... In the eyes of the world and the media he's presented as some kind of terrifying figure - which I don't think he takes any trouble to dispel... His life is ruined by something and I don't think anyone quite knows what. Maybe he doesn't either. The result is he constantly doubts the purpose of the things he's involved in. He always wants to have his own way and has grown accustomed to getting it. I've worked with him for 25 years... and I feel as though I don't know him at all."

Ronnie James Dio commented: "I saw him go through a succession of people who

Chapter 5

wanted more from him than he was willing to give, and those people were just about banished for ever... Ritchie always needed a person to anchor his avant-garde leanings to a more down-to-earth level. He needs someone to talk to him, to drag him here and there, to pat him on the back and tell him [they care]. To a man of such incredible talent something like that is important. Having the level of talent Ritchie possesses means you are bound to suffer in other areas, perhaps on a personal level... It must have been difficult to come to terms with his own fame... he needed the rest of us all the time to back him up."

Joe Lynn Turner views it differently: "We had chemistry. I guess Ritchie had a similar chemistry with Ronnie Dio. That's why it worked so well. He just has this way of pulling the best out of people. There was no question who was top dog. You showed him respect. I think it was to my credit that I did that because he showed me an awful lot of respect in return. Okay, I'd give him a hard time over something I believed in and I may have been a little cocky at times but I knew my place. I think my psychology in dealing with Ritchie worked, in terms of trying to understand this guy, because I've always been flattered by what he's had to say about me. Ninety per cent of the time I spent in Rainbow I consider to be great. The other ten per cent isn't worth bearing any malice or hatred over. All I can say is I feel privileged to have been in the position I was in the early eighties. They were great times."

Driven by a burning ambition in Rainbow's early days to eclipse his work with Deep Purple, Ritchie's newly found musical freedom gave rise to some excellent, original studio product along with some incendiary live shows. But, all too soon, the burden of responsibility that came with being Rainbow's principal player and focal point, further multiplied by the perceived failure of successive band members to perform to his exacting standards, began to exact a price.

The need for Rainbow to become financially self-sustaining via US record sales meant ploughing an increasingly commercial and unfulfilling furrow. Although Blackmore and his cohorts initially continued to broaden Rainbow's commercial appeal and would go on to further success, as the eighties rolled on the critical and artistic perception of the band gradually decreased. Attempts to establish a true group identity were doomed as repeated line-up changes meant continual re-establishment from one album to the next.

Thus - as we were forever reminded by the press - each studio offering was recorded by a different line-up. During their initial nine-year existence no less than 17 musicians came and went. But this turnover in personnel was hardly unique - witness Whitesnake, with 17 members over 12 years, MSG's 12 in 8 years, Black Sabbath's 18 in one 10-year period and Uriah Heep's 22 in 16. From the early days, it was firmly stated that the main emphasis of the group remained the time-honoured empathy between singer and guitarist (Page and Plant, Jagger and Richards, etc). As with many rock bands, other members proved (or were perceived to be) merely supporting players to this duality. It is therefore logical that these musicians should come and go as the sound evolved. Rainbow proved no exception to the rule.

Yet it speaks volumes of those musicians chosen that, despite the internal machinations, Rainbow still managed to produce product of such quality that the group consistently sustained popularity and profile worldwide. It may even be argued that the line-up changes kept the material fresh and contemporary (that was undoubtedly Blackmore's opinion). Thus each successive Rainbow album had its own distinct sound and direction - a situation uncommon in heavy rock, where relentlessly reproducing the same successful formula is the norm.

A good proportion of these ex-members owe a great deal to Blackmore. Having been brought into the spotlight often as unknowns many proceeded to achieve further success outside the band, either with their own projects or with other acts. (Joe Lynn Turner, for instance, has been involved in post-Rainbow projects that have globally shifted over three million units.) In the fullness of time, many now openly admit they regard their time in Rainbow as a peak in their careers.

What had the man himself personally achieved? Commercially, by the time of *'Bent Out Of Shape'*, Blackmore was arguably within an ace of achieving the American breakthrough he seemingly desired so much. Yet, perversely, it was at this very time his focus switched back to Deep Purple.

The dilemma facing Ritchie by late 1983 was one which history suggests he never fully resolved. Keep total creative control within one's own group of hirelings, or

Chapter 5

sacrifice absolute power in favour of working with musical equals better attuned to your aspirations? With the reformation of Deep Purple in 1984, Blackmore appeared to favour the latter, returning to what most considered to be his spiritual home. However, succeeding years saw even Deep Purple strive vainly to reach anything approaching the heights of their previous popularity. Consequently the subsequent debate over the band's ability to hack it centred around the commitment of their main creative force.

Five years after reforming, it was obvious that not only were the successes of 1970-74 unattainable, but that 'musical differences' could no longer be easily resolved. Ritchie had gone into the reunion firmly set on pushing the band, forcibly, down his own defined musical path. Inevitably the battle renewed between (particularly) singer and guitarist, yet once Gillan had departed things were to prove no easier for Blackmore, as his attempts to further impose what was conceived as an overly commercial direction continued to cause further friction with the rest of Deep Purple.

Yet while the rifts opened up again, the continued popularity of Blackmore's overall corpus of work remained undiminished. If proof was ever needed of Blackmore's enduring influence, then witness the undeniable popularity of the numerous retrospectives that were (and continue to be) periodically released. 'Purple Rainbows', nothing more than a run-of-the-mill compilation of Deep Purple, Rainbow and related standards, became one of the Top 10 selling UK rock albums of 1991, some 10 to 20 years after some of the material had been recorded. The 1997 re-issue of 'Made In Japan' re-entered the UK album charts, while even the low-key 'Blackmore Rock Anthology' on Connoisseur sold a healthy 30,000 units.

Ritchie Blackmore's influential legacy to rock music, through both Purple and Rainbow, can be traced directly to numerous metal combos of the eighties, and even to several contemporary indie-rock outfits of the nineties. The Smashing Pumpkins, Kula Shaker, Stereophonics and Dinosaur Jr are just a few examples of more mainstream rock acts whose personal homage to Ritchie has been recently documented. A lasting influence is also clear in the music of Stratovarius, Ten, Royal Hunt, Axel Rudi Pell and Dream Theater, examples of successful artists who boast neo-classical or melodic nuances directly traceable to the Blackmore sound.

As far as most long-standing fans are concerned, Rainbow's golden age was undoubtedly the 1975-78 era. Disillusionment with subsequent efforts meant that, with the passage of time, the 1976 Rainbow line-up has assumed an almost legendary status. To say many Rainbow fans still find the prospect of a 'classic' line-up reformation exciting is an understatement (sadly no longer possible since the death of Cozy Powell).

Perhaps it is best to let sleeping myths lie. A periodic blast through *'Rising'* or *'Live In Germany'* will suffice in reminding ourselves of a legendary band at the very peak of their powers.

Chapter 6

RAINBOW REVIVAL

(1994-1997)

DEEP PURPLE'S 1984 COMEBACK *'Perfect Strangers'* went triple-platinum and they, amazingly, enjoyed a hugely successful, lucrative (and nearly strife-free) world tour. But by the time of the 1987 follow-up, the old personality conflicts that had rent Purple asunder in the past were again coming to the fore.

"None of us got it right," admitted Ian Gillan. "There was no spirit in the group and I was appalled by some of this record (*'House Of Blue Light'*). I couldn't deal with Blackmore at all... (he) started getting cranky again and I could see the nervousness creeping into everyone's eyes. Roger and I did a lot of preparation only to find Ritchie wasn't interested in listening. It's hard to deal with that sort of thing and I didn't. Suggestions and half-worked ideas were strangled, but so long as Ritchie was happy with the guitar parts the lads were happy. I wasn't and said so. But let's not blame everything on Ritchie, I was a wanker too."

Ritchie gave his version of events: "I would stick to my guns, not cause trouble for its own sake. Ian had a hang-up; if any idea about what we should do was to Ritchie's way of thinking, then it was wrong." The relative commercial failure of *'House Of Blue Light'* forced a reappraisal of the band's objectives. Gillan demanded a more progressive hit-and-miss approach without regard to commercialism. ("I was rocking the boat hard because I thought the band was stagnating. I wanted us to become more creative and aggressive.") On the other hand, Ritchie pushed for the more lucrative immediacy of a melodic direction that had worked with Rainbow in 1980. This dichotomy led to the first rumours of a split - initially denied by management - in mid-1988.

Polarisation of opinion, irrespective of who was right or wrong, became so acute that at this stage Ritchie contemplated reactivating Rainbow. Whether this was planned as a permanent alternative to Purple or purely as an individual outlet to vent his creative frustrations is unknown. Ritchie was quoted as saying he considered the Purple reunion was only for one album and a tour, and Rainbow was simply on hold. But he got lazy for four years or so.

What is known is that discussions were reported between Blackmore and various vocalists throughout the year, including Robert Plant soundalike Lenny Wolf (Kingdom Come), close friend Brian Howe (Bad Company) and, naturally enough, Joe Lynn Turner. Faced with the possible loss of their main creative force and a splitting-up of the band, the other members took what they saw as the only course of action open to them and the subsequent turn of events led to the

Chapter 6

sacking of Ian Gillan in the spring of 1989.

His role now assured, at least for the moment, Blackmore and the band drew up a list of candidates as possible vocalist. Among those rumoured to have been on the short list were Doug Pinnick of Kings X and old Rainbow colleague Ronnie James Dio. Those reportedly auditioned but deemed unsuitable included Aussies John Farnham (ex-Little River Band) and former Cold Chisel singer Jimmy Barnes, Brits Kal Swann (a Coverdale soundalike, ex of Lion and Tytan) and (once again) Bad Company's Brian Howe.

Those who came closest, however, were unknown American Terry Brock (of Scottish AOR band Strangeways, who was reportedly signed up but booted out after only three days!) and ex-Survivor/Cobra frontman Jimi Jamison. Jamison, an undoubtedly powerful singer, was provisionally offered the job but turned it down on management advice in favour of a solo career (singing the 'Baywatch' theme and not much else). On Ritchie's suggestion, Joe Lynn Turner was reconsidered and he joined in December 1989. "There's Purple in the corner, all set up," Turner reminisces about his audition. "I walked in, and Ritchie just started playing 'Hey Joe' by Hendrix. I immediately picked up the mike without saying hello and started singing. We started getting into this really long jam. We ended that, started slapping five and everything, and made our introductions."

By 1992 Glover, Lord and Paice's urgings backed by the record company meant Turner was out and Blackmore persuaded to agree to Gillan rejoining the band. (Joe: "BMG went: 'How about two million dollars to start your own solo project? We'll put that on the side if you let Gillan come back.' So Ritchie went: 'Two mil? Okay. Put it on paper, wire it into my account.'") Gillan did come back but the musical and creative relationships between singer and guitarist were at best strained, at worst downright hostile. Although 1993's album *The Battle Rages On'* turned out little more than average, the supporting tour became a veritable Blackmore tour-de-force with the increasingly peeved guitarist seemingly determined to blow the rest of the band off stage. With Ritchie's volatile performances pushing the others on, fans witnessed some of the best concerts Blackmore and Purple had been involved with since the reunion. The basic problems behind the personality clashes with Gillan could not be resolved however, and during the European tour, with the Japanese leg of the tour in December 1993 still outstanding, Ritchie resigned from the band.

While Purple soldiered on to the Far East with stand-in Joe Satriani and then more permanently with Dixie Dregs' Steve Morse, Ritchie took up the solo option with BMG which had been in place for some time. (The whole band - excepting the singer, naturally - had signed to the label as individual artists in the late eighties.) The project was once again named Rainbow, though against Ritchie's wishes: "I wanted to call it Moon, after my grandfather's surname, but the record company said it has to be called Rainbow 'for sales' - you know what record companies are like."

Ritchie initially considered both Ronnie James Dio and Joe Lynn Turner again as front men for the band: "I thought about the old guys, but for not more than a couple of seconds. I felt I'd done as much as I could with them in that style. I wanted someone to have a combination of maybe Ronnie Dio with Joe Lynn Turner, and a more bluesy kind of voice, like a Paul Rodgers type of thing too." Joe's response at the time appeared - understandably - guarded: "He called me and asked if I wanted to work with him again. I didn't really think he was serious and said 'yes'. We had such big problems before that I didn't mean it - in fact Ritchie didn't ask me again and I was quite happy about it." Ritchie did find someone but his identity has not been traced and initial rehearsals proved disappointing. "The original singer, once we started playing, I realised couldn't improvise. He had a great voice, similar to Bryan Adams, but when we'd do a blues or something he couldn't improvise at all. It turned out he was a copy vocalist. Great guy, great voice, but I couldn't take him."

By the summer of 1994, relative tyro Douglas (or 'Doogie' as he prefers) White had been chosen as singer. Doogie had forwarded a demo tape to Ritchie's management some time before. Ritchie's girlfriend Candice Night had found the tape and played it to an impressed Blackmore, who arranged a try-out. White flew to the States for the audition. "It was kinda nervy. Ritchie was just my favourite guitarist and composer. Strangely I wasn't as nervous as when I had done the Maiden audition. You see I knew everything, every song that Rainbow ever played. I just started singing 'Rainbow Eyes' and Ritchie said 'I know that' and started playing. I knew then that it was going to be special. We just hit it off. We jammed, we wrote, we fooled around with the old stuff... awesome."

The initial three-day audition was extended to over a week as Doogie met and exceeded each of the demanding criteria set in turn by the Rainbow main-man.

Chapter 6

"I got a call from Jim, Ritchie's roadie, and he said that it was good news as Ritchie wanted me to stay for a few more days and jam some more. So I went to the rehearsal hall and Paul Morris, the keyboard player, started to jam out a couple of ideas with John O. Reilly, the drummer, and Rob, the bass player. Ritchie came in and fired up the Marshalls and we wrote a huge tune called 'Judgement Day'. We never recorded it for the album as we had other epic tunes to do." Doogie officially became the new singer on 20th April 1994.

Scotsman Doogie had formed La Paz in 1984, playing pubs and clubs around Scotland for four years. In 1988 he joined Midnight Blue, cutting one eponymous LP of good hard-edged AOR (released on Zero Records exclusively in Japan). Although a capable debut, a proliferation of similar rock outfits at the time meant record-company apathy was hard to overcome and led to the eventual break up of the band. A trip to Japan followed in 1991 singing with Praying Mantis in a NWOBHM revival tour.

A chance meeting with Blackmore's entourage at a Purple show in London resulted in the aforementioned demo tape being forwarded to Ritchie's office with a note to contact him if ever he needed a singer. White had also auditioned for German metal band Pink Cream 69 and come within an ace of being the new vocalist with Iron Maiden, only losing out in the final choice to Wolfsbane's Blaze Bayley. Just before the Rainbow job, Doogie had been lined up to lay down tracks with Cozy Powell and Neil Murray for a Powell solo project.

The rest of the band came together during the summer. Although Virgin Steele's Rob De Martino was the initial bassman for rehearsals in August, Ritchie's dissatisfaction soon meant American Greg Smith (Wendy O'Williams, Americade, Alice Cooper, Red Dawn and Joe Lynn Turner's band) joined the band. Paul Morris (ex-Warlock) on keyboards, who had previously auditioned for Rainbow over 10 years earlier, drummer John O. Reilly (from Mother's Army and - again - another of Joe Lynn Turner's bands) and occasional backing vocalist Candice Night completed the line-up.

A stunningly attractive former model, Candice Night had no performing background in music, and was working for an American radio station in the early nineties when she first met the guitarist (Ritchie was still in Deep Purple). By the time of the Rainbow album the couple were engaged, Candice had begun to write lyrics and sing for the upcoming album and the seeds of a future musical career together were beginning to be sown.

Ritchie told reporters: "I wanted to do more of a blues thing, but Doogie doesn't really have a bluesy voice, he's into the old classic hard rock and he loves Ronnie Dio. So as soon as he puts his vocal stamp down its naturally curved more toward a hard rock sound. There's nothing wrong with that. He can sing a hard rock song and then a ballad and then some old Scottish folk song - he has a broad spectrum as far as his voice goes. It's nice to have a singer that can sing different ways. John's not a showy type of drummer but more of a time-keeper - it's very hard to find a drummer these days that plays in time. Greg plays a very punchy right hand - he hits hard and its very rock'n'roll."

Ideas for the album were written over a seven-week period during the late summer of 1994 in an old colonial house called Tahigwa located in Cold Spring, New York. Doogie: "We worked every day for six weeks just jamming, gigging in local biker bars and Bavarian Inns, playing football and recording. Just getting to know each other. I taped everything and ended up with hours of cassettes of riffs and ideas. I had to keep a record of it or some of the ideas would have got lost. We wrote 'Stand & Fight', 'Black Masquerade' and 'Silence' during those sessions. Other tunes that failed to make the album from those times were 'Ask God For That', a very heavy riff-based song with a cracking melody and powerful lyrics. Very Rainbow.

"'Pagan Love Song' was going to be the ballad 'I Have Crossed Oceans of Time'. It was cracking. We actually recorded it for the album, but it had lost the mood it had at Tahigwa and Ritchie decided not to finish it. 'There Was a Time When I Called You My Brother' was a special song for me as it was the first we wrote together. I can still hear it in my head... 'Wrong Side Of Morning' was a reworking of a Midnight Blue tune that I had included on the audition tape I gave to Ritchie. There were several versions of songs recorded at that time. Ritchie made sure that no one escaped with any copies, and I had to hand over all the tapes to him. They probably still lie in his garage in the corner in a box."

The album itself was recorded between January and April 1995 at Long View Farm Studios in the heart of New England. Several tracks were credited to the Blackmore/Night partnership. Former Purple producer Pat Regan was chosen to control proceedings, as Ritchie reasoned: "He knew how to keep Doogie in line, whereas sometimes I wouldn't know quite what to tell Doogie as far as approaching a song - but Pat would always know what angle would be best."

Released in late 1995, the album broke little new ground and held no real surprises, although the style and content thankfully leaned more towards the late Dio era than the lighter material of the early eighties. Apart from the guitar the other instrumental performances proved workmanlike and, essentially, offered solid support. Most arrangements reprised the established 'Rainbow Sound', albeit with a punchy production and a welcome touch of a slightly heavier, aggressively British flavour courtesy of White's vocals.

Such was the singer's versatility that aspects of the styles adopted by each of his three predecessors could occasionally be heard. Doogie, in hindsight, remains critical of the album sound: "When we played the songs live there was an energy that perhaps is missing from the album. When I met the producer at a gig in L.A. he said, 'now that's what I was trying to capture.' I think Pat Regan is a tremendous producer and we always got on personally but I think we maybe lost the raw power that we had live. Its always a fine line between the American radio friendly sound and the British rock sound."

Left-right: Paul Morris, Chuck Bürgi, Scott Hazell (Ritchie's then guitar tech), Greg Smith, Doogie White, Blackmore

Much of the album revisited Rainbow's glorious past, with standout track 'Ariel' very much in the spirit of a 'Gates Of Babylon', its highlight a Candice Night vocal whispered over some archetypal Blackmore doodling in a spine-tingling finale. 'Too Late For Tears', by Ritchie's own admission, was a recycled 'Can't Happen Here'. 'Hunting Humans' was a relatively simple idea expertly done - a moody, dark number lyrically inspired by recent serial killings in the UK. Doogie: "That song just came so naturally. Ritchie just started the riff, the guys joined in and I warbled my way through it. I had my wee tape running and knew it was special. That night I made up a highlight of the day tape and rushed to Ritchie's apartment and played him the tune. It never changed from that arrangement, riff or melody. The whole thing took about 45 minutes to write."

From 'Ariel' video shoot: Doogie White, Candice Night, Blackmore

The plodding 'Cold Hearted Woman' originally had a Zeppelin style guitar-vocal opening section dropped from the final version. 'Black Masquerade', an otherwise rather average uptempo effort, stood out due to a breathtaking flamenco-style guitar solo that had a story behind it: "I played acoustic on that track, and that posed a unique problem when it came to recording the solo. When I play I hum along - I sing the notes as I'm playing. We got that particular solo down first take. Pat was really pleased with it, and I thought 'Great!' Then he played it back and said 'What's that noise in the background? Are you singing?' So we had to keep going over it. And I couldn't play without humming it. Finally, we had to mike it in such a way that the mike wouldn't pick up my humming while I was playing."

'Stand And Fight' was a bluesy romp harking back to a 'Slaves And Masters' era groove, while the hard-hitting 'Silence' was based around the theme from 'The Man With The Golden Arm' with the vocal melody line blatantly copped from Purple's 'You Fool No One'. The track was also originally to feature a different vocal style. "We wanted to do this twin vocal thing," Doogie explained, "because Ritchie was a fan of Jack Bruce and Eric Clapton doing that twin vocal thing that he also sort of covered in the Coverdale-Hughes era of Deep Purple." Grieg's 'Hall Of

Chapter 6

The Mountain King' received a similar Rainbow treatment as Beethoven's Ninth, albeit with improvised lyrics. (Ritchie: "I used to play it now and again on stage, we put a vocal onto it, and then going to an instrumental and speeding up towards the end. Very much like the actual classical version. I thought, 'This could be a bit corny,' but the more I got into it, playing with the band, the more I thought this could sound really good.")

Apart from the aforementioned tracks like 'Judgement Day', several tracks remained in the can in demo form, and included titles reported as 'Treason And Pain', and 'Emotional Crime' - though the latter was originally intended for the album but instead turned up as the obligatory bonus track on the Japanese CD release. The re-recording of 'Still I'm Sad' - originally intended to be the bonus track - was mistakenly included by the record company on the standard European version. "We were playing it at rehearsals," revealed Ritchie. "The bass player and drummer said it might be a good idea to do it again, and we did it very quickly." Apart from a fabulous minute-long guitar intro, this version - now with lyrics - paled in comparison with the 1975 cover.

Commercially, things were always going to be difficult. By now the emerging rap-derived 'nu-metal' was the flavour of the month for all metal cognoscenti, almost to the exclusion of all else. This meant there was little room for Rainbow's characteristic brand of sophisticated melodic hard rock, particularly in Britain and North America where the viability of AOR and traditional heavy metal prominent for the past 20 years was, in the eyes of the music industry at least, dead and buried.

Doogie dealt with unbelievers in a traditional Rainbow-esque fashion: "Some of the journalists wanted to know if I thought that Rainbow music was still relevant in the '90s. I always said that it was and gave my reasons. One guy wouldn't let it lie, he kept on about how music had changed and how we were old farts living off past glories. All this crap while drinking our beer and eating our food in our dressing room. So I picked him up and threw him out the dressing room, took his pass off him and had a security guard throw this 'intruder' out the building."

Despite its perceived shortcomings, the album showed enough promise to sell well in Blackmore's traditional foreign strongholds, racking up sales of over 350,000. In Scandinavia the album peaked at No. 8 and in Germany it hung around the thirties and forties, selling steadily for several months. In Japan the release went straight in at No.3.

After a week of rehearsals in Copenhagen during late September, the promotional tour commenced in Helsinki on 30 September 1995. Most dates were in 1,000-3,000-seat theatre venues, finishing in Japan in late November. After Reilly had been injured playing soccer, Chuck Bürgi was drafted in as replacement (at Greg Smith's suggestion). He returned to the band - after completing a jobbing session with Blue Öyster Cult - in mid-September 1995, initially for the first few live shows only but soon became a permanent member of the touring band.

Such was the positive impact of the Japanese tour that Burrn magazine's 1995 poll awards featured Ritchie or the band in no less than seven categories, including Best Group, Best Songwriters, Best Live Show and Best Song (for 'Black Masquerade'). Several concerts were broadcast in various media formats - the Stockholm show from 2nd October 1995 was aired on Swedish radio and German satellite channel WDR video-taped the band at the Düsseldorf gig on 9th October for TV transmission over the Christmas period.

Both shows featured heavily in an extensive bootleg catalogue; with the advent of DAT and CD-R, over two dozen recent performances became generally available. The Japanese even put out an extortionately priced 10-CD box set featuring all of the Far Eastern tour! An edited version of 'Ariel' was released as a single in many European countries, backed with a gloriously majestic version

Chapter 6

of 'Temple Of The King' taken from the Stockholm concert.

The shows were based around the new material bolstered with a collection shrewdly biased towards the ever-popular Dio songs. Set lists were changed regularly, rather ironically since Blackmore had been criticised in the past for resisting such changes with Deep Purple. Blackmore had the final say regarding what they would play live and, while White's suggestions to include 'Temple Of The King', 'Mistreated' and 'Burn' were accepted, he pushed in vain for ever more varied inclusions. "I wanted 'Kill The King', I wanted to do 'Tarot Woman', I wanted to have a go at 'Stargazer' or 'Gates Of Babylon'. He has certain things he likes and certain things he doesn't like - he won't be persuaded one way or the other."

Not everything worked. In Doogie's words, "Anything by Graham Bonnet (was) impossible for me to sing. He tracks his voice and that's what gives it this huge scary sound. We tried 'All Night Long' and I can still hear the band's laughter as I spluttered through it - it was in my range but sounded unconvincing." 'Rainbow Eyes' was another oldie aired in rehearsals but never performed in its entirety, although a verse or two did feature occasionally. Purple tracks included the obligatory 'Smoke On The Water', along with a welcome return later in the tour for 'Mistreated'.

'Burn' was taken at a ferocious pace, the music whipped along by Bürgi's drums, and featured Hughes-Coverdale style twin vocals, Greg Smith proving well able to handle the harmony parts. 'Perfect Strangers' was performed much as the original 1984 studio version and fans were also treated to the occasional romp through 'Black Night'.

Doogie, in particular, acquitted himself well on stage. Unlike some of his predecessors he was more than capable vocally with the entire range of Rainbow catalogue, equally at home belting out rockers or ballads. He was also able to bring an emotional range to the newer songs far more than he managed (or maybe was allowed to) in the studio. The rest of the band came across as able if rather anonymous players, projecting little in the way of stage presence, seemingly subordinate to the efforts of the guitarist everyone had paid their money to see. The band pulled out the stops on the UK dates at the Hammersmith Apollo. Doogie: "That first Hammy show was just the best.

The best vibe, the most fun and certainly the longest we ever played. I think it was over two and a half hours long. We played a lot of things we had not played before - indeed we didn't really know some of them. At the end of the gig Ritchie did a big finale and dramatically laid the guitar on the edge of the stage feeding back. The crowd was going mad and he said we should go back on and do another. We got out there and his guitar was gone. The synth was still feeding back with a drone like a set of bagpipes but the guitar was nowhere to be seen. So I made up a sort of Scottish folk song about wanting to do a song but someone had nicked Ritchie's guitar.

"There was a huge cheer as two blokes came back into the hall holding the guitar above their heads like it was a football trophy. Ritchie calmly took the guitar which was still in tune, gave the guys passes for the party and let rip. Awesome."

Rather than arrange the usual intensive ongoing tour schedule, things were taken at a more leisurely pace from the outset, with short bursts of dates punctuated with several weeks off. (Many shows were soundboard-recorded onto DAT with a view to a live album sometime in the future.)

Some bizarre scheduling followed which meant many areas played in Europe in 1995 were revisited less than a year later. Ritchie had the singer's monitors turned off during the Copenhagen gig, Doogie's response to which apparently led to the singer's sacking after the show, although things were patched up the day after. "He was dicking around with me. I took exception to him turning my monitors off and then blaming me for singing flat or sharp or whatever. It was just so idiotic to have 15,000 people or whatever and to cut out the singer's vocals. I asked him to come and talk to me if he had a problem with me. He never did."

During 1996 Ritchie agreed to do a rare session, playing (albeit rather restrained) guitar on 'Apache' for *'Twang - A Tribute To The Shadows'*. He also reprised 'Smoke On The Water' for MOR singer Pat Boone's bizarre set of hard rock covers *'In A Metal Mood'*, recording the guitar parts right after the Vienna show in July.

The next round of live shows included a nine-date visit to South America, undertaken in June and early July 1996 - the first visit by Rainbow to this newly discovered hotbed of hard rock. For Doogie and the rest of the band though, things were starting to unravel, primarily with their relationship with the administration. (Former schoolteacher Carole Stevens - Candice's mother - was now also Ritchie's business manager.) "South America was the last time that we had THAT vibe. Ritchie's new management started making life difficult when there was no need. We were all doing well and getting on famously in '95 but I think Carole Stevens had a different plan that did not involve Ritchie being in Rainbow. So he became more isolated and insular. It was very difficult to talk with him and it did not lead to a happy band."

Indeed, Ritchie's announcement at around this time of his intention to work on a solo album may perhaps explain the growing isolation between band and guitarist. Ignoring the opportunity to write the killer instrumental album most fans would have voted for. ("A singer is important. It's like an orchestra without the lead violin. I like instrumentals - but not all the time.") The material was described as acoustic renaissance-style songs, with the vocals handled by Candice.

The American release of *'Strangers In Us All'* was delayed until January 1997, in order to co-ordinate promotion and to coincide with a low-key tour throughout February and March. Chuck Bürgi had by this time departed for more financially lucrative pastures (drumming for Enrique Iglesias). Former Sabbath/Gary Moore/Kiss jobber Eric Singer was initially in the frame though Bürgi had recommended 34 year-old New Yorker John Micelli. Ex of Meatloaf and Marchello, Micelli who was stylistically more in the Cozy Powell mould of an economic, hard-hitting power drummer, had replaced Bürgi in Blue Öyster Cult.

Programme from the 1997 Esbjerg Festival, Rainbow's last ever gig

With just nine days in which to rehearse before the first of the American dates, initial shows were not the best, the band sounding a touch rusty although the latter concerts proved excellent. Overall performance

was also hindered by periodic bouts of illness that hit all in the group at various times. The concerts were also dogged with sound problems. Without the budget to justify playing the larger venues the tour achieved little in terms of extra sales (even distribution of the album throughout the US remained sporadic) and the lack of co-ordinated promotion meant the tour slipped by largely unnoticed in the music press.

These problems notwithstanding, positive future plans were laid for the group. At this time the intention was to take a break before a series of summer festival appearances through the summer of 1997, along with some European dates (including Poland and Russia) already pencilled in. Ideas for the next Rainbow album would then be worked up in the early autumn. However, events surrounding the Blackmore's solo album meant the US tour would ultimately prove the swansong of this particular incarnation of Rainbow.

Chapter 7

RENAISSANCE MAN
(1997-2002)

IN SEPTEMBER/OCTOBER 1996, Ritchie embarked on recording the solo album. The Renaissance project had long been an ambition of Blackmore's, often citing this musical style and period of history as one of his favourites. "It's taken me the last 25 years to get a grip on the acoustic guitar [sic]. I was hesitant about it, but now I can play it well. It's the type of stuff you can imagine people in Europe playing around a castle when the full moon's out. I'm quite excited about it because its different - there's not going to be any Marshalls."

Several tracks had been written by Blackmore and Night in free time up to and during the sessions for the Rainbow album (indeed, 'Ariel' had originally been written for this project). *'Shadow Of The Moon'*, recorded at Ritchie's Long Island home, was released under the Blackmore's Night name in Japan in April 1997 (RCA), with Europe (Edel Records) following in August.

This was obviously a world away from Rainbow and Deep Purple fare and showed another side to the 'rock god' guitarist. Ritchie's acoustic efforts proved to be the most rigidly structured studio work of his career. Away from the pressure of writing-to-order in the studio that became the norm with both previous groups, the tunes here were written at a more leisurely pace and had that much more room to develop. Candice's vocals, although lacking a rock-singer's range, had a wistful folk feel reminiscent of Maggie Reilly or Sally Oldfield, perfectly complementing the mood of the album.

Ritchie's empathy and love for the style of the music shines through, though said styles proved to be rather more eclectic than the medieval-orientated release described. 'Writing On The Wall', with its programmed disco drum-beat, even showed a bizarre Euro-pop sensibility not apparent in any previous rock directions ('Blackmore's Abba', anyone?). Opinions tended to be polarised over the track, it was loved or loathed in equal measure. The moody, Pink Floyd-esque vibe of 'No Second Chance' and 'Wish You Were Here' (a cover of a Rednex song), along with the title track itself, were the most impressive cuts, and the instrumentals too proved excellent. At least 18 tracks were recorded, including the acoustic version of 'Ariel' that was not used on the final album. Jethro Tull's Ian Anderson contributed flute on 'Play Minstrel Play'.

Despite the deliberate intention to keep the project distinctly low key, the album was received so well in some quarters it sold beyond all expectations and peaked at 14 in the Japanese album charts during May, shifting a impressive 100,000 units in the first fortnight of release alone. In some countries it even matched sales of the recent Rainbow effort.

Rainbow played the annual Esbjerg rock festival in Denmark in May 1997. Cozy Powell, at the event with Peter Green's band, agreed to guest during the encore for 'Smoke On The Water' but unfortunately the set overran the strict curfew imposed by the festival promoter and the plan was nixed. Although the band was in great demand throughout Europe and further tours were pencilled in for the autumn, it had been decided (even before the US tour) to concentrate on the acoustic project. Doogie: "Ritchie, myself, Cozy Powell and a couple of others shared stories and some wine and had a great night. On the day of the gig Ritchie was in a good mood. It was after the show that I knew I would not be doing any more gigs with him. It was business stuff. I waited a couple of weeks after the show to see if the waters would calm, but no-one from his side would talk to me. Not him, not his management, nobody. I had no choice but to call their bluff and see if they still wanted me as part of the set-up. On Friday 13th July, I called Carole and handed in my notice."

Each of the Rainbow band members were offered retaining contracts by Carole Stevens' Minstrel Hall Management, but none considered the offers to be financially sufficient until such time as the band was reformed so the musicians went their separate ways. From comments by the man himself in various interviews it seemed Blackmore's interest in pursuing a heavy rock direction was over, at least in the short term. Even though his tenure was now over, Doogie White had no regrets: "He gave me something that only three other guys have ever had. I was the singer in Rainbow. And it was brilliant."

Meanwhile, 'The Very Best Of Rainbow' was put out by Polydor during August 1997 primarily to fill the niche in the US market for a general collection. Originally planned as a double, the eventual single CD consisted of already available material, albeit in supposedly remastered form.

Despite Ritchie being wholly committed to the acoustic project, the impending 21st anniversary of 'Rising' in 1997 saw the spread of Internet-led rumours regarding a reformation of the classic seventies line-up for a one-off album and tour. Ritchie had mentioned in recent interviews that he would consider working with both Ronnie and Cozy again in some capacity in the future. The involvement of Tony Carey appeared unlikely ("Ronnie needs Rainbow more than I do") though the participation of Bob Daisley's manager in early negotiations suggested he was a probable bassist. However, a tragic turn of events meant provisional plans got no further.

Then the whole affair assumed a wholly new character. On 5th April 1998, Cozy crashed his Saab on the M4 motorway near Bristol in Southwest England and died from head injuries on the way to hospital. Opinions on the causes for the tragedy varied; he had been travelling at over 100 mph and was talking on his mobile phone to his girlfriend around the time of the crash. Post mortem results also revealed his blood alcohol level was just over the legal limit. Whatever the reasons, Cozy's dreadful loss brought forth a wave of emotional tributes that exemplified his prominent standing within the music world.

Ritchie stated: "The news of his death was a great shock to us all. His friendship was always valued, his music immortalised." Roger Glover: "His challenging, lop-sided grin and easygoing charm endeared him to everyone during our time in Rainbow. We shared many a laugh and adventure. He did nothing in half measures."

Ronnie James Dio: "The rock world has lost a legend and I have lost a friend. His brilliance as a drummer was evident to anyone who knew him. But it will always be his irrepressible spirit and full appetite for life that will be remembered by those who knew him personally."

Ritchie seemed to lose interest in any reunion thereafter: "We'd thrown the idea around, and Ronnie and I sent each messages back and forth, and we spoke to Cozy, but it was never followed up properly. It sounded a good idea over a drink, but Ronnie's very busy and so am I, and after what happened to Cozy it all fizzled out."

Never one to mince words, Dio saw Ritchie's management as the stumbling block: "For me, the timing was right because I had divested myself of my then band, but I suspect Ritchie's management felt I wasn't worthy to be in that band again, that my stature was not as big as Ritchie's... which is bullshit. I sold a helluva lot more records than Ritchie did for years. Sure, he did well with the reformed Purple. But, hey, I did pretty well with Dio and pretty damn well with Sabbath."

The ever-candid Ronnie disparaged Blackmore's new direction in acoustic music:

"It's so idiotic for this man who has set himself up as being this god of hard rock. If you want my opinion, he's being led around by the nose by his missus. It's all about getting her a career."

Given the turnover of personnel over the years, it perhaps comes as a surprise that there seems little long-term animosity preventing most ex-band members being receptive to some sort of Rainbow reformation, Joe Lynn Turner for one: "I think if we put Rainbow back together with a line-up that also contained Chuck Burgi, Greg Smith and David Rosenthal, we would come out and kill! Actually we all tried to get hold of Ritchie one time on a conference call but we couldn't get past Carole Stevens. She's Candice's mother, and between the pair of them they intercept any attempt to get through to Ritchie these days."

Whatever the official stance from all interested parties, rumours of moves to bring together various ex-members have continued into the new millennium. Airey, Dio, Bain and Blackmore have all reportedly expressed interest in reuniting for one of a series of classic band specials, called One Night Only, organised by Polygram. Provisionally to take place in Japan sometime in 2002, Aynsley Dunbar is mooted for drum duties with the show to be recorded for CD and DVD/video release.

At the time of writing Rainbow's profile remains surprisingly high, the entire Polydor back catalogue was released in 1999 in re-mastered form (alas with no outtakes, lyric sheets, expanded booklets, etc.) and continues to sell around six figures annually. From Rainbow royalties alone, Blackmore's accountants need not fear for their jobs. With the resurgence of classic hard rock, several Rainbow tribute albums (albeit of variable worth) from Germany and Japan have done the rounds, while unauthorised bootleg recordings from Rainbow's entire concert history still proliferate.

In 2001, the band were nominated for inclusion in the Rock'n'Roll Hall of Fame. Recent polls in several hard-rock magazines have shown Rainbow among the top ten 'most missed bands', and Ritchie remains firmly positioned in the Best Guitarist listings.

Another Blackmore's Night CD *'Under A Violet Moon'* (featuring a delightfully fragile take of Rainbow's debut LP track 'Self Portrait') was released in 1999 and a tour of European castles was followed by their first eagerly-awaited British dates in the summer of 2000. The third release, *'Fires At Midnight'*, saw the light of day in June 2001 via the German SPV label. Rainbow, though, is still on hold - until The Man in Black gets a hankering for cranking out those fabulous hard-rock riffs just one more time.

To Blackmore, the last word: "I have to give it a rest for a while. This music's so fulfilling and different I just have to get it out of my system. Maybe further down the line, when my batteries are recharged... it's a definite possibility."

Chapter 8

AFTER THE RAINBOW

SO WHAT HAPPENED to the score or so of musicians and singers formerly a part of the Rainbow?

Don Airey

Contributed keyboards or musical arrangements (live and in the studio) to a veritable multitude of acts throughout the eighties, including Bernie Marsden's Alaska, UFO, Gilbert O'Sullivan, Jethro Tull, Gary Moore, Fastway, Irish rockers Mama's Boys, ELO and Brian May. Studio sessions included, most significantly, Whitesnake's multi-million seller *'1987'*, while he arranged the winning 1997 Eurovision song 'Love Shine A Light' for Katrina And The Waves.

He also set up Don Airey Music, which provides corporate ID and soundtracks. A solo concept comprising orchestral pieces and instrumentals called *'K2'* was also released, and featured Colin Blunstone and Gary Moore with Cozy Powell (who else?) on drums. In mid-1996 Don collaborated on Tony Iommi's eponymous solo album (released in 2000) and the reformed Quatermass II CD release *'Hard Road'*. He toured in 1999 as part of Blunstone's band, and with Moody, Murray and Marsden's Company of Snakes, parting company in June 2001.

Don recently linked up with Graham Bonnet to tour a Rainbow-based set around Europe and the UK before replacing the retiring Jon Lord in Deep Purple in early 2002.

Jimmy Bain

Stepped in at short notice to tour Europe with John Cale and later appeared with Ian Hunter's Overnight Angels. Demos were also recorded with Procol Harum's Matthew Fisher that remain unreleased to this day. Jimmy then got together with ex-Thin Lizzy guitarist Brian Robertson, with a view to putting a band together. Wild Horses was the result, releasing two LPs on EMI in the early eighties (*'Wild Horses'* and *'Stand Your Ground'* - both 1999 reissues on Zoom Club). Understandably the material resembled Thin Lizzy in style, although Bain's vocals were a little on the weak side.

At the turn of the punk decade, Bain was a regular participant in a bibulous and good-time collective featuring members of Lizzy, The Damned, The Sex Pistols, The Boomtown Rats and various others, playing sporadic club dates under the moniker The Greedies, or more often The Greedy Bastards. In 1983, Jimmy linked up again with Ronnie in his band Dio. Jimmy had just finished touring as part of Phil Lynott's solo band and had contributed bass parts to The Scorpions' platinum-selling *'Blackout'* album.

A central figure within Dio, Jimmy helped craft some of the finest heavy-metal anthems of the eighties, as well as playing a central part in writing 'Stars', the heavy rock world's contribution to the famine relief charity started by Bob Geldof and Live Aid.

By 1989, however, Ronnie Dio dismissed his band in an effort to rejuvenate fortunes. Jimmy Bain took his sacking particularly badly, some acrimonious comments in the press regarding Dio fuelling a rift between them. Jimmy's personal circumstances were further complicated with his ongoing struggles with alcohol and drugs.

He had signed a solo deal with Atco Records in mid-1988 and, in autumn 1989, Jimmy formed a band with American vocalist Jesse Bradman (a former keyboard player in an early version of Night Ranger) and ex-Kingdom Come guitarist Danny Stag. With the recruitment in March 1990 of Mandy Lyon on vocals, Tracey G on guitar, and old colleague Vinnie Appice (in November 1990) the group evolved into what would become known as World War III. Their passable 1991 eponymous debut album sank without trace, however, the band floundered and Appice rejoined Black Sabbath.

By the mid-nineties, Jimmy, having now thankfully conquered his addictions, had started work on a new venture. The Key utilised a far more melodic and commercial approach. Guitarist on the project was again Tracey G, borrowed from Dio's then band. Ronnie's concept project Magica then saw Bain return to the Dio story: "Jimmy came into the picture after we'd written it. He called to tell me that he'd been completely 'rehabbed' now. And step 10 of the rehab was to call people and apologise for the bad things you've done to them. He called Wendy and apologised and asked if I would speak to him after some of the horrible things he said about me when he was drugged out.

"He's on the right road now. He called me and said: 'I'm sorry for whatever happened.' And I said, 'Jimmy, I'm just glad you sorted yourself out. I'm not gonna have a go at you now; I'm gonna be on your side.' So we got the best of everything. Jimmy came back - the best bass player I ever worked with... He's exactly the same as he was before except he remembers everything now!"

Graham Bonnet

As if his departure from Rainbow wasn't enough, his personal management then rapidly disappeared over the horizon with much of Bonnet's cash, leaving the singer with just $12,000 to show for his time with Rainbow. (Thereafter Bonnet would handle his own business affairs.) He went on to release his solo album, *'Line Up'*, on Vertigo which included such luminaries as Jon Lord, Status Quo's Francis Rossi, guitarist Micky Moody and Cozy Powell. Bonnet returned the favour by singing on Moody's TV commercial for Levi jeans around this time.

Despite the first single 'Night Games' (a hard-rock number written by Ed Hamilton) making the UK Top 10 and the follow-up 'Liar' (a Russ Ballard cover) also doing well, the album sold in modest numbers. Ranging from fifties pastiche 'Anthony Boy' to the bar-room boogie of 'Out On The Water', it suffered from a lack of a cohesive direction and a watered-down mix. "It became a pop album though it started out as basic rock. The guy who produced it (Guy Eden) got in keyboard players from Toyah's band and made it flowery."

After attempts to retain Moody, Powell and Lord as a touring band ended in failure, Graham followed Cozy's lead in early 1982 by joining the Michael Schenker Group, though the drummer had left before the recording of *'Assault Attack'* later that year. By August 1982 the pressure told with some bizarre behaviour during a warm-up gig just days before a Reading Festival headlining appearance, splitting his trousers and forgetting lyrics. Possible causes were many and varied, and the incident remains to be fully explained to this day. Excuses included alcoholic excess coupled with Bonnet's diabetes.

What was in no doubt was Bonnet slagging off Schenker to the bemused audience, dragging hidden rhythm guitarist Steve Casey from behind the stage amps ('This is the guy who plays the parts Michael can't manage!') before finally storming off stage. An immediate parting of the ways occurred directly afterward, Graham fleeing to the States with his professional reputation severely dented.

Although rumours abounded that he had recently turned down an offer from Black Sabbath, Bonnet's only real option left was to bring in others and put together his own group. He formed Alcatrazz in early 1983, going on to produce three studio albums and a live mini-album, initially on Rocshire Records before the label's collapse meant a move to Capitol for the second LP. Attempts to co-opt Sensational Alex Harvey Band guitarist Zal Cleminson and ex-Jethro Tull drummer

Chapter 8

Barriemore Barlow came to nought and he initially employed ex-Iron Maiden drummer Clive Burr, although he was replaced by Alice Cooper drummer Jan Uvena after only a few weeks.

Other recruits to the group were a 19 year-old Swedish guitar virtuoso Yngwie Malmsteen from Steeler and two former members of a well-respected AOR band called New England: bassist Gary Shea and Jimmy Waldo on keyboards. Initially things went well and Bonnet was pleased with the band, especially his guitarist: "He was perfect... a heavy sort of Blackmore guitarist... but I think he's probably better!"

The material presented on the debut album *'No Parole From Rock'n'Roll'* was indeed very much in the recent Rainbow and MSG mould, particularly with Malmsteen's input - tracks like 'Hiroshima Mon Amour' and 'Jet To Jet' borrowed heavily from the style first pioneered on *'Down To Earth'*. With Bonnet's Far Eastern popularity following the last Rainbow tour, it came as no surprise that the album did extremely well in Japan. It did not however, secure a UK release (on RCA) until almost a year later.

A tour of Japan met with further success. (The *'Live Sentence'* mini-LP was recorded at this time, but proved a poor representation of their abilities.) The singer enthused: "The band is very, very big in Japan... we're something like second top band at the moment." Conflicts over musical direction between vocalist and guitarist soon saw Yngwie quit for an ultimately successful solo career in mid-1984. Bonnet, now having revised his opinion of the Swede, commented sourly: "He's an ignorant little sod, a star-struck little arsehole... He was very fortunate to be in this band, and he's fortunate to be out of it too."

Yngwie responded: "He was a very unstable sort of person - in many ways a manic-depressive. But I don't actually dislike the guy at all." Steve Vai was recruited in time for the second LP, *'Disturbing the Peace'*, which sounded far less derivative, instrumentally at least, and things progressed nicely, even though Vai's extraordinary axe-work tended to overshadow other aspects of the LP. A one-off talent like Vai was always going to be sought-after by higher profile artists and it came as no surprise that Steve left in late 1985 for a job with David Lee Roth. His replacement was former Axis, Rick Derringer and Rod Stewart guitarist Danny Johnson.

After the third album, *'Dangerous Games'*, the band were dropped by the record company and split soon after amid a welter of debt. To make ends meet, Bonnet sang backing vocals on Pretty Maid's *'Future World'* opus. There followed a co-operation with shredder Chris Impellitteri and a series of forgettable Forcefield albums through the late eighties.

'Here Comes The Night' was a 1991 album of pop-chart material done in Bonnet's inimitable style, including yet another take on 'Only One Woman'. In June 1991 he contributed vocals on four songs for the live performance of Eddie Hardin's *'Wind In The Willows'* in Germany, an enjoyable live CD following on Angel Air. In the early nineties Bonnet and Jimmy Waldo linked up with former Meatloaf guitarist Bob Kulick and Quiet Riot's rhythm section of Chuck Wright and Frankie Banali as the super-group project Blackthorne. 1993's *'Afterlife'* (on Music For Nations) was a fair reflection of each member's past with some archetypal classic (and at times classy) hard rock.

Bonnet then released a low-key solo effort *'Underground'* (Victor Entertainment) in 1997. This time co-opting in Danny Johnson, former Firm/Blue Murder bassist Tony Franklin and drummer Kevin Valentine, it was more of the same, yet again boasting a Rainbow remake; this time a creditable stab at 'Lost In Hollywood'. Late 2000 saw Bonnet rejoin Impellitteri for the album *'Seek And Destroy'*, while he also linked briefly with the Japanese metal band Anthem for its reunion tour and CD, *'Heavy Metal Anthem'*.

Some European dates were arranged through 2001 with Don Airey, Voodoo Hill guitarist Dario Mollo and Thunder's rhythm section of Harry James and Chris Childs. This coincided with the European release of the previously Japanese-only *'The Day I Went Mad'*, again with Franklin and Valentine and with guest appearances from ex Guns'N'Roses six-stringer Slash, Def Leppard's Vivian Campbell and former Kiss member Bruce Kulick.

With the benefit of hindsight some twenty years on, Bonnet recently related how he regretted his departure from the Rainbow fold. "I should have stayed - I wish I had. I should have stayed for another year. I left too soon. My ego was a bit too over-the-top... Ritchie was a real influence. My career took a huge leap forward with Rainbow. He was always a good guy to me, and a great guitar player. I'd love to sing with him again given the opportunity." Over to you, Ritchie.

Chapter 8

Chuck Bürgi

After a recommendation by Meatloaf guitarist Bob Kulick (who had been in Balance with the drummer) Chuck became an integral part of Meatloaf's group for a five-year succession of albums and tours. Other work included recording with over-hyped German rockers Zeno on their mediocre 1986 eponymous debut, Kulick's own band project Skull in 1987 (for one album in mid-1989) and Bobby Messano's self-titled solo LP of July 1988. Chuck also appeared on Glen Burtnick's 1987 album *'Heroes and Zeroes'*.

A lengthy four-year stint with Blue Öyster Cult ensued through the nineties before his return to Rainbow, following this with a spell backing Latin-pop lothario Enrique Iglesias.

Tony Carey

Forged a successful career for himself as a singer-songwriter and multi-instrumentalist, issuing a series of sophisticated middle-of-the-road rock albums (1982's *'Tony Carey'*, 1984's *'No Tough City'* and 1986's *'Blue Highway'* are the pick). Carey and his band opened for Night Ranger on their summer 1984 US tour. He also produced other artists in Germany, as well as writing for film and television, and guested on Pat Travers' 1977 LP *'Puttin' It Straight'*.

A mid-eighties studio project, Planet P, yielded two albums (*'Planet P'* and *'Pink World'*, on Geffen and MCA respectively) consisting of complex, conceptual prog-rock coupled with a state-of-the-art production. In 1984 the single 'Fine Fine Day', lifted from *'No Tough City'*, even crept into the US Top 50. By 1985 he owned and ran his own recording facility, the Hot Line Studios in Frankfurt. Tony also co-wrote with Aussie singer Jimmy Barnes, appeared on Max Carl's *'Circle'* (on MCA - a Sammy Hagar-type rocker and former Tommy Bolin band member) and worked with (among many others) Peter Maffay, Debbie Bonham and John Mayall. In 2000 a third Planet P album was in the process of being recorded.

Mark Clarke

Resurfaced with the Henry Gross Band, before the start of a long association of producing and writing with American rocker Billy Squier in 1981. He was also briefly part of Tony Carey's backing group. He joined guitarist Leslie West in a reformed Mountain during the mid-eighties, supporting Deep Purple at Ritchie's specific request on part of their 1985 reunion tour. (Their 1984 LP *'Go For Your Life'* is recommended.) Clarke also made the final short-list as Bill Wyman's replacement in The Rolling Stones. Writing, production and performing credits include work with such diverse artists as Michael Bolton, Cher, Ian Hunter, The Monkees and Stephen Stills.

A 1994 reformation of Colosseum resulted in a very successful 60-date tour and yielded the 1995 album *'Colosseum Lives'*. This was followed up in late 1997 by the excellent *'Bread And Circuses'*. Mark continues to record and perform live with both Colosseum and Mountain.

Bob Daisley

Became a much sought-after jobbing bass-player. An encounter with a forlorn Ozzy in Camden early in 1981 meant Bob became a founding member of Ozzy's Blizzard Of Oz, along with hotshot guitarist Randy Rhoads. Although Bob and drummer Lee Kerslake were dumped in favour of the more visually acceptable Rudy Sarzo and Tommy Aldridge in November 1981, Daisley maintained a writing agreement with the singer for several years. Bob allegedly contributed most of the lyrics (albeit uncredited) on albums like *'Blizzard Of Oz'*, *'Bark At The Moon'*, *'Ultimate Sin'* and *'No Rest For The Wicked'*.

In 1982, Daisley took both Jet Records and Ozzy's then manager, (the infamous) Don Arden, to court for unpaid royalties deriving from his work on the first two albums. Recent proceedings, started in 1999, saw both Daisley and Kerslake (along with other ex-Ozzy musicians) renew attempts to legally force outstanding payments. A stint with the revitalised Uriah Heep (for eighties album releases *'Abominog'* and *'Head First'*) was followed by a spell with Gary Moore on a succession of LP's (*'Run For Cover'*, *'Wild Frontier'* and *'Still Got the Blues'*). Other sessions for numerous and varied acts also took place, most interestingly with Yngwie Malmsteen (for 1987's *'Odyssey'*) and Black Sabbath (*'Eternal Idol'* in 1989). In the early nineties he co-founded the Mother's Army project, helping to write a series of releases with an American-flavoured hard-rock direction.

Ronnie James Dio

Initially intended to embark on a solo career, and he started to consider musicians with which to form a band. Meantime he recorded vocals for a couple of tracks (*'Mask Of The Great Deceiver'* and *'To Live For The King'*) on Kansas guitarist Kerry

Chapter 8

Livgren's CBS solo LP *'Seeds of Change'* released in 1980. The Sweet was at the time singer-less after Brian Connolly's departure and reportedly approached him, but they decided to carry on as a trio. Other proposed options involved Bob Daisley on bass, but a call from Black Sabbath's management in the late spring of 1979 radically changed Dio's career strategy from that point on.

With their current singer Ozzy Osbourne about to be sacked, Dio was invited to try out with the band. Ronnie takes up the story: "I received a phone call from Tony Iommi... Sabbath were currently doing their 'farewell' album. They had a house in Beverley Hills and he asked me to go up and meet Geezer and Bill. I was a bit doubtful considering Ozzy was still around but I went and it proved a fruitful evening! Tony took me into the rehearsal studio, which was in fact a garage, and played me the beginning of 'Children Of The Sea'. We finished the song that night and I was asked to join."

This new and highly productive partnership led to the hugely impressive *'Heaven And Hell'* opus of April 1980, which rejuvenated the band's fortunes (making Number 9 in the UK album charts and selling well over a million in the US alone) and re-established their credibility. Perhaps most importantly, it brought them to the attention of a new generation of fans. Ronnie's efforts confounded critics and fans alike, proving without doubt that Sabbath could remain viable without Ozzy. Former Elf/Rainbow bassist Craig Gruber assisted with pre-production when the disenchanted Geezer Butler quit the band. Gruber even went as far as inspiring the characteristic bass line of the album's title track. (It is said that once Butler heard the fruits of the initial album sessions, he wisely decided to rejoin!)

Recently Ronnie expanded on the problems during recording: "Geezer went home due to personal reasons, after just a day. Who did that leave to write? Look at the four-way credits on the album and then tell me the songs that Geezer Butler wrote. I can tell you on two fingers." The rest of 1980 and early 1981 was taken up with extensive touring to promote the album, at times co-headlining with Blue Öyster Cult (BÖC guru Sandy Pearlman managing both outfits at the time).

For the final leg of the US tour, drummer Vinnie Appice replaced the ailing Bill Ward, struggling with severe drug and alcohol addiction. Dio: "Someone gave us a tape of Vinnie, and we listened to it, and said, 'This kid's great!' Brought him down for rehearsal, and the rest was easy. He's just a great player." Vinnie (brother of famed Vanilla Fudge/Rod Stewart drummer Carmine Appice) had previously worked with Rick Derringer and co-formed Axis in the mid-seventies. Appice's recruitment prompted Ozzy to christen the line-up 'Geezer and the three Wops'.

While on the road, tracks for the follow-up LP *'Mob Rules'* were written. The songs were recorded at the Record Plant in L.A. and the album released in late 1981. The *'Mob Rules'* material was again impressive (check out the expansive 'Falling Off The Edge Of The World' and the intense 'Sign Of The Southern Cross'), but at the time the album ended up unfairly overshadowed by its awesome predecessor.

With such strident personalities involved, egos invariably clashed and things came to a head with a bitter row over mixing of the forthcoming live album, taped on the world tour. By October of 1982, the inevitable and acrimonious split had occurred, leaving Dio to finally embark his planned solo career. The double *'Live Evil'* album was released in January 1983 and (over-long guitar solos apart) remains arguably the best live record of any Sabbath line-up. Sandy Pearlman was also ditched at the time (in favour of the infamous Don Arden) and told the press: "Sabbath had an ability to consume large amounts of money... Dio and I got on pretty well... he knew what money was worth and he wanted to make it... Dio was not a problem - it was the others."

Ronnie's original intention to record a solo LP meant a record deal with Warner Brothers had been in place for some two years. He had already written some material, including early versions of what became 'Holy Diver' and 'Don't Talk To Strangers'. It was already agreed that Vinnie Appice and brother Carmine would drum together on one - unspecified - track. David Stone, now playing with Le Mans, had also been approached to assist, but did not appear on the album.

The result was *'Holy Diver'*, released during May 1983. Cynics anticipating an egocentric and dated offering backed by sycophantic hirelings were proved profoundly wrong. The opus confounded those who saw Dio as simply the perennial sideman and had doubted his ability if left to his own devices. Ronnie had distilled what he started with Rainbow and Sabbath and refined it one stage further. The album clicked with consumers and sold extremely well throughout the world. In the US it soon went platinum, and in Britain became the best-selling heavy-metal release of 1983.

Two more popular, well-crafted albums along similar lines to the debut followed in succeeding years. Second album *'Last In Line'* (July 1984) highlighted the Egyptian majesty of the title track and a new crowd-pleasing anthem in 'We

Rock'. Extensive touring supported each release in turn, the band now including former Rough Cutt keyboard player Claude Schell. *'Sacred Heart'*, released in August 1985, proved one of the year's Top 10 rock sellers in the UK, with sales approaching even that of recent Clapton and Springsteen product. The LP spawned a Top 30 UK single in 'Rock'n'Roll Children'. 'Hungry For Heaven' formed part of the soundtrack to the science-fiction feature film 'Vision Quest' (as did the non-album cut 'Hide In The Rainbow' for the shoot-em-up action adventure Iron Eagle II).

After successfully touring Europe, America and the Far East, Dio and the group took a well-earned rest after almost three years on the 'album-tour-album' merry-go-round. Tony Iommi approached Ronnie to contribute to his proposed solo album (which became - controversially - a Sabbath album, *'Seventh Star'*). The plan was for Ronnie, Judas Priest's Rob Halford and Glenn Hughes to sing on selected songs. News leaked out and was interpreted in sections of the press as a tentative approach to reform the Dio line-up of Black Sabbath. Said Dio at the time: "My initial reaction was - 'Are you joking?' It made no sense to me as not enough time had elapsed for a proper resurrection."

However, by the release of the comeback LP *'Dream Evil'* in August 1987 Dio's star was on the wane with critics and public alike. The album was less well received (and sold less) compared to the previous releases, the reason cited as that oft-quoted cliché 'lack of progression'. The worsening economic situation in the US and elsewhere did not help matters, with weak ticket sales hitting numerous major tours. The 'Sacred Heart' tour had sold out all its arena venues but still lost nearly $500,000, while the 'Dream Evil' trek in early 1988 played to 10,000-seaters up to a third empty. (Even established stadium acts like Van Halen and Aerosmith struggled. In the future, corporate sponsorship of tours would rescue many major music acts from potentially ruinous costs.) The expensive visual aspects of the shows (at various times a fire-breathing dragon and huge marauding spider) meant a further serious drain on resources.

Ronnie defended the use of extravagant props: "I was comfortable with it all until we brought in the spider. It was supposed to come down from the ceiling but only worked on the ground by the end. And the press? That hurt because I personally had spent half a million dollars to put that show on the road, and if that isn't giving it back to your audience then nothing is. But no, 'Ah, the little bastard's got a dragon up there, but we only want to see the band.' So you take the dragon away and those fuckers moan about that as well. You can't win."

So what had gone wrong? As the eighties ticked on, the emerging generation of young music fans grew tired of the increasingly recycled brand of rock force-fed to them by the major labels. The metal boom reached its commercial zenith with Whitesnake's *'1987'* and Guns'N'Roses' *'Appetite for Destruction'*, after which there was nowhere else to go except more of the same. The disenchanted turned to the grunge movement gathering pace, with its garage-band integrity and predilection for more serious - or miserable, depending on your view - emotional issues.

The press were not slow to reflect this shift in public taste. Dio's escapist Gothic schtick, so appropriate earlier in the decade, now brought bile beyond imagining. Ronnie himself admitted, with disarming honesty: "I've made myself a bit one-dimensional in terms of lyrics... I've always enjoyed writing about castles, rainbows, etcetera because these things lead me into a world I love and relate to... but there comes a time you can no longer write that way, and you have to be clever enough to understand this."

In the wider scheme of things, the shift in tastes led ultimately to the break-up in the broad church of styles that had come to define 'heavy rock', splintering it into more extreme underground genres less acceptable to a more mainstream audience. The rap-heavy and angst-ridden 'nu-metal' of the late nineties resulted, with few exceptions far removed from the broad mass appeal of previous decades.

Precious few rock bands even saw the wall, let alone the writing on it, and even fewer had the nous to adapt. By the early nineties the demise of the more superficial of the thrash, 'big-hair' or melodic rock outfits was already assured. The real tragedy was that those more traditional-sounding metal collectives with still something valid to offer ended up in as much of a commercial wilderness as their less worthy peers. In some cases, personalities as well as the music proved an all too tempting target for sections of the rock press.

Dio stood for all that was now deemed obsolete, and in shifting into a campaign of ridicule (via irrelevancies like Ronnie's short stature and age) previously supportive rock journalists were demonstrating their rejection of traditional heavy metal. Ronnie Dio was not the only one to suffer but, taken all together, this criticism reflected on many an artist's credibility.

The time when Dio was perceived as a central figure in rock had passed and, to halt further decline, a contemporary album approaching the quality of the debut was needed. Soon after they reconvened in late 1988 to start work, Ronnie sacked Craig

Chapter 8

Goldie. Explaining why, Dio said: "Craig's playing was too bitty... he isn't a street kind of player... he didn't quite link up the chain and we didn't really gel as a writing partnership. You could take Goldie out of Giuffria but you couldn't take the Guiffria out of Goldie!"

The highly-rated Doug Aldrich (of Lion) was touted as replacement, but turned the job down. After further unproductive sessions and rehearsals (using Fire guitarist Mike Gray as stand-in) it became obvious a radical rethink was necessary. By mid-1989 the rest of the band had also parted company.

Ronnie recruited a new batch of musicians over the next six months, but ultimately the influx of new blood didn't improve matters, and the band failed to revitalise fortunes to any great degree with May 1990's higher-calibre but largely ignored *'Lock Up The Wolves'*. A shift towards a much more basic, riff-orientated Sabbath-tinged direction held some promise, but the songs were simply not strong enough. Dio returned to Sabbath for one more pay-day. Arrangements were agreed for an initial album and tour, after which the members would review the situation.

A two-month spell of rehearsals with Iommi, Butler and Cozy Powell ('Black Rainbow' anyone?) strangely failed to gel, although things improved with the return of Vinnie Appice, resulting from Powell's enforced lay-off following a horse-riding accident. Ronnie gave his side of the story recently: "Cozy was perfect for Rainbow, but he was absolutely the wrong choice for the Black Sabbath I was in. Geezer felt the same way too. When Cozy played with us, we got nothing done, but Vinnie was a drummer who was there to play and think."

Even during the 'Dehumaniser' world tour, Sabbath's management were quietly hatching plans for a Black Sabbath-Ozzy reunion. To test the waters a four-song set featuring the original Sabbath line-up was planned for the encore on the second night. To Ronnie this was a clear indication of the lack of commitment on the part of the whole Sabbath organisation to the present line-up. The final straw came when instructions were given not to perform any Ozzy-era material during the Sabbath set.

Ronnie tendered his immediate resignation prior to the gig. ("I refused to share a stage with this clown... I did not rejoin that band just to open up for a guy who had said nothing but bad things about me, and who had even called Tony a homosexual.") This led to the slightly bizarre scenario of Judas Priest vocalist Rob Halford stepping in at a few hours' notice to front Sabbath on the night. Ironically, the planned reunion fell apart, allegedly over Ozzy's exorbitant demands, and was not finally realised until the late nineties.

Dio - the band project - was resurrected during 1993. Ronnie's attempts at a more 'today' sound learned the lessons of bands like Rage Against The Machine and Nine Inch Nails. The heavy, dense industrial flavour of 1994's *'Strange Highways'* resulted. To the dismay of some and the relief of others, the mystical lyrical references were again minimal. This revised direction was taken a stage further with *'Angry Machines'* (1996), the increasingly dour and darkly forbidding aura of which made for some decidedly depressing listening. Ronnie: "It was a very disjointed, confusing album... but maybe we needed that failure to generate the success of our new album." Both LPs were released through Mercury to a muted response.

The group soldiered on in one guise or another through the nineties with most touring centred around the emerging markets of Eastern Europe, South America and the familiar Far East. By 1998 they were supporting Iron Maiden, then suffering something of a commercial hangover after the departure of Bruce Dickinson. Dio's set, shrewdly biased towards the early favourites, often went down better than the headliners and did much to raise profile once more.

The concept album *'Magica'*, released on Spitfire Records in March 2000, returned towards the mid-eighties sound. This reprise was helped in no small measure by the return of Jimmy Bain, Craig Goldie and Simon Wright (Warrant's Scott Warren was on keys). Dio: "When I decided to revert to the classic Dio sound I felt that I had to get in those musicians who could make it work best... this is our first attempt at doing a concept album, although I wouldn't compare it to something like *'Tommy'*."

Ronnie was special guest for Deep Purple's 'Concerto' performances at the Royal Albert Hall in September 1999 and he accompanied the band on the series of concerts around Europe. A world-girdling support tour with Alice Cooper then took up most of 2001. In addition to his heavy-rock endeavours, plans were afoot to reform Elf. Reuniting Dio with Mickey Lee Soule, Dave Feinstein and with Manowar's Joey DiMiao as guest bassist, plans were drawn for an album and a few shows around the US.

Ronnie summed up his current attitude thus: "So long as you're doing what you do well, you should be able to do it for as long as you wish. I fully appreciate that each generation wants its own artists, and that many people who used to come to our shows are now married with children and can't chuck their money away on a concert, so music is now marketed towards a generation that can. Now many of those older fans have fulfilled their social obligations and are coming back, I see them all the time... I'm gonna keep on until people want me to stop, but I'll still be able to sing when I'm on my deathbed!"

Gary Driscoll

Went on to drum with Dakota, then Starcastle - soft-rockers who somehow achieved a cult status via four rare and now much sought-after LPs on Epic, even though they sounded like a sicklier version of Styx - some achievement. In the late seventies he started his own group called Bible Black. *'Thrasher'* was a heavy metal project recorded in New York that included Driscoll and various members of Riot, Savoy Brown, The Rods and Blue Cheer. A rather mundane self-titled 1985 LP on Music For Nations resulted. Tragically, Driscoll was shot dead (aged 41) during a burglary at his home in 1987.

Roger Glover

His solo album *'Mask'* finally came out in June 1984. Response was muted, primarily because the release was just a few weeks after the news of the Purple reformation had broken. Consequently media emphasis concentrated on the reunion to the detriment of what was in retrospect an interesting and entertaining work. The title track 'Mask' itself, 'Hip Level' and 'You're So Remote' were excellent, along with several other contemporary and commercial songs in a mature pop vein far removed from Rainbow's sound, veering more towards an XTC or Police styling at times. A 1990 production credit for Danish metal band Pretty Maids' *'Lethal Heroes'* remains his only other major work outside Purple since the reunion, although at the time of writing a bass session for a forthcoming Gov't Mule album has been reported.

In the early nineties, some solo material was worked up but remains unreleased, including an instrumental featuring Gary Moore. Roger also turned his attention to the Deep Purple back catalogue, co-ordinating the impressive re-mixing of the classic early-seventies' albums that have been periodically reissued throughout the nineties. The recruitment of guitarist Steve Morse has seen Glover's long-standing writing partnership with Ian Gillan rejuvenated, and the powerful new albums (along with the reissues) have seen Deep Purple's profile on the up again, particularly since the resurgence of interest in hard rock during the late nineties. A new Purple opus was promised for 2002, as was another Glover solo set.

Craig Gruber

Later went on to join Greg Parker's *'Ninja'*, thereafter linking up with Dio again in pre-production on Black Sabbath's *'Heaven And Hell'* album. By December 1983 he had joined Gary Moore's band in time for the 'Victims Of The Future' dates. (Craig features on the live double *'We Want Moore'*). A spell with Dave Feinstein's Rods during the mid-eighties followed.

John Micelli

Returned to Meatloaf's band and teaching at Long Island Drums & Guitar Centre.

Paul Morris

Along with Greg Smith, was involved with Joe Lynn Turner's band for a while in the late nineties, as well as backing Mountain guitarist Leslie West. Most recently Paul has been involved with Melodica, a five-piece formed by former Danger Danger singer Ted Poley, and featuring drummer Jonathan Mover (ex-Marillion/Satriani). Their *'Lovemetal'* opus was released in mid-2001.

Cozy Powell

It was widely rumoured Cozy was lined up as the late John Bonham's successor with Led Zeppelin, as well as being linked with replacing Bill Ward in Black Sabbath. He was also touted (bizarrely) as possible replacement for the outgoing Peter Criss in Kiss (it's interesting to speculate what cosmetically-enhanced persona Powell might have adopted!) Money was not a problem for Cozy at the time, as drum clinics and kit endorsements meant he could indulge his racing interests for a while. He temporarily put the music side of things on hold to concentrate on motor racing. He returned to record another solo album, this time for Polydor, at the Britannia Row studios during spring 1981.

The second solo outing, *'Tilt'*, was again very successful in Japan, going gold, and reached 58 in the UK charts during September 1981. This time the album showcased several vocal tracks, courtesy of ex-Bedlam vocalist Frank Aiello and Stretch singer Elmer Gantry. Again, guest appearances from alumni like Jeff Beck, Jan Hammer,

Bernie Marsden, Jack Bruce and Gary Moore helped heighten the album's profile.

Given the options available, it seemed strange Powell's next move was to join up with erratic German guitarist Michael Schenker, thereby effectively reprising a situation not dissimilar to that he had so recently left. Cozy contributed to the disappointing 'MSG' on Chrysalis (almost coming to blows with producer Ron Nevison over the recording of his drumming) and the live double 'One Night At Budokan' from the equally patchy world tour. If you can tolerate the terrible singing and the erratic material, the excellent production highlights as fine an example as any of the sheer gut-wrenching drive of Cozy's on-stage drumming.

Cozy left MSG in mid-1982 and went on to guest on solo albums by Robert Plant ('Pictures At Eleven') and Jon Lord ('Before I Forget'). Around this time, a proposed collaboration with Gary Moore and Glenn Hughes was talked about but unrealised. A link-up with Graham Bonnet in Alcatrazz seemed on the cards before Cozy finally succumbed to the latest of David Coverdale's offers and a stint with Whitesnake ensued, joining the band in the autumn of 1982. "David kept phoning me up but at the same time, Tony wanted me to join Black Sabbath."

Another solo effort 'Octopuss' (Coverdale's nickname for Powell) in May 1983 saw a return to purely instrumentals, with interpretations of orchestral film themes ('633 Squadron' and 'The Big Country') and a take of a David Coverdale-penned tune aptly entitled 'The Rattler'. Cozy's powerhouse drumming on Whitesnake's January 1984 LP 'Slide It In' was an indication of how much he was considered an integral part of the desired heavier direction.

By spring 1985 Cozy had left a bickering band. His next move was to join up with Keith Emerson and Greg Lake in the launch of a new ELP. It was mischievously speculated in certain quarters that first choice Simon Phillips had declined to join so Cozy was the only other alphabetically suitable choice. Cozy recalled: "I had to learn everything in a couple of months - musically the most exciting thing I've ever done, and I specifically wanted that job because at the time everyone was putting me into a certain bag, saying, 'Oh, he can only play heavy rock.' It was great, possibly the most enjoyable part of my career." Problems between Lake and Emerson ended the trio; Powell's hard-hitting interpretations were considered by the other two to be inappropriate to the more subtle parts of their classical workouts.

Powell remained very much in demand and regular - if unexciting - work came in.

Sessions were undertaken for Tom and Mel Galley's conceptual *'Phenomena'* project. The initial idea showed promise but, as with most concepts of this sort, enthusiasm defeated pragmatism and it ballooned into something far too ambitious. On listening to the album, the songwriting limitations were all too obvious and, in any case, the proposed tour and feature film were eventually undermined by the financial collapse of record label Bronze.

Powell's long-standing friendship with guitarist Ray Fenwick resulted in guest appearances on a series of rather mediocre albums released from 1987 through to 1990 under the Forcefield moniker (*'Forcefield'*,*' The Talisman'*, *'To Oz And Back'* and *'Let The Wild Run Free'* on President Records with oddball guitar virtuoso Jan Akkerman of Focus also guesting) that did little other than pay the bills.

A session helping on Cinderella's bluesy *'Long Cold Winter'* opus was a little more creatively worthwhile. A proposed co-operation with former Whitesnaker John Sykes (in what eventually became the excellent *'Blue Murder'*) fell through owing to disagreements over financial arrangements, soon after demos were started in late 1987. ('They wanted me to sign a five-year contract which is far too long and restricting for me.')

The still-open invitation to join Black Sabbath was then accepted, although pressing financial problems resulting from the commercial failure of his last few undertakings prompted Cozy into temporarily joining up with Gary Moore while business arrangements concerning Sabbath were thrashed out. Powell recorded drums on six tracks for Moore's final dalliance with the hard-rock genre, the inconsistent *'After The War'*.

Two campaigns with Tony Iommi's version of Black Sabbath duly followed. However, an enforced lay-off after a serious horse-riding accident cut short this mutually beneficial involvement with Sabbath. Cozy sat out Sabbath's renewed collaboration with Ronnie James Dio, who was not prepared to wait around for the drummer to recuperate. This was something that was to rankle with Powell: "Ronnie had come back in, and he didn't want me. He'd been kicked out of Rainbow and had asked me to play on his solo album to spite Ritchie, but I turned him down. He's hated my guts ever since."

The drummer also contributed to Hale And Pace's Comic Relief charity chart-topper 'The Stonk' of 1991. A fourth Powell solo album, the mediocre *'The Drums Are Back'* (EMI) from August 1992 was greeted with general apathy, although it did feature a potentially formidable Murray, Lord, Airey and Fenwick line-up. Now invariably linked with bassist Neil Murray, the duo became the 'hired guns' of heavy rock, ready to step in wherever anyone needed a ready-made rhythm section. (This included the likes of Steve Vai, Paul Rodgers, Yngwie Malmsteen, Robert Palmer, Jimmy Barnes and Ian Gillan.) Late 1992 even saw Hammer reformed for a short spell of dates around Europe, featuring Murray, Sabbath singer Tony Martin and guitarist Mario Parga, presenting a set that included several Whitesnake and Rainbow covers.

An appearance as part of the house-band with Brian May during the Expo' 92 Guitar Greats concerts in Seville preceded further work for the duo with the Queen guitarist. May's 1993 album, the highly successful *'Into The Light'* was followed by a supporting tour, which included a creditable version of the supposedly dreaded 'Since You Been Gone'. (An entertaining live CD entitled *'Live At The Brixton Academy'* resulted.) October 1994 marked a brief return (along with Murray) to the Black Sabbath ranks for the mundane *'Forbidden'* album and associated tour, though Cozy left the band part-way through the dates in July '95 with exhaustion.

He next lent a guiding hand to the stage comeback of the legendary (but still mentally fragile) Fleetwood Mac guitarist Peter Green, as part of his backing band The Splinter Group. As much an emotional support to Green as a musical one, their low-key blues approach through 1996-97 gave Cozy a chance to show an altogether more subtle side to his playing - the monogrammed double bass drum set-up was noticeably absent.

Leaving the band after disagreements with Green's management, Cozy next worked on Judas Priest guitarist Glenn Tipton's 1997 solo CD *'Baptism Of Fire'*, Malmsteen's *'Facing The Animal'* and Colin Blunstone's *'The Light Inside'* during early 1998. Arrangements were made to tour with Brian May again late in that year, and sessions for May's upcoming album *'Another World'* featured Powell. Work also continued - when time allowed - on demos for a future solo release (which became the posthumous 1999 Japanese-only CD entitled *'Especially For You'*, with Murray, guitarist Mike Cresswell and impressive vocals from ex-Artension and future Royal Hunt vocalist John West).

John O. Reilly

Linked up with Ritchie again for the early Blackmore's Night tours. The drummer then jobbed with Blue Öyster Cult, parallel to involvement with a band called Westworld comprising former TNT singer Tony Harnell, Riot's Mark Reale and ex-JLT's band bassist Bruno Ravel. Reilly backed an excellent self-titled album of melodic hard-rock on Roadrunner in 1999, and an even better follow-up entitled *'Skin'* that reprised a vaguely similar early-eighties' Rainbow sound.

Bobby Rondinelli

The Scorpions, who were having trouble recording with their drummer, called in Bob to assist on the *'Love At First Sting'* album sessions. He then returned to teaching in New York. A 1984-85 solo project - aptly titled *'Rondinelli'* - featured brother Teddy on guitar and sister Dorothy on keyboards. The future Black Sabbath and Badlands vocalist (the late) Ray Gillen was also briefly involved.

The band recorded a few demos but at the time did not release any material (these demos and a few live recordings formed the basis of the 1996 CD release *'War Dance'*). The drummer remained very much in demand; offers at various times to join Whitesnake, Cinderella and The Scorpions were all turned down. A job with former Warlock singer Doro Pesch's solo band in 1989-90 (recording *'Force Majeure'* on Vertigo) was followed by a couple of stints with Black Sabbath. A year was spent supporting the 1993 IRS album *'Cross Purposes'* and in July 1995 he replaced Cozy Powell mid-tour on the 'Forbidden' dates.

A session for a project entitled 'Sun Red Sun' saw a self-titled release on Angel Air in 1998, in addition to some recording with ex-Gillan bassist John McCoy. Live work was undertaken meantime with both Blue Öyster Cult and Zebra (Bob also appearing on the BÖC's 2001 album *'Curse Of The Hidden Mirror'*).

By the turn of the millennium, Rondinelli had replaced Chuck Bonafante in The Sign, an AOR supergroup put together around Strangeways singer Terry Brock (briefly in Deep Purple!), ex-Touch/Drive She Said musician Mark Mangold and former Journey/Zebra bassist Randy Jackson. Their debut, *'Signs Of Life'*, was released in late 2000 to critical and commercial acclaim. A group including Teddy Rondinelli, Neil Murray and vocalist Tony Martin was rumoured to be recording - again under the Rondinelli banner - in late 2001.

David Rosenthal

Played on Little Steven and The Disciples Of Soul's 'Voice Of America' world tour through 1984-85, before teaming up with Cyndi Lauper for her *'True Colours'* album and tour. An exhaustive live trek as part of Robert Palmer's band followed in 1988. He was also in demand session-wise with Whitesnake (the double platinum *'Slip Of The Tongue'*), Steve Vai's *'Passion And Warfare'* and Dream Theater's prog-metal classic *'A Change Of Seasons'*. He then began a lengthy association with Billy Joel, initially for the 18-month tour promoting *'River Of Dreams'*.

Rosenthal's own ambitions were realised with an interesting studio-based project, *'Red Dawn'*. Recording a rich brand of keyboard-orientated symphonic progressive rock with Chuck Bürgi, vocalist Larry Baud and guitarist Tristan Avakarian, the 1993 *'Never Say Surrender'* album was initially released solely in Japan.

David also appeared on Yngwie Malmsteen's *'Inspirations'* CD of covers and worked for nine months on the 300-page orchestral scoring for Malmsteen's foray into classical orchestral composition, *'Concerto For Electric Guitar And Orchestra'* released in February 1998. He also got involved with nineties' progressives Departure, the eponymous up-beat pomp debut being followed by 1999's more melodically accessible *'Open Your Mind'* (on the Escape label). Other recent ventures include contributions to Bruce Kulick's band Good Rats for *'Cover Of The Night'* and the reformed seventies prog combo Happy The Man. David currently lectures in music at Berkeley and runs his own recording studio, Sonic Adventures.

Greg Smith

Initially re-joined Joe Lynn Turner's band and appeared on the album *'Nothing's Changed'*. Greg also contributed to Rosenthal's *'Red Dawn'* project. Smith also formed part of guitarist Stuart Smith's 'Heaven And Earth' touring band during 1999 before returning to Alice Cooper for his highly successful 2000-01 'Brutal Planet' world tour.

Mickey Lee Soule

Worked with first Roger Glover through late 1975 and then Ian Gillan in his *'Shand Grenade'* project early in 1976. On leaving in September 1976, he concentrated on session work. He recently renewed his acquaintance with both Purple musicians as the keyboard roadie for Deep Purple in 1996. Some rare live performances came guesting on piano during the 'Deep Purple Concerto' shows at the Royal Albert Hall in September 1999 and the subsequent series of dates around the world in 2000.

David Stone

After a brief sojourn with Le Mans, Stone appeared on the Max Webster Band's 1980 album *'Universal Juveniles'* (Phonogram). Thereafter he disappeared from sight.

Joe Lynn Turner

Embarked on a solo career as planned, although things didn't start off too well. Turner's initial demos (recorded with guitarist Bob Kulick) interested David Geffen enough to propose a project involving Joe, Kulick, and Starship guitarist Craig Chaquico. Inquiries also came in from Tommy Aldridge and Rudy Sarzo requesting Joe front their band project 'Driver', and such high-profile outfits like Survivor and Toto were also said to interested in recruiting Turner. Joe also started working on advertising and commercial soundtracks - initially rather reluctantly.

Solo work was deemed the main priority however. Joe wrote and recorded a fresh set of demos through mid-1984 in New York with former Foreigner and Spys keyboardist Al Greenwood, with Chuck Bürgi and Aldo Nova guitarist Stephen Dees helping out with recording. These quickly led to a record deal with Elektra in April 1985. A moderately successful solo album, *'Rescue You'*, was released in October 1985. The recording personnel formed the touring band, along with Pat Travers' bassist Barry Dunaway. They secured a support slot to Pat Benatar on her US dates through the spring of 1986. (In mid-1999 an interesting live CD surfaced. Originating from a radio broadcast of a Boston gig, it revealed a more harder-edged, guitar-biased take on the *'Rescue You'* material. Rainbow songs performed were limited to 'Stone Cold' and 'Street Of Dreams'.)

Later that year a 'supergroup' comprising Turner, guitarist Viv Campbell and former Asia/ELP drummer Carl Palmer was proposed by record bosses David Geffen and John Kalodner but came to nought. Joe then contributed backing vocals to John Waite's superb 1987 EMI LP *'Rover's Return'*. Offers from other groups continued to come in; Joe turned down both Foreigner and drummer Jason (son of John) Bonham's group project.

Further recording continued - without any formal deal - through mid-1987 with Greenwood, guitarist Tony Bruno (formerly of Long Island band Swift Kick) drummer Chuck Bonafante and bassist Bruno Ravel. Said Joe in September 2000: "I recently had an offer from a European label to re-record all this stuff, but the money wasn't good enough, to be honest. I still don't know whether or not

Chapter 8

I'm going to release this stuff as it was laid down originally or really go for it and re-record it all."

Then came a brief team-up in June 1987 with Blackmore clone Yngwie Malmsteen. This was at the decree of Polygram, who desperately wanted someone who could help break the Swede commercially by imparting a more contemporary sheen to Malmsteen's impressive but often over-indulgent guitar work. Joe joined on the understanding that, after an album and world tour, Polygram would then negotiate a long-term solo deal for the singer. Initially Bob Daisley and former Gary Moore drummer Eric Singer were in the band, although by the time of recording Anders Johanssen was on drums and Bob had left before any live dates.

The result was *'Odyssey'* (Polydor) which one critic dubbed 'the finest album Rainbow never made.' Certainly the ingredients were all there for a potentially huge seller. 'Heaven Tonight', the single lifted from the album, got some serious airplay and all the signs were good. The LP sold 360,000 units in the first week and debuted at 40 in the US Billboard charts. Unfortunately, lack of back-up and co-ordination meant the release made no further headway and dropped down after just two more weeks.

A groundbreaking tour of the then Soviet Union duly followed. Malmsteen was one of the first Western rock acts to tap the potential market in Russia, and was therefore soon one of the most popular artists. The band played twenty shows to huge enthusiastic crowds totalling over a quarter of a million people. *'Trial By Fire - Live In Leningrad'* CD and concert video of October 1989 marked the commercial high point of Malmsteen's career.

Given the Swede's volatile personality, the band was always living on borrowed time and, once the album had opened the US market up to Malmsteen's satisfaction, the inevitable split with the vocalist occurred in 1989. ("Malmsteen and I broke up over religious reasons... He thought he was God, and I didn't agree... Blackmore's God!" joked JLT.) Meanwhile, the US rock scene had seen the emergence of a clique of songwriters possessing an enviable knack for churning out very formalised but nevertheless hugely popular soft-rock hits for a succession of acts requiring a successful radio-friendly single. In the wake of this trend, many other outside writers found themselves co-opted by record companies and management to write that big 'rock ballad' that could open the door to considerable commercial success.

Although of a lower profile than the likes of Desmond Child, Diane Warren, Holly Knight, 'Mutt' Lange and Jim Steinman, Joe Lynn Turner's compositional talent meant he found gainful employment with an eclectic array of artists with just these objectives in mind. Numerous sessions writing and recording for other people followed. For a while, Joe became in effect an in-house writer and backing singer for Geffen Records, his compositions and performances appearing on a series of label releases (including platinum-seller Michael Bolton's album *'The Hunger'*, Cher's self-titled LP, and Jimmy Barnes' magnificent opus *'Freight Train Heart'* - specifically 'Walk On'). A Coca-Cola jingle with Robyn Beck also helped pay the bills - a jingle which would go on to be an international hit, 'First Time'.

Parallel to all this activity, attempts to once again kick-start his solo aspirations resulted in the formation of a new backing band based around Al Greenwood, guitarist Al Pitrelli and ex-Kingdom Come drummer James Kottak (now with The Scorpions). Turner remarked: "This will feature a lot of blues, plus a certain trashy element." The band was provisionally called Jolt (geddit?). However plans soon fell apart, as in the winter of 1989, the call from Deep Purple came (see above) and Pitrelli joined Alice Cooper soon after.

Turner's Purple reign was relatively successful but dismissal in August 1992 was, with hindsight, inevitable. Ritchie recalled: "Joe's voice started cracking and he didn't come up with any ideas... Joe, to me, is very much like Glenn Hughes. He's a funny character, full of life. But his identity was fading... He wanted to copy other bands. The rest of the band wanted Ian back in. I wanted to bring someone else in, but I was outvoted, so I said 'I'll go along with that...' They needed a scapegoat - and Joe was it."

After the sojourn with Purple, Turner's next major project was 1993's *'Mother's Army'*. Originally a Japan-only release, the undertaking was co-ordinated and co-written by the ubiquitous Bob Daisley and starred the strong line-up of ex-Night Ranger guitarist Brad Gillis and drummers Bobby Blotzer (Ratt) and Carmine Appice. *'Nothing's Changed'* was billed as a bona-fide solo effort and released on Music for Nations in the UK during late 1995. It proved a typically melodic AOR offering, though following the virtual extinction of melodic rock post grunge, what little commercial potential the album enjoyed was limited to the more traditional markets of Japan (where Turner's projects continue to sell around 30,000 units).

A series of jobbing sessions on other releases followed - Joe contributed to several covers albums, including a couple of Deep Purple tributes and to Yngwie

Chapter 8

Malmsteen's collection (1997's surprisingly good *'Inspirations'*) in addition to a lead vocal for the AC/DC tribute *'Thunderbolt'*. The year also saw Joe's own set of covers released as *'Under Cover'* in the US (for which a version of 'Street Of Dreams' was re-recorded). The late nineties saw more 'Mother's Army' contributions. *'Planet Earth'* (1997) was another enjoyable if rather formulaic hard-rock outing featuring Daisley, ex-Night Ranger guitarist Jeff Watson (who co-wrote the album with Daisley) and Carmine Appice.

1998's much better (read heavier) *'Fire On The Moon'*, again featured Turner (who thankfully co-wrote the tracks this time), Daisley and Watson, this time with veteran drummer Aynsley Dunbar. Joe also sang on several tracks for British-born guitarist Stuart Smith's excellent *'Heaven And Earth'* album (Smith is also a close friend of Ritchie Blackmore). 1997 also saw the start of an ongoing co-operation with guitarist Nikolo Kotzev's Brazen Abbott. *'Eye Of The Storm'* and *'Bad Religion'* showcased some polished, classically influenced hard rock with a slight nod towards late-era Rainbow.

Other ventures include a Nikolo Kotzev concept album based around the life of Nostradamus, and another volume of covers released in March 1999 (on Pony Canyon) that proved very popular in Japan. *'Under Cover 2'* was a heavier collection than the previous, including some straight-ahead attempts at Deep Purple's 'Lady Double Dealer', Rainbow's 'Lost In Hollywood' and Whitesnake's 'Fool For Your Lovin'. The summer of 1999 also marked the next solo release; the strident and bluesy *'Hurry Up And Wait'* (MTM) was more in a Paul Rodgers/Bad Company vein and had contributions from Al Pitrelli, Greg Smith and Paul Morris.

A collective enterprise called 'Voices Of Rock' was set up by Turner and various other vocalists, and toured featuring a rotating base of musicians including (among others) Mike Reno (Loverboy), Jimi Jamison (Survivor) and Mickey Thomas (Starship). Each singer had their own featured slot in the show. Appearances on more tribute releases followed, including those for Van Halen and Randy Rhoads. A bizarre hip-hop version of AC/DC's 'Back In Black' with Def Leppard's Phil Collen (for an AC/DC tribute of the same name on Cherry Red Records) showcased his vocal flexibility, Joe's throaty efforts sounding more like Brian Johnson than Johnson himself!

His next solo collection *'Holy Man'* (MTM) was released in August 2000. The 13-track album presented a further progression toward more blues-edged retro-rock with a sparser, stripped-down sound that complimented Turner's more abrasive vocal tone. 'Holy Man', 'Wolves At The Door' and 'Midnight In Tokyo' were of particularly high quality, with some excellent guitar work courtesy of Akira Kajiyama and blues guitarist Joe Bonamassa (Pitrelli, Smith and Morris again guested).

The supporting tour of Japan in October 2000 saw Turner and Kajiyama recruit (somewhat bizarrely) the keyboardist and drummer from Japanese Rainbow tribute band Niji Densetsu. Interest in the tour was cranked up further once Glenn Hughes stepped in on bass for the shows, even singing a few old Purple numbers and a couple of his own solo songs. The recent *'Slam'* (September 2001) took this 'retro' direction a step further. As workaholic as ever, Joe is presently hard at work on several more solo and outside projects, one a studio album with Glenn Hughes entitled *'HTP'* for release in March 2002.

Doogie White

Immediately started work on a set of demos with former Midnight Blue guitarist Alex Dickson (spotted in the late nineties as part of Robbie Williams' band!) with a view to securing a solo deal. He kept his hand in by singing with covers band The Barnstormers, while White recently secured a UK release (on Phoenix Music) of his 1994 recording sessions as part of Chain, entitled *'Eros Of Love And Destruction'*. Doogie could also be heard on TV, singing on the recent set of Action Man toy adverts!

Sessions on several tribute releases were next, the Whitesnake tribute *'Snakebites'* and several tracks included on *'666 - Number Of The Beast'*, a two-volume tribute to Iron Maiden out on Deadline (making a better job of some Maiden classic than Blaze Bayley, in the author's opinion!). Doogie also appeared on Nikolo Kotzev's *'Nostradamus'*. A contribution to Royal Hunt bassist Steen Morgensen's fine solo project *'Arrival'* (under the name Cornerstone) was released in late 2000.

Such was the positive critical and commercial response that a further series of albums were mooted, this time with Doogie's creative input. Further fruitful, interesting projects and an increasingly high profile career were surely just around the corner.

APPENDICES

Rainbow UK/US Chart Placings	**166**
Discography	**167**
Details of Equipment	**177**
Tour Programmes	**182**
Gig List	**185**
Songs Rainbow Performed Live	**215**
Bootleg Discography	**216**
Websites, Societies and Publications	**248**

RAINBOW CHART PLACINGS - ALBUMS

Title	Release Date	UK Chart Position	US Chart Position
'Ritchie Blackmore's Rainbow'	Aug '75	11	30
'Rainbow Rising'	May '76	11	40
'On Stage' (2LP)	Jul '77	7	65
'Long Live Rock'n'Roll'	Apr '78	7	89
'Down To Earth'	Aug '79	6	66
'Difficult To Cure'	Feb '81	3	50
'Ritchie Blackmore's Rainbow' (reissue)	Aug '81	91	-
'Straight Between The Eyes'	Apr '82	5	30
'Bent Out Of Shape'	Aug '83	11	34
'Live In Germany' (2LP)	Sept '91	49	-
'Stranger In Us All'	Oct '95	-	-
COMPILATIONS:			
'Monsters Of Rock' (2 live tracks)	Oct '80	16	
'Best Of Rainbow' (2LP)	Nov '81	14	-
'Finyl Vinyl' (2LP)	Mar '86	31	83
'The Best Of Rainbow'	Oct '97	-	-

RAINBOW CHART PLACINGS - SINGLES

Title	Release Date	UK Chart Position	US Chart Position
'Kill The King' (live)	Sept '77	44	-
'Long Live Rock'n'Roll'	Mar '78	33	-
'L.A. Connection'	Sept '78	40	-
'Since You Been Gone'	Aug '79	6	57
'All Night Long'	Feb '80	5	-
'I Surrender'	Jan '81	3	-
'Can't Happen Here'	Jun '81	20	147
'Stone Cold'	Mar '82	34	40
'Street Of Dreams'	Aug '83	52	60
'Can't Let You Go'	Oct '83	43	-

THE RAINBOW DISCOGRAPHY

Listed below is a brief chronological summary of the major official album, EP and single releases made by the band over the years. Note that this listing is by no means exhaustive and that numerous reissues continue to appear, particularly in Eastern Europe and the Far East.

■ *Ritchie Blackmore's Rainbow*
Side 1: Man On The Silver Mountain/Self Portrait/Black Sheep Of The Family/Catch The Rainbow. Side 2: Snake Charmer/Temple Of The King/16th Century Greensleeves/Still I'm Sad.
Recorded at Musicland Studios in Munich Feb-Mar 1975. Mixed by Martin Birch. Produced by Blackmore, Birch and Dio.
UK Gatefold Aug 1975 - Oyster OYA2001
UK reissue 1978 - Polydor 2490 141
UK reissue 1983 - Polydor SPELP 7
Ger 1975 - Oyster 1C 062 96787
Ger reissue 1978 - Oyster 2391 190
Ger reissue 1981 - Oyster 2929 096
Fra 1975 - Oyster 2C 068 96787
Hol 1975 - Oyster 5C 062 96787
Jap 1975 (limited edition with poster) - Oyster MP2502
Arg 1978 - Polydor 2391190
Jap reissue 1978 - Oyster MP1144
Jap reissue 198(?) - Oyster MPX402
Jap reissue 198(?) - Oyster 23MM 0021
US/Can 1975 - Polydor PD6049
Can reissue 198(?) - MIP 1 9325
Rus 1993 - AnTrop/Santa 00531 (pirate)
Worldwide reissue (CD) 1987 - Polydor 825 089-2
Jap 199(?) Polydor POCP-2289 (CD)
Jap Dec 1998 - Polydor (Cardboard Jacket Series CD) POCP-9155
USA Remastered reissue 1999 - Polydor 314 547 360-2 (CD)

● **Man On The Silver Mountain**/Snake Charmer (single): UK Oct 1975 - Oyster OYR 103
● **Man On The Silver Mountain**/Snake Charmer (single): US - Polydor PD 14290
● **Man On The Silver Mountain**/Snake Charmer (single): Jap Dec 1975 - Polydor PD 1996
● **Man On The Silver Mountain**/Snake Charmer (single): Ger - Oyster 1C 006 97061
● **Man On The Silver Mountain/Snake Charmer/If You Don't Like Rock'n'Roll/16th Century Greensleeves** (EP): Ger 1975 - Polydor Club 2835 035
● **Man On The Silver Mountain/Black Sheep Of The Family/Temple Of The King/16th Century Greensleeves** (EP): Thai 1975 - 4 Track Records FT 313 197
● **Temple Of The King/Self Portrait/Man On The Silver Mountain/Snake Charmer** (EP): Thai 1975 - Express Songs EXP 225
● **Still I'm Sad**/Temple Of The King (picture sleeve single): Italy 1975 - Oyster 3C 006 97224

■ *Rainbow Rising*
Side 1: Tarot Woman/Run With The Wolf/Starstruck/Do You Close Your Eyes.
Side 2: Stargazer/A Light In The Black.
Recorded at Musicland Studios, Munich Feb 1976. Produced by Martin Birch.

UK May 1976 (gatefold) - Polydor Deluxe 2490 137
UK reissue (single sleeve) 1984 - Polydor SPELP 35
US/Can 1976 - Oyster OY 1 1601
US/Can reissue 198(?) - Oyster MIP 1 9339
Jap Jun 1976 - Polydor/Oyster MWZ1004
Ger 1976 - Polydor 2391 224
Rus 1993(?) - 00221292098 (pirate)
Worldwide reissue (CD) 1987 - Polydor 823 655-2
Can 1987 - Polydor 823 655-2 Y-1 (CD)
Jap 1995 Polydor POCP-2290 (CD)
Jap Dec 1998 - Polydor (Cardboard Jacket Series) POCP-9156
Remastered CD reissue USA May 1999 - Polydor 314 547 361-2

● **Starstruck**/Run With The Wolf (picture sleeve single): Ger 1976 - Polydor/Oyster 2066 709
● **Starstruck**/Run With The Wolf (picture sleeve single): Jap Sep 1976 - Polydor/ Oyster DWQ 6010
● **Tarot Woman** (edit): Jap Feb 1976 - (flexi-single free with music magazine) FR144

■ *Ritchie Blackmore's Rainbow/ Rainbow Rising*
(2LP) UK Sep1978 Gatefold reissue - Polydor 2683 078

■ *On Stage*
Side 1: Kill The King/Man On The Silver Mountain. Side 2: Catch The Rainbow. Side 3: Mistreated. Side 4: 16th Century Greensleeves/Still I'm Sad.

Edited tracks derived from Japanese and German dates 1976. Produced by Martin Birch Mar 1977.
UK Jul 1977 - Polydor 2657
Ger 1977 - Polydor 2675 142
US/Can 1977 - Polydor/Oyster OY-2-1801
Jap Jul 1977 - Polydor/Oyster MWZ 8103/4
Eur gatefold reissue 1984 - Polydor SPDLP 6
Remastered (?) reissue on CD UK 1987 - Polydor 823656-2
Jap 199(?) - Polydor POCP-2291
Jap Dec 1998 - Polydor (Cardboard Jacket Series) POCP-9157
Remastered CD reissue May 1999 Polydor 314 547 362-2

● **Kill The King/Man On The Silver Mountain** (edit)/**Mistreated** (edit) (maxi-single): UK Aug 1977 - Polydor 2066 845
● **Kill The King/Man On The Silver Mountain** (edit)/**Mistreated** (edit) (maxi-single): reissued Jul 1981 - Polydor POSP 274

■ *Long Live Rock'n'Roll*
Side 1: Long Live Rock'n'Roll/Lady Of The Lake/ L.A. Connection/Gates Of Babylon.
Side 2: Kill The King/The Shed (Subtle)/ Sensitive To Light/Rainbow Eyes.
Produced by Martin Birch. Recorded at Château d'Herouville, France using the Rolling Stones' Mobile studio May-Jul, Dec 1977.
UK (gatefold plus lyrics insert) Apr 1978 - Polydor POLD 5002
Ger 1978 - Polydor 2391 335
US/Can 1978 - Polydor PD1 6143
Jap May 1978 - Polydor MPF 1156

UK vinyl reissue (single sleeve) 1983 - Polydor SPELP 34
Eur 1987 - Polydor 825090-2 (CD)
Jap 199(?) - Polydor POCP-2292
Jap Dec 1998 Polydor (CD Cardboard Jacket Series) POCP-9158
CD remastered reissue 1999 - Polydor 314 547 363-2

- **Long Live Rock'n'Roll**/Sensitive To Light (single): Eur Mar 1978 - Polydor 2066 913
- **Long Live Rock'n'Roll**/Sensitive To Light (single): Jap May 1978 - Polydor DPQ 6086
- **Long Live Rock'n'Roll**/Sensitive To Light (single): US May 1978 - Polydor PD 14481
- **Long Live Rock'n'Roll**/Sensitive To Light (single): UK reissue Jul 1981 - Polydor POSP 276
- **L.A. Connection**/Lady Of The Lake (single on red vinyl): UK 1978 Polydor 2066-968
- **L.A. Connection**/Lady Of The Lake (single): UK reissue Jul 1981 Polydor POSP 275

■ *Down To Earth*
Side 1: All Night Long/Eyes Of The World/No Time To Lose/Makin' Love.
Side 2: Since You Been Gone/Love's No Friend/Danger Zone/Lost In Hollywood.
Recorded at Château Pelly de Cornfeld, France using the Maison Rouge Mobile Studio. Vocals recorded at Kingdom Sound Studios, New York. Engineered by Gary Edwards. Produced by Roger Glover.

UK Aug 1979 - Polydor POLD 5023
UK (inner sleeve, merch.insert, clear vinyl) Aug 1979 - Polydor Deluxe POLD 5023
UK reissue 1984 - Polydor SPELP 69
Ger/Eur 1979 - Polydor 2391 410
US/Can 1979 - Polydor PD-1-6221
Yugoslavia 1979 - Polydor 5968 (pirate LP)
UK/Ger 1986 - Polydor 823 705-2 (CD)
Jap 1986 - Polydor POCP-2293 (CD)
Jap Dec 1998 - Polydor (CD Cardboard Jacket Series) POCP-9159
Remastered CD reissue May 1999 - Polydor 314 547 364-2

- **Since You Been Gone**/Bad Girl (single): Eur 1979 - Polydor POSP 70
- **Since You Been Gone**/Bad Girl (single): US 1979 - Polydor
- **Since You Been Gone**/No Time To Lose (single): Ger 1979 - Polydor 2095 104
- **All Night Long**/Weiss Heim (single): Eur 1980 - Polydor 2095 196
- **All Night Long**/Weiss Heim (single): UK 1980 - Polydor POSP 104
- **All Night Long**/Weiss Heim (single): Jap 1980 - Polydor DPQ 6181
- **All Night Long**/ No Time To Lose (pic. single): Hol 1980 - Polydor 2095 188

■ *Difficult To Cure*
Side 1: I Surrender/Spotlight Kid/No Release/Magic/Maybe Next Time.
Side 2: Can't Happen Here/Freedom Fighter/Midtown Tunnel Vision/ Difficult To Cure.
Recorded and mixed at Sweet Silence Studios, Copenhagen. Engineered by Flemming Rasmussen, assisted by Clay

Hutchinson (Kingdom Sound Studio) and Thomas Brekling. Mastered by Greg Colby at Sterling Sound. Produced by Roger Glover.
UK Feb 1981 - Polydor POLD 5036
Eur 1981 - Polydor 2391 506
US/Can 1981 - Polydor PD1 6316
Jap 1981 - Polydor 28MM 0018
Eur CD reissue 1987 - Polydor 800018-2
Jap 1987 - Polydor POCP-2294
Jap Dec 1998 - Polydor (CD Cardboard Jacket Series) POCP-9160
Remastered CD reissue May 1999 - Polydor 314 547 365-2

● **I Surrender**/Vielleicht Das Nachste Mal (single): Eur 1981 - Polydor 2095 339
● **I Surrender**/Vielleicht Das Nachste Mal (single): UK 1981 - Polydor POSP 221
● **I Surrender**/Vielleicht Das Nachste Mal (single): Jap 1981 - Polydor 7DM 0013:81
● **Can't Happen Here**/Jealous Lover (single): UK 1981 - Polydor POSP 251
● **Can't Happen Here**/Jealous Lover (single): Eur 1981 - Polydor 2095 381
● **Magic**/Freedom Fighter (picture sleeve single): Jap 1981 - Polydor 7 DM 0033
● **Difficult To Cure/Can't Happen Here/Jealous Lover** (EP): Hol 1981 - Polydor 2141 373
● **Jealous Lover/Weiss Heim/Can't Happen Here/I Surrender** (EP): US 1981 - Polydor PX 1 502

■ *Straight Between The Eyes*
Side 1: Death Alley Driver/Stone Cold/Bring On The Night(Dream Chaser)/Tite Squeeze/Tearin'Out My Heart.
Side 2: Power/Miss Mistreated/Rock Fever/Eyes of Fire.
Recorded at Le Studio, Morin Heights, Montreal, Canada during Dec 1981. Engineered by Nick Blagona, assisted by Robbie Whelan. Digital mixing by Roger Glover and Nick Blagona. Digital master by Greg Calbi at Sterling Sound, New York. Produced by Roger Glover.
UK Jun 1982 - Polydor Deluxe POLD 5056
US 1982 - Mercury SRM-1-4041
Can 1982 - Polydor PDS-1-8348
South America 1982 - Polydor 2391 542
Eur/Can 1987 - Polydor 800028-2 (CD)
Jap 199(?) - Polydor POCP-2295 (CD)
Jap Dec. 1998 - Polydor (CD Cardboard Jacket Series) POCP-9161
Remastered CD reissue May 1999 - Polydor 314 547 366-2

● **Stone Cold**/Rock Fever (single): UK Apr 1982 - Polydor POSP 421
● **Stone Cold**/Rock Fever (single): Eur Apr 1982 - Polydor 2095 451
● **Stone Cold**/Rock Fever (single): US 1982 - Mercury 76146
● **Stone Cold**/Rock Fever (single on blue/black vinyl): Jap 1982 - Polydor 7DM 0044
● **Death Alley Driver**/Power (single): Jap 1982 - Polydor 7 DM 0059

■ *Bent Out Of Shape*
Side 1: Stranded/Can't Let You Go/Fool For The Night/Firedance/Anybody There?
Side 2: Desperate Heart/Street Of Dreams/Drinking With The Devil/Snowman/Make Your Move.
Recorded at Sweet Silence Studios,

Copenhagen, May-Jun 1983. Engineered by Flemming Rasmussen, assisted by Thomas Brekling. Mixed by Nick Blagona at Bear Track Studios, New York. Mastered by Greg Colbi at Sterling Sound, New York. Produced by Roger Glover.
UK Sep 1983 - Polydor/Oyster POLD 5116
Ger 1983 - Polydor 815 305-1
USA 1983 - Mercury 815 305
Can 1983 - Polydor PDS-1-6378
Jap 1983 - Polydor 28MM 0300
Rus 1993 - AnTrop/AnTrop 00525
UK/Ger 1987 - Polydor 815395-2 (CD)
Jap 199(?) - Polydor POCP-2296 (CD)
Jap Dec 1998 - Polydor (CD Cardboard Jacket Series) POCP-9162
Remastered CD reissue May 1999 Polydor 314 547 367-2

● **Street Of Dreams**/Anybody There (single): UK Aug 1983 - Polydor POSP 631
● **Street Of Dreams**/Anybody There (pic. single): UK 1983 - Polydor POSPP 631
● **Street Of Dreams**/Anybody There (single): Eur Aug 1983 - Polydor 815 2657
● **Street Of Dreams/Anybody There/ Power** (EP): UK 1983 - Polydor POSPX 631
● **Can't Let You Go**/All Night Long (live) (single): UK 1983 - Polydor POSP 654
● **Can't Let You Go**/All Night Long (live) (picture single): UK 1983 - Polydor POSPP 654
● **Can't Let You Go**/Drinking With The Devil (single): Spain 1983 - Polydor 821369-T
● **Can't Let You Go/All Night Long** (live)/ **Stranded** (live) (EP): UK Oct 1983 - Polydor POSPX 654

■ *Finyl Vinyl*
Side 1: Spotlight Kid/I Surrender/Miss Mistreated. Side 2: Jealous Lover/Can't Happen Here/Tearin'Out My Heart/Since You Been Gone/Bad Girl. Side 3: Difficult To Cure/Stone Cold/ Power. Side 4: Man On The Silver Mountain/ Long Live Rock 'n'Roll/Weiss Heim. (Extra track on cassette version - Street Of Dreams.)
Compiled and produced by Roger Glover. Mixed at White Plains, USA. Executive producer Ritchie Blackmore.
Eur Feb 1986 - Polydor PODV 8
US 1986 - Mercury 422 827 987 (CD - all initial CDs omitted 'Tearin' Out My Heart')
Eur 1986 - Polydor 827 987-2 (CD)

● **Bad Girl/Spotlight Kid** (live)/**Man On The Silver Mountain** (live) (EP): Ger 1986 - Polydor 883 970-1
Jap 199(?) Polydor P38P-20040 (CD)
Eur remastered 2CD reissue May 1999 (now incl. 'Street Of Dreams' and 'Tearin' Out My Heart') - Polydor 314 527 368-2
Jap Dec 1998 - Polydor POCP-9163

■ *Rainbow - Live In Germany*
Disc 1: Kill The King/Mistreated/16th Century Greensleeves/Catch The Rainbow. Disc 2: Man On The Silver Mountain/ Stargazer/Still I'm Sad/Do You Close Your Eyes.
Live tracks recorded during German dates in 1976: 25th Sep (Cologne), 27th Sep (Dusseldorf), 28th Sep (Mannheim) and 29th Sep (Munich). The first 10,000 copies included colour photo booklet. Sleeve notes by Simon Robinson.

UK 1990 - Connoisseur DP VSOP CD 155 (2CD)
UK (gatefold vinyl with picture booklet) 1990 - Connoisseur DP VSOP LP 155
Jap 199(?) Teichiku TECX-30850-1 (2CD)

■ *Rainbow - Live In Europe*
(2CD) US 1996 Mausoleum Classix/King Biscuit Ent. 71278-60024-2
The US version of *'Live in Germany'*.
Bruce Pilato wrote the US sleeve notes.

■ *Stranger In Us All*
Wolf To The Moon/Cold Hearted Woman/ Hunting Humans (Insatiable)/ Stand And Fight/Ariel/Too Late For Tears/ Black Masquerade/Silence/Hall Of The Mountain King/Still I'm Sad.
(Extra track on Japanese release - 'Emotional Crime'.)
Recorded at Long View Farm Studios, North Brookfield MA. Overdubs recorded at Cove City Sound Studio, Long Island, New York, Sound On Sound, Unique Studio, and Soundtrack Studios, all in New York City. Mixed at Time Machine in Landgrove, Vermont. Engineered and mixed by Pat Regan, assisted by Jesse Henderson, Doug, John Reigart, Ed Miller, Fran Flannery, David Shackney, Steve Moseley and Steve Sisco. Mastered at Sony Music Studios, New York City by Vlado Meller. Produced by Pat Regan and Ritchie Blackmore.
Eur Sep 1995 - RCA/BMG 74321-30337-2 (CD)
Jap Sep 1995 - BMG Victor BVCP-862 (CD + bonus track)

USA 1998 - Fuel 2000 FLD-1010 (different back cover)

● **Hunting Humans**/Stand And Fight/ Black Masquerade (promo): Eur Sep 1995 - RCA/BMG 74321-30336-2
● **Ariel** (radio edit)/Ariel (Album version)/ The Temple Of The King (live) (CD single): Eur Nov 1995 - RCA/BMG 74321-32982-2

COMPILATIONS

■ *Monsters Of Rock*
(LP) (Donington Aug 1980, live tracks incl. two by Rainbow) - UK 1980 Polydor

■ *The Best Of Rainbow*
Side 1: All Night Long/Man On The Silver Mountain/Do You Close Your Eyes/Lost In Hollywood/Since You Been Gone. Side 2: Stargazer/Catch The Rainbow/Kill The King. Side 3: 16th Century Greensleeves/ Still I'm Sad/Long Live Rock'n'Roll/ Eyes Of The World/Starstruck. Side 4: A Light In The Black/Mistreated (live).
Jap Feb 1981 Polydor MPZ 8139/40 (2LP)

■ *The Best Of Rainbow*
Side 1: All Night Long/Man On The Silver Mountain/Lost In Hollywood/Jealous Lover/Long Live Rock'n'Roll. Side 2: Stargazer/Kill The King/A Light In The Black. Side 3: Since You Been Gone/ 16th Century Greensleeves/Catch The Rainbow/ Eyes Of The World.
Side 4: I Surrender/Gates Of Babylon/ Can't Happen Here/Starstruck.

UK Nov. 1981 - Polydor PODV2 (2LP)
Jap 1982 - Polydor 38MM 0114/5 (2LP)
Eur 1987 - Polydor 800 074-2 (2CD)

■ *Ansambji Rainbow*
(LP): Rus 1990 Polydor/Melodija C60-27023-005

■ *The Rainbow Family Album*
Deep Purple - Speed King/**Cozy Powell** - Dance With The Devil/**Elf** - Wonderworld/ **Rainbow** - Kill The King (Live 1976)/ **Rainbow** - 16th Century Greensleeves (Live 1976)/**Colosseum II** - Am I/**Roger Glover** - 1st Ring Made Of Fire/ **Fandango** - I Would Never Leave/**Wild Horses** - Face Down/**Tony Carey** - A Fine Fine Day/**Alcatrazz** - Will You Be Home Tonight/**Dio** - Don't Talk To Strangers.
UK 1994 - Connoisseur RP VSOP CD 195

■ *Rainbow - The Very Best Of...*
Man On The Silver Mountain/Catch The Rainbow/Starstruck/Stargazer/Kill The King/Long Live Rock'n'Roll/Gates Of Babylon/Since You Been Gone/All Night Long/I Surrender/Can't Happen Here/ Jealous Lover/Stone Cold/Power/ Can't Let You Go/Street Of Dreams.
USA Jul 1997 - Polydor 31453-7687-2

■ *Rainbow - The Millennium Collection*
Man On The Silver Mountain/Catch The Rainbow/Stargazer/Mistreated (live)/Kill The King/Rainbow Eyes/Since You Been Gone/All Night Long/I Surrender/Stone Cold/Power/Street Of Dreams
US 2000 - Polydor 31454-9138-2

■ *Classic Rainbow*
All Night Long/Catch The Rainbow/Since You Been Gone/I Surrender/Stone Cold/ Kill The King/Stargazer/Starstruck/ Sixteenth Century Greensleeves/ Man On The Silver Mountain/Long Live Rock'n'Roll/Run With The Wolf/Lost In Hollywood/If You Don't Like Rock'n'Roll/ Miss Mistreated/Death Alley Driver.
(1CD) Eur Dec 2001 Polydor 589 157-2

■ *Rainbow - An Introduction To...*
All Night Long/Catch The Rainbow/ Since You Been Gone/I Surrender/Stone Cold/Kill The King/Stargazer/Starstruck/ 16th Century Greensleeves/Man On The Silver Mountain/Long Live Rock'n' Roll/Lost In Hollywood/If You Don't Like Rock'n'Roll/Miss Mistreated/Death Alley Driver.
Europe 2002 - Universal Masters Collection 589157-2

■ *Rainbow - Pot Of Gold*
Still I'm Sad/Stargazer/Kill The King/ L.A. Connection/Rainbow Eyes/Since You Been Gone/Makin' Love/Danger Zone/ Veilleicht Das Nachste Mal/Eyes Of Fire/ Stone Cold/Fire Dance/Fool For The Night.
Europe Feb 2002- Spectrum 5446512

RADIO PROMOS - ALBUMS

■ *The Ritchie Blackmore Rainbow Radio Special*
1975 Polydor SA13 (LP): Interviews with Blackmore and Dio. 4 tracks off first LP.

On Stage Special Edition
1977 Oyster 2808 010 010 (LP) Edited clips from *'On Stage'* with Blackmore and Dio, Australian interview with DJ Trevor Smith (41 mins).

BBC Rock Hour
1978 (LP) Rare 60 mins edit transcription disc for US radio, Atlanta 24/6/78 show.

The Source - The Rainbow Concert
1981 AchCM V47919 (2LP) Recording of Boston Orpheum 7/5/81. Radio promo with adverts included.

King Biscuit Flower Hour
1981 BOB45 (2LP) Edited Boston Orpheum 7/5/81 with Pat Travers. Fourth side blank. Better mix than The Source.

King Biscuit Flower Hour
1983 (2LP) Soundtrack from video, aired on US radio, with ads. Fourth side blank.

Rainbow Captured Live
1984 RKO Radio CL184, CL284 (two 2LP albums), St David's Hall 14/9/83 gig. Pressed for US radio with jingles and introductions, etc.

Ritchie Blackmore - The Sound And The Fury
1981 Modern Music 24 (2LP) 5 mins interview interspersed with edited Deep Purple track, 4 by Rainbow and Cozy's 'Dance With The Devil'.

Jim Ladd Hosts 'Rainbow'
1981 series 16 Prog 5 (LP) Interview with Roger Glover with Rainbow and Deep Purple studio tracks.

Off The Record - Ritchie Blackmore
1981 Westwood One OTR 7.81 (2LP) Interview with Blackmore, assorted DP and Rainbow tracks over 4 sides.

Radioactive - 1981 London
Wavelength (LP)
11 short interviews with various artists, including Blackmore and JLT.

Off The Record
1983 OTRSP 83 46 (2LP)
Old Blackmore/Glover interview with new questions dubbed in. 12 Rainbow studio tracks plus commercials.

King Biscuit Flower Hour
1986 (2LP)
Three sides with Glover, Dio and Payne interviews. All tracks from *'Finyl Vinyl'*.

RADIO PROMOS - SINGLES

- **Man On The Silver Mountain**/Man On The Silver Mountain
1975 stereo/mono white label US radio promo single.
- **Starstruck**/Starstruck
1976 stereo/mono white label US radio promo single.
- **Long Live Rock'n'Roll**/Long Live Rock'n'Roll
1978 stereo/mono white label US radio

promo. Polydor PD14481
- **Since You Been Gone**/All Night Long 12" German radio promo single. Polydor 120 002
- **All Night Long**/All Night Long 1980 stereo/mono white label US radio promo single. Polydor PD2060
- **All Night Long**/Danger Zone USA jukebox single (imported into UK)
- **I Surrender**/I Surrender 1981 stereo/mono white label US radio promo single. Polydor 2163.
- **I Surrender**/Spotlight Kid USA 12" white sleeve promo, 33rpm. Polydor PRO 147
- **Can't Happen Here**/Spotlight Kid/ Freedom Fighter 1981 USA 12" white sleeve promo. Polydor PRO156.
- **Extracts from 7 tracks off *'Straight Between the Eyes'*** 1982 clear vinyl flexi issued free with French music mag 'Vinyl'. Vinyl 004.
- **Stone Cold**/Stone Cold 1982 USA blue vinyl promo 7". Mercury 76146DJ
- **Stone Cold**/Stone Cold 1982 USA blue vinyl promo 12". Mercury MK 195
- **Power** (live)/Power (studio) 1982 12" USA promo. 33rpm. Mercury MK 232
- **Street Of Dreams**/Street Of Dreams 1983 stereo/mono white label US radio promo single. Mercury 815 660.7
- **Can't Let You Go**/Street Of Dreams- 1983 French promo. Polydor 821 257.7
- **Stranded**/Stranded

1983 USA 12" promo. Mercury PRO 242
- **Bad Girl**/Bad Girl US 1986 12" promo. Mercury PRO 404-1
- **Hunting Humans**/Stand And Fight/ Black Masquerade Europe CD promo Sep 1995. RCA/BMG74321-30336-2

VIDEOS

■ *Live Between The Eyes*
Spotlight Kid/Miss Mistreated/ I Surrender/It Can't Happen Here/ Tearin' Out My Heart/All Night Long/ Stone Cold/Power/Blues Interlude-Beethoven's Ninth: Ode to Joy/Long Live Rock'n'Roll/ Smoke On The Water.
Concert from San Antonio, Texas, 18th Aug 1982. Directed by Nigel Gordon. Produced by Aubrey Powell.
UK 1982 - PolyGram/Spectrum 790587-2 (75 mins, VHS/Betamax)
Jap - 200(?) Released on DVD

■ *Live Japan 1984*
Spotlight Kid/Miss Mistreated/Can't Happen Here/I Surrender/Catch The Rainbow/Power/Street Of Dreams/Fool For The Night/Difficult To Cure/Blues-Stranded/Death Alley Driver/Firedance/ Maybe Next Time/All Night Long/Since You Been Gone/Smoke On The Water.
Final concert recorded at Tokyo.
Jap 1984 - TEM 585 (115 mins, VHS/Betamax)
Jap - 200(?) Released on DVD Budokan, 14th Mar 1984.

■ **The Final Cut**
Spotlight Kid/Death Alley Driver/
I Surrender/All Night Long/
Can't Happen Here/Difficult To Cure/
Can't Let You Go/ Power/Since You Been
Gone/Stone Cold/ Street Of Dreams.
A collection of promo videos.
Produced by Len Epland, Claude
Borenzweig and Don Bernstine.
Audio producer was Roger Glover.
US/Eur 1985 - Polygram/Spectrum 041
385.2 (VHS/Betamax)
Jap - 200(?) Released on DVD

PROMOTIONAL VIDEOS

1976: Poor quality footage of snippets of Mark II Rainbow performing 'MOSM'/'Stargazer'/'LITB'/'Do You'. Switches back and forth with no continuity, shot from mixer area. (Approx 15 mins.)

1977: 'L.A. Connection', 'Long Live Rock'n'Roll', and 'Gates of Babylon'. 'Live'-style promos shot 1977-78. Slight lyrical changes by Dio.

1979-80: 'Since You Been Gone' and 'All Night Long'.
Stage-performance-style promos shot in New York and Stockholm, interspersed with 'story' footage. Grainy.
Little attention is paid to Ritchie, more to Bonnet and Glover.

1981: 'I Surrender'.
Another grainy stage performance. 'Can't Happen Here' features appropriate environmental footage, with group superimposed at times.

1982: 'Death Alley Driver' promo features a biker chased by a car containing the grim reaper (actually Ritchie). Also 'Stone Cold'.

1983: Promos for 'Street Of Dreams', 'Can't Let You Go'.

1995: 'Ariel' promo, filmed at Meiningen, Germany. Blackmore walks through a field guitar in hand, then footage concentrates on Dougie, Ritchie and occasionally Candice).

DETAILS OF EQUIPMENT USED

Don Airey

Always more of a 'hired gun' or one-off session-man, Airey's keyboard set-ups were many and varied, reflecting the large range of sounds and effects he may be expected to provide.

Thus it is difficult to assign particular keyboard arrangements to the various eras of his career. Continuing advances in electronic technology has rendered many types of keyboard redundant within a couple of years and has led to a bewildering array of hardware (not forgetting associated software).

In Rainbow he inherited a lot of the band equipment (see Tony Carey) but in 1988 gave his current set-up as: Roland D300 piano, Roland JX10 synthesiser, Roland D110 (multi-timbral), Casio F21 sampler, Two Memory Moogs, Mini Moog, Yamaha DX711D, Yamaha TX802, Yamaha TX16W sampler, Akai Linn MPC 60 drum machine and sequencer.

Jimmy Bain

Guitars - Main live and studio guitar through his Rainbow tenure was a 1961 Fender Telecaster bass with Schaller machine heads, with a 1975 Fender Precision and a 1963 Gibson Thunderbird as back-ups. Strings were Rotosound.

Amps - A JBL 5306 mixer and Auri 5273 graphic equaliser was used with two Crown DC300E power amps.

Ritchie Blackmore

Guitars - Ritchie's long-standing preference for Fender Stratocasters and Marshall stacks is well documented. (His original black Strat was given to him by Eric Clapton.) Less well-known, however, is the subtle variations to his guitar set-ups over the years. Since changing to Fender from Gibson around 1969-1970, Ritchie has modified his Stratocasters to his own personal requirements.

Unlike some other name players, Ritchie prefers the quality and sound of newly manufactured Stratocasters to the more venerated vintage models. The most fundamental modification is that he personally grooves out the wood between the frets to personally-suitable concavities. This allows better finger grip for note-bending. Frets are also changed to the thicker Gibson type. The middle pick-up was screwed down and never used. A thicker, more robust tremolo arm is fitted, as were Schaller heads. The necks are glued firmly in to prevent any potential movement.

On the back of the guitar the tremolo access plate is moved back a few inches to allow ease of string-changing. A standard model Fender

Telecaster was also used occasionally for studio work, as was a Yamaha acoustic (used for 'Temple Of The King') and a Fender bass guitar. Picato or Clifford Essex strings were used (of gauges .010, .011, .014, .026, .036 and .042) along with hard tortoiseshell picks (squared at one end, pointed at the other) which are more suited to Ritchie's fast right-hand picking technique than the more pliable plastic types.

Amps - Modified Marshall Major 200W stacks were used until the mid-nineties, with an extra stage built in to boost output to almost 300W and give more distortion at high sound levels - the most powerful Jim Marshall ever built. Ritchie usually had no bass set at all on his amp and treble setting at mid-range. Guitar tone controls was kept full up, with a half-volume setting for the quieter solos.

By the mid-nineties Blackmore's dissatisfaction with current Marshall build quality meant the set-up was replaced with a Blackmore Signature kit custom-built by German manufacturer Engl, based on their Savage 120 amps. Usual set-up is two 60W combos made up of two 4 by 12 cabinets and amp. These are said to give better sound quality at lower volume levels.
Effects are kept to a bare minimum. A wah-wah pedal was sometimes used in the studio (e.g. on 'Snake Charmer').

In the mid-seventies a Hornby Skewes treble booster was utilised to achieve more sustain. Live echo effects were achieved through a suitably modified Aiwa two-spool tape recorder. A fuzz effect can be obtained by turning up the output of the tape recorder. A simple foot pedal activates these effects.

Additionally, Ritchie often used a Moog Taurus pedal synthesiser. Resembling a box with two sliding, pedally-operated plates on top that control tone and volume, with seven on-off buttons below operating pre-set 'voices' or tones (bass, tuba, phase, decay, etc). Thirteen foot-pedals stick out rather like organ pedals and cover an octave from C to the C above. Three other button controls can change the octave settings. Ritchie was particularly partial to long thunderous bass crashes during concerts circa 1977-78.

Chuck Bürgi

His most recent Pearl Masters custom kit includes: One MMX 212DI 10x12-inch tom, one MMX 213DI 11x13-inch tom, one MMX 214DI 12x14-inch tom, and one MMX 215DI 14x15-inch tom. One MMX 224DX 16x24-inch bass drum.

Tony Carey

Carey's keys arrangement was largely

dictated by the fact that the equipment was purchased by and owned by the Rainbow 'organisation'. For the 1976 tour this consisted of: Hammond B3 organ* (specially modified cut-down version for ease of handling), three model D Mini Moogs, ARP String Ensemble series 28 with pedal, Polyphonic Orchestron and pedal, two Hohner Clavinettes model D6.

*Later utilised by Jon Lord on Deep Purple's 'The Battle Rages On' Tour.

Bob Daisley

Fender Precision bass guitars (rosewood necks), Picato bass strings, Marshall (more recently Ampeg) amplification.

Ronnie James Dio

Though the singer never played guitar live with Rainbow, for the record he used a Gibson SG bass and Sunn amplification while with Elf.

Gary Driscoll

The former Elf drummer had a powerful traditional rock'n'roll style that belied the simplicity of his kit set-up: Black Gretsch kit with a 24-inch bass drum, two floor toms, single racked tom and 6 inch snare. Cymbals included an 18-inch crash, 16-inch crash-ride, 14-inch hi-hat, 6-inch splash and two 14-inch crashes. Sticks were huge 2Bs. Driscoll also wore a glove on his left hand for better grip.

Roger Glover

Unlike Blackmore's equipment set-up, Roger was never totally content with his guitar sound and chopped and changed regularly (he still does, to a certain extent).

Guitars - He used a Gibson Thunderbird during the *'Down To Earth'* period, then switched briefly to an Ovation Magnum. He was given a white Fender Precision Special by Fender Japan which became his preferred guitar in the early eighties, used extensively live and in the studio (as seen in *'Live Between The Eyes'*). He also purchased a cheap Hondo Longhorn which he liked the sound of so much he used it for studio work coupled with a Alembic pre-amp. During recording he also used a Polytone Mini Brute Three.

Amps - Roger initially inherited the Rainbow back-line of Crown DCA 300 speakers and Gauss cabinets. By 1983 Glover had added a back-line of specially-made Bagend (Illinois) speakers. As for the tambourine sometimes used on stage, I'm still researching the model and make!

Craig Gruber

Fender Precision bass guitars.

John Micelli

Sonor Designer series with 5000 series hardware.

Paul Morris

Kurzweil PC-88, Roland JP-8000, Alesis QS6, Korg 01RW, and a Roland 1080.

Cozy Powell

The main change in Cozy's drum set-up while with Rainbow was the switch from Ludwig to Yamaha late in his tenure - the build quality and on-tour durability of the Yamaha being the main reasons. His tom-tom set-up was unusual in that both his racked and floor toms respectively were the same size. This set-up gradually evolved until the late eighties, by which time his racked arrangement had expanded to four differing-sized toms.

In 1975 Cozy was one of the first drummers to take his own customised monitor system on the road. Robert Simon at Pirate Sound developed and built the first of several sound systems Cozy used right through his career. Listed below are three examples of Cozy's kit set-up:

CIRCA 1977 (RAINBOW):
Ludwig red sparkle: Two 26-inch bass drums with Premier 250 pedals, two 14-inch racked tom-toms, two 16-inch floor toms. 6-inch metal symphonic snare. Cymbals (All Paiste): 24-inch ride (formula 602), 18-inch china, 18-inch crash-ride, 20-inch ride, 18-inch crash, two 16-inch crashes, 6-inch splash and a 15-inch hi-hat. Ludwig 35 sticks.

CIRCA 1983 (WHITESNAKE):
Yamaha custom in natural wood finish: Two 26-inch bass drums, two 15-inch racked tom-toms, an 18-inch floor tom and a 20-inch floor tom. 6-inch metal snare. Cymbals (Paiste 2000 series): 24-inch ride, 18-inch china, 20-inch crash-ride, 20-inch crash, 18-inch crash, 6-inch splash and a 15-inch hi-hat.

CIRCA 1989 (BLACK SABBATH):
Yamaha 9000 series custom in black and silver: Two 26-inch bass drums, four racked tom-toms: a 16 x 6-inch, 18 x 8-inch, 13 x 9-inch and a 14 x 10-inch. An 18-inch and a 20-inch floor tom. 6-inch metal snare. Cymbals (Paiste 3000 series): 24-inch ride, 18-inch china, 20-inch crash-ride, 20-inch crash, 18-inch crash, 6-inch splash and a 15-inch hi-hat and a 36-inch gong.

Bob Rondinelli

CIRCA 1981:
Yamaha and Sonor custom drums (including double bass drums), Paiste Cymbals, Remo drum heads, Paiste 52-inch gong, Capella sticks.

CIRCA 1995 (BLUE OYSTER CULT):

GMS drums, including 10x13-inch rack, 16x16-inch and 16x18-inch floor toms, 24x16-inch bass drum, 6x14-inch Ludwig Black Beauty snare, 6x14-inch GMS snare, Gibraltar kick pedal and hi-hat pedal, LP Roughrider cowbell and 52-inch gong. Cymbals are all Paiste Signature; 10-inch splash, 12-inch trash set, 15-inch crash, 17-inch crash, 18-inch New Dimensions crash, 18-inch china, 20-inch upside down china, 20-inch crash, 20-inch ride and 20-inch china. 8-inch Visions hi-hat, 14-inch Sound Formula hi-hat or a 14-inch New Dimensions hi-hat were all utilised. 1A Vater sticks and a MAE in-drum mike system with AKG D112 mikes.

David Rosenthal

During the 'SBTE' tour a Hammond B3 (through two 122 Leslie cabs), 2 MiniMoogs, a Oberheim OB-Xa, a Roland P505 string synthesiser, a Hohner D6 clavinet and Taurus bass pedals were used. For the 'BOOS' tour the same Hammond/Leslie set-up, with one Mini Moog, a Memory Moog, an Emulator I, Oberheim OB-Xa, Hohner D6 Clavinet, Roland P505 String Synthesiser and Taurus Bass Pedals.

For the Billy Joel tours David utilised a Kurzweil K2000, Roland JD800, Yamaha KX76, and a Korg CX3 through a Leslie 147 cab.

For the more rock-orientated efforts a more analogue approach is preferred.

For the *'Red Dawn'* recordings a Memory Moog, Roland MKS70, Roland JD800, Oberheim OBXa and Taurus bass pedals were employed.

Greg Smith

Guitars - A 1957 Fender Precision with maple neck, a 1972 Fender Precision with rosewood neck. Also used are an early-1980s red Spector NS2, a 1976 Music Man Sabre, two 1984 Guild Pilot basses, an Ibanez 5-string and assorted Kramer basses. Strings are Fender and pick-ups are EMG.

Amps - Two Ampeg SVT 4/10 1/15 cabinets, two Hartke 4/10-s, two 4.5 cabinets and one Hartke 15 cab.

Joe Lynn Turner

Joe holds the unique position of being the only other six-string guitarist to feature live with Rainbow. During 1981-82 the later stages of the *'Difficult To Cure'* tour saw Joe don a mahogany finish Gibson SG for rhythm work, though it was always difficult to make any judgement of his efforts as the mix invariably meant you could hardly hear him!

Other guitars used for composing and studio work over the years include a rare '57 Peavey and a Les Paul Junior, along with a standard Fender Telecaster and several Stratocasters.

RAINBOW TOUR PROGRAMMES

In these days of desk-top publishing its easy to forget that during the seventies provision of tour programmes was not that common, and good ones were the exception rather than the rule. Listed below are the good, the bad and the ugly publications relating to Rainbow's live tours.

UK TOUR (1976)
Basic black cover with a 'rainbow' in four colours. Advert for *'Rising'* on page 2, and an introduction with tour dates. A group shot plus individual shots of the members coupled with brief biographies of each. Centre spread is an out-of-focus US-sourced live picture. Also included is a US concert review, equipment information and a page on support band Stretch. Inside back cover was a form for ordering band merchandise.

AUSTRALIAN TOUR (1976)
A4 two-colour black/red design, 16 pages. This is based on the UK programme. Seven pages are in black and white. There is a full-page advert for *'Rising'*, along with three pages of general adverts. Support band Buffalo get a page for themselves. Back cover features a nice shot of Ritchie.

JAPANESE TOUR (1976)
10" by 14" 36-page effort for the Japanese tour. Front cover features repeated images of the *'Rising'* artwork with thumbnails of the band, all bordered with silver. Back cover is a group shot. Advert for the tour included. Four colour pages, two of Ritchie and a centre spread of live photos. 22-odd pages contain black and white photos, and eight of advertising (two are for the band). A nice all-round effort, quite rare.

LONG LIVE ROCK'N'ROLL TOUR (1977)
A4 sized 24-page, with colour front and nine pages in colour. Eight pages of ads, including full page for *'Rising'*. Centre spread features on-stage photo with album sleeves inset. Five pages carry sepia photos of band members with a detailed biog. Support act Kingfish have a page feature. Also includes details of band's equipment from the previous year's

programme. A couple of group pictures in version one were said to have been rejected by Blackmore, and these were changed mid-tour, hence this exists in two versions (the former is much rarer).

JAPANESE TOUR (1978)
10" by 14" 40-page Japanese-only programme. Eight colour pages. Cover is a collection of live shots. Most pages simply have a small picture and little else. Nine pages of advertising, including centre-page spread (for coffee!).

RAINBOW (1980)
9" by 12" 24-page programme for the European *'Down to Earth'* tour. Front photo of band imposed on a sunset ('All Night Long' picture sleeve), back catalogue ad on back. Four pages of ads for Picato strings, Yamaha drums, Panache music and Southern Comfort. Mixture of small b/w and colour photos, mostly on-stage imposed on rainbow background format. Strangely, also includes two pages of pictures of the Rainbow road crew.

JAPAN TOUR (1980)
An LP-sized 36 page Japanese-only programme. Six pages of colour. Design features small square pictures of the band. Centre pages feature (you've guessed!) a coffee advert, along with five other pages of ads to the back.

MONSTERS OF ROCK (1980)
A4 sized 24-page festival programme by Concert Publishing. Covers all bands on bill, three pages on Rainbow by Steve Gett of Melody Maker, using pictures taken for the earlier tour programme. Picato strings advert with Ritchie, and merchandise page, along with page on how to join the fan club. (Note: a cheap-looking pirate programme was also printed for festival, in black with a two-colour cover. Now rare.)

RAINBOW FAN MAGAZINE (1980)
Although not strictly a tour programme, this is a first edition A4 sized 12-page publication from the short-lived fan club, celebrating the Monsters Of Rock appearance. Sparse in content: a brief report on the tour by Sounds' Pete Makowski follows Ritchie's responses to fans' (rather trite) questions. One page has a poorly reproduced hand-written letter to the fan club from Ritchie. Several nice on-stage

colour shots of Blackmore, especially on the cover.

DIFFICULT TO CURE (1981)
28-page 10" by 14", put together by Concert Publishing. Unexciting photo of band sitting on a wall on the front cover. Back catalogue advert on back. Includes a resume of band events up to the tour, with colour pictures throughout. Recent tour dates listed on the inside back cover. A whole two pages are wastefully taken up by credits for just 12 people! Surprisingly, no adverts.

JAPAN TOUR (1981)
LP-size 36-page Japanese-only programme. Ritchie photo on front and live group shot on back. Black and white photos with six-page colour middle section. An ad for car tyres features Sean Connery! Two-page discography. Nice effort.

STRAIGHT BETWEEN THE EYES (1982)
A4 sized 24-page in full colour. Pictures of each member inset into the eyeball design from the album cover. Live photos of Blackmore, great shot on cover.

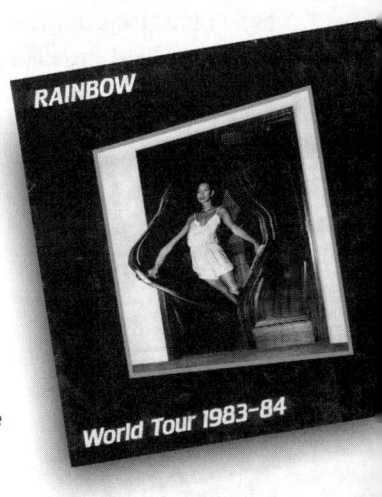

RAINBOW WORLD TOUR (1983-84)
20-page 10" by 10". Album cover on front (black surround), repeated on back. Colour photos on black background throughout. Advert for the fan club and merchandise on one page. One page on the new album and the new members, written by Steve Gett. The rest of the programme is taken up with 2-page spreads of each band member's photo and their responses to standard questions (likes, dislikes etc). Rumours persist of a tour programme for final three Japanese dates, but is unconfirmed.

JAPANESE TOUR (1995)
28 pages with the cover several shades of dark grey with no pictures. Inside pictures mostly out of focus.

LIST OF GIGS (1975-1997)

Over 600 shows were played by Rainbow during the periods 1975-1984 and 1995-1997, of which 593 are included in this listing. Gig entries set out in the following format: Date (dd.mm.yy); Venue; Country; Notes. Some unresolved dates included where venue, or even date, remains unconfirmed.

1975 'RAINBOW' TOUR

After rehearsals at Pirate Sound, Rainbow eventually played their debut concert in Canada, after the initial four shows were rescheduled and two replacement gigs were delayed as well.

Date	Venue	Country	Notes
05.11.75	Pittsburgh, Syria Mosque, Pennsylvania	USA	Rescheduled for 18th Dec.
06.11.75	Allentown, Fairgrounds Agricultural Hall, Pennsylvania	USA	Rescheduled for Dec.
07.11.75	Boston, Orpheum Theater, Massachusetts	USA	Rescheduled for Dec.
08.11.75	Upper Darby Tower Theater, Pennsylvania	USA	Rescheduled for 15th Nov.
10.11.75	Montréal, Forum Concert Bowl, Québec	Canada	Supported by Argent. Despite sizeable venue, only approximately 1,500 saw the show.
12.11.75	Beacon Theater, New York	USA	Supported by Argent. After Boston and Pennsylvania concerts rescheduled, this gig advertised for 6th Nov - as debut gig - but put back to following week.
13.11.75	Waterbury Palace Theater, Connecticut	USA	Supported by UFO. Again, after initial concerts rescheduled, gig advertised for 8th Nov but put back to following week.
14.11.75	Hempstead, Calderone Concert Hall, Long Island, New York	USA	
15.11.75	Upper Darby Tower Theater, Pennsylvania	USA	Supported by Argent. Rescheduled from 8th Nov. Performance delayed for a few hours, crew tackling problems of buzz interference from the rainbow's lights.
16.11.75	Akron, Civic Theatre, Ohio	USA	Support The Mutants, though Argent advertised support.
18.11.75	Detroit, Ford Auditorium, Michigan	USA	
19.11.75	Milwaukee, Uptown Theater, Wisconsin	USA	
20.11.75	St. Louis, Ambassador Theater, Missouri	USA	
22.11.75	Chicago, Auditorium Theater, Illinois	USA	Support band Rush cancelled.
26.11.75	Fresno, Warnors Theatre, California	USA	Not included in original tour advert. Fresno Selland Arena has also been mentioned but - with a 10,000 seat capacity -

28.11.75	Berkeley, Community Theater, California	USA	seems too large as this was predominantly a theatre tour.
29.11.75	Santa Monica, Civic Auditorium, California	USA	Argent didn't play. 'Still I'm Sad' was dedicated to the recently deceased racing driver Graham Hill.
12.75	Portland, Paramount Theater, Oregon	USA	
12.75	Seattle, Paramount Theatre, Washington	USA	
12.75	Vancouver, Queen Elizabeth Theatre, British Columbia	Canada	Rescheduled from 7th Nov.
12.75	Boston, Orpheum Theater, Massachusetts	USA	Rescheduled from 5th Nov. All of these first five Dec shows listed as 'date TBA' in a press advert.
12.75	Pittsburgh, Syria Mosque, Pennsylvania	USA	
12.75	Allentown, Fairgrounds Agricultural Hall, Pennsylvania	USA	Rescheduled from 6th Nov.
12.75	Tampa (venue unknown), Florida	USA	Referred to in article in Beat Instrumental as where the tour was due to end.

Whilst in Munich, in February 1976, the band played an impromptu set at an ice-skating rink that they visited during a break from recording, using the resident band's gear. An interview in New York, from Nov 1975, had mentioned a tour of France in March - this never happened.

24.03.76	Santa Monica, Civic Auditorium, California	USA	Ritchie jams with The Sweet on 'All Right Now', in tribute to Paul Kossoff who had died the previous week.

1976 'RISING' TOUR

During May 1976, tour rehearsals were captured on tape, including a new track 'Kill The King', and Deep Purple's 'Mistreated'. Press reports referred to planned tour activity for late-May and early-June supporting Jethro Tull (who had just played some European dates) being blown out, as well as plans to go out supporting Alice Cooper being cancelled after Alice got hepatitis. Dates in Texas, the Mid-West and on the West Coast were cancelled. Thin Lizzy (who had played US dates in May) were the support act on a couple of shows before Phil Lynott was taken ill. Press reports had referred to a 40-date tour by Rainbow and it is likely that more dates have yet to be identified, particularly in July. These summer dates included return trips to several of the places played at the end of 1975, including Allentown, New York, Hempstead, Boston, Milwaukee, Chicago and Montréal - though the last two were in different venues.

06.06.76	Stateline (venue unknown), Idaho	USA
11.06.76	Columbus (venue unknown), Ohio	USA

Appendices

Date	Venue	Country	Notes
13.06.76	Allentown, Fairgrounds, Pennsylvania	USA	Supported by Max Webster. Cancelled. Possible that tickets were never put on sale. Rescheduled for 20th July.
14.06.76	Montréal, Le Theatre St. Denis, Québec	Canada	Thin Lizzy cancelled, there was no replacement support. Support Southside Johnny And The Asbury Dukes. Ritchie smashes his first guitar with Rainbow at this show.
15.06.76	Cleveland, Allen Theater, Ohio	USA	
17.06.76	Beacon Theater, New York	USA	
06.76	Hempstead, Calderone Concert Hall, Long Island, New York	USA	
06.76	Boston, Orpheum Theater, Massachusetts	USA	
22.06.76	Dayton, Hara Arena, Ohio	USA	
24.06.76	Milwaukee, Uptown Theater, Wisconsin	USA	
25.06.76	Chicago, Aragon Ballroom, Illinois	USA	Supported by Heart and Mahogany Rush.
26.06.76	Indianapolis (venue unknown), Indiana	USA	Unconfirmed.
27.06.76	Davenport, Orpheum Theater, Iowa	USA	
02.07.76	Rochester, Masonic Temple, New York	USA	With Gentle Giant and Angel. Some tapes are incorrectly dated 6th July.
03.07.76	Asbury Park, Boardwalk Casino Arena, New Jersey	USA	
07.76	An outdoor gig (possibly on 4th July)		Remains unconfirmed.
07.76	Burbank, Starlight Bowl Amphitheatre, California	USA	Vetoed by Burbank council but rearranged for early Aug.
08.07.76	Dallas, SMU McFarlin Memorial Auditorium, Texas	USA	
10.07.76	Houston, Music Hall, Texas	USA	Promotional film recorded, including 'Over The Rainbow' and excerpts from 'Man On The Silver Mountain', 'Stargazer', 'A Light In The Black', 'Still I'm Sad' (drum solo only) and 'Do You Close Your Eyes'.
15.07.76	Miami, Jai Alai Fronton, Florida	USA	
07.76	Jacksonville (Civic Aud. or Veterans' Mem. Coliseum), Florida	USA	Review included in UK tour programme.
20.07.76	Montréal, Le Theatre St. Denis, Québec	Canada	Supported by Max Webster.
26.07.76	Pittsburgh, Civic Arena, Pennsylvania	USA	Supporting Jethro Tull. This date does not seem to appear on Tull lists. Around this time, Tull believed to have played Philadelphia, Boston, New York, Detroit, Cincinnati and Louisville.
27.07.76	Indianapolis, Market Square Arena, Indiana	USA	Supporting Jethro Tull. This date does not seem to appear on Tull lists.
03.08.76	Burbank, Starlight Bowl Amphitheatre, California	USA	

Rainbow RISING

Date	Venue	Country	Notes
26.08.76	Orange, Theatre d'Antique d'Orange	France	'Orange Festival' - the festival was cancelled.
28.08.76	Nimes, Arénas Romaines	France	'Rock And Pop Festival' - the festival was cancelled.
31.08.76	Bristol Hippodrome	UK	Guitar demolition during encore. UK support were Stretch.
01.09.76	Leicester, De Montfort Hall	UK	Guitar demolition during encore.
03.09.76	Liverpool, Empire Theatre	UK	
04.09.76	Edinburgh Playhouse, Scotland	UK	Start delayed due to a problem with the generators - guitar demolition during encore.
05.09.76	Manchester, Free Trade Hall	UK	Guitar demolition during encore.
07.09.76	London, Hammersmith Odeon	UK	No encore. Neil Murray and Don Airey saw the show.
08.09.76	London, Hammersmith Odeon	UK	Guitar demolition during encore. Glover, Lord, Paice and Coverdale were in attendance.
09.09.76	London, Hammersmith Odeon	UK	Provisional date reported in press but never put on sale.
10.09.76	Cardiff Castle, Wales	UK	There were full-page adverts for this show, billed as special guests supporting Queen - Rainbow didn't appear. The concert went ahead in virtually monsoon conditions. The bill would have been: Queen, Rainbow, Andy Fairweather Low, Frankie Miller's Full House.
11.09.76	Birmingham, Odeon	UK	Guitar demolition during encore. Glover watched the show.
12.09.76	Southampton, Gaumont Theatre	UK	Venue mistakenly referred to as the Odeon in adverts in UK music weeklies. Cozy's car broke down on the way to this gig and he had to thumb a lift!
13.09.76	Cardiff, Capitol Theatre, Wales	UK	Cancelled when the festival appearance was booked.
14.09.76	London, Soho, The Speakeasy	UK	Ritchie, with Ian Hunter, guests with The Fabulous Poodles.
15.09.76	Newcastle, City Hall	UK	Guitar demolition during encore.
16.09.76	London, Soho, The Speakeasy	UK	Ritchie guests with Screaming Lord Sutch.
17.09.76	Lund (venue unknown)	Sweden	Cancelled, the rainbow wouldn't fit into the venue.
20.09.76	Stockholm, Konserthuset	Sweden	Guitar demolition during encore. Support AC/DC.
22.09.76	Copenhagen, Tivolis Koncertsal	Denmark	Support AC/DC.
23.09.76	Hamburg, Musikhalle Grosser Saal	Germany	Support AC/DC. Filmed in part by Oyster.
24.09.76	Bremen, Stadthalle	Germany	Support AC/DC.
25.09.76	Cologne, Sporthalle	Germany	Recorded for live album. 'Sixteenth Century Greensleeves', 'Stargazer' and 'Still I'm Sad' included on 'Live In Germany'

Appendices

Date	Venue	Country	Notes
27.09.76	Düsseldorf, Philipshalle	Germany	1976'. 'Man On The Silver Mountain' included on *Rock Profile Volume Two*. Support AC/DC.
28.09.76	Nuremberg, Messezentrum Halle A (not Mannheim Multihalle)	Germany	Recorded for live album. 'Catch The Rainbow' included on *Live In Germany 1976*. Support AC/DC.
29.09.76	Munich, Circus Krone	Germany	Recorded for live album. 'Man On The Silver Mountain' included on *Live In Germany 1976*. Support AC/DC. Recorded for live album. 'Kill The King', 'Mistreated' and 'Do You Close Your Eyes' included on *Live In Germany 1976*. 'Sixteenth Century Greensleeves' included on *Rock Profile Volume Two*. Support AC/DC.
01.10.76	Wiesbaden, Rhein-Main-Hallen	Germany	Support AC/DC.
02.10.76	Dortmund, Westfalenhalle	Germany	With Van Der Graaf Generator and Procol Harum.
03.10.76	Geneva (venue unknown)	Switzerland	Unconfirmed.
04.10.76	Bern, Casino	Switzerland	Support AC/DC.
05.10.76	Zürich, Volkshaus	Switzerland	Support AC/DC.
06.10.76	Frankfurt, Jahrhunderthalle	Germany	Support AC/DC.
08.10.76	Hoensbroek, Luxor Theater	Holland	Support AC/DC.
11.10.76	Le Mans (venue unknown)	France	Support AC/DC.
12.10.76	Le Havre (venue unknown)	France	Support AC/DC.
13.10.76	Paris, Porte De Pantin Pavillon	France	Support AC/DC.
15.10.76	Rouen (venue unknown)	France	Support AC/DC.
16.10.76	Marseille (venue unknown)	France	Support AC/DC.
17.10.76	Brussels, Koninklijk Circus (Cirque Royal)	Belgium	Support AC/DC.
18.10.76	Den Haag, Congresgebouw (also known as Congrescentrum)	Holland	Support AC/DC. During the European dates Carey was fired, but was rehired after rehearsals with another keyboard player didn't work out.
28.10.76	Erlangen Stadthalle	Germany	Unconfirmed, doubtful. A tape recording exists purporting to be this show but is actually Nuremberg on 28th Sep.
04.11.76	Perth, Entertainment Centre, Western Australia	Australia	Support group Buffalo.
09.11.76	Melbourne, Festival Hall, Victoria	Australia	Support group Buffalo.
11.11.76	Sydney, Hordern Pavilion, New South Wales	Australia	Support group Buffalo.
12.11.76	Newcastle, Civic Theatre, New South Wales	Australia	

13.11.76	Brisbane, Festival Hall, Queensland	Australia	Support group Buffalo.
16.11.76	Sydney, Hordern Pavilion, New South Wales	Australia	Support group Buffalo. No encore, a press report said that Ritchie had planned to set fire to a guitar but, due to an oil strike, couldn't get any petrol!
19.11.76	Adelaide, Festival Theatre, South Australia	Australia	Additional 5pm show - support group Buffalo.
19.11.76	Adelaide, Festival Theatre, South Australia	Australia	Support group Buffalo.
20.11.76	Adelaide, Festival Theatre, South Australia	Australia	Support group Buffalo - no guitar demolitions in Adelaide.
22.11.76	Melbourne, Festival Hall, Victoria	Australia	
11.76	Countdown Club	Australia	Ritchie jammed with Ross Wilson's Mondo Rock Band at the Countdown Club one night whilst in Australia.
02.12.76	Tokyo, Taiikukan Gymnasium, Honshu	Japan	
04.12.76	Nagoya, Shi Kokaido, Honshu	Japan	
05.12.76	Osaka, Koseinenkin Kaikan (Festival Hall), Honshu	Japan	
07.12.76	Nagoya, Shi Kokaido, Honshu	Japan	
08.12.76	Osaka, Koseinenkin Kaikan (Festival Hall), Honshu	Japan	Recorded for live LP. 'Mistreated' dedicated to Tommy Bolin.
09.12.76	Osaka, Koseinenkin Kaikan (Festival Hall), Honshu	Japan	Recorded for live album.
13.12.76	Kyoto, Kaikan Daiichi Hall, Honshu	Japan	
14.12.76	Fukuoka, Kyuden-Kinen Taiikukan, Kyushu	Japan	
16.12.76	Hiroshima, Kenritsu Taiikukan, Honshu	Japan	3pm show. Recorded for live album. No encore.
16.12.76	Tokyo, Budokan, Honshu	Japan	Recorded for live album - guitar demolition during encore.
	Tokyo, Budokan, Honshu	Japan	

1977-78 'ON STAGE' TOUR

Ritchie and Cozy jammed with some local bands in Paris whilst over there finding a suitable place to record the next album. Mark Clarke later recalled that he played live with Rainbow in Los Angeles, in a club in Paris and on one other occasion. With nothing more than these vague details and given that these would seem to have been less than full shows, these have not been listed. UK dates for July were scrapped as the album wasn't finished. US dates starting at the end of July to September were referred to in interviews but had also been scrapped. These would have included the following two dates:

13.08.77	Buffalo, Rich Stadium, New York	USA	Cancelled.
09.09.77	Los Angeles, Shrine Auditorium, California	USA	Cancelled.

Appendices

Tour rehearsals held in September at Shepperton Studios, UK, during the week prior to Scandinavian dates. Support on European tour were Kingfish.

Date	Venue	Country	Notes
18.09.77	London, Finsbury Park Rainbow Theatre	UK	Rescheduled for November.
19.09.77	London, Finsbury Park Rainbow Theatre	UK	Rescheduled for November.
20.09.77	London, Finsbury Park Rainbow Theatre	UK	Rescheduled for November.
21.09.77	London, Finsbury Park Rainbow Theatre	UK	Rescheduled for November.
23.09.77	Helsinki, Finlandia Hall	Finland	Cancelled after the gear was held up at Customs.
25.09.77	Stockholm, Konserthuset	Sweden	Start delayed by an hour, no guitar demolition.
26.09.77	Gothenburg, Scandinavium	Sweden	
27.09.77	Oslo, Château Neuf	Norway	
28.09.77	Trondheim, Nidarøhallen	Norway	The show started half an hour late and was done without the rainbow which hadn't arrived from Oslo.
30.09.77	Vejle, Idraettens Hus	Denmark	
01.10.77	Copenhagen, Falkoner Teatret	Denmark	
02.10.77	Aarhus, Vejlby-Risskov Hallen	Denmark	
04.10.77	Den Haag, Congresgebouw	Holland	
05.10.77	Münster, Münsterlandhalle	Germany	Cancelled.
06.10.77	Essen, Gruga-Halle	Germany	Not on original itinerary. During the demolition, one guitar goes into the audience intact!
07.10.77	Berlin, Eissporthalle	Germany	Cancelled.
08.10.77	Cologne, Sporthalle	Germany	Encore with guitar demolition.
09.10.77	Dortmund, Westfalenhalle	Germany	Cancelled.
10.10.77	Bremen, Stadthalle	Germany	
11.10.77	Ludwigshafen, Friedrich-Ebert-Halle	Germany	
12.10.77	?	Germany	It is thought that a gig was played in Friedrichshafen. This appears very doubtful and seems most likely to simply be a misinterpretation of the previous night's entry.
13.10.77	Stuttgart, Sporthalle	Germany	Band not on stage in time for the 'over the rainbow' intro tape ending. No encore. Originally scheduled for 15th Oct.
14.10.77	Hanover, Sporthalle	Germany	
15.10.77	Berlin, Deutschlandhalle	Germany	Replaced Berlin Eissporthalle, originally scheduled 7th Oct.
16.10.77	Hamburg, Congresszentrum	Germany	

Date	Venue	Country	Notes
17.10.77	Wiesbaden, Rhein-Main-Hallen	Germany	Rescheduled.
18.10.77	Vienna, Stadthalle	Austria	Ritchie arrested after show and jailed after alleged scuffle resulted in security man getting broken jaw. He was later fined over £5,000.
19.10.77	Munich, Olympiahalle	Germany	Postponed, rescheduled for 20th Oct.
20.10.77	Munich, Olympiahalle	Germany	Originally scheduled for 19th Oct but, with bail refused in Vienna, Munich show had to be rearranged. Ritchie was late arriving from Austria and start was considerably delayed. After Kingfish's set, refunds were offered. It wasn't until midnight Rainbow finally took the stage. Filmed.
21.10.77	(location/venue unknown)	Yugoslavia	Cancelled.
21.10.77	Nuremberg, Messehalle	Germany	Originally scheduled for 18th Oct but rescheduled to fit in the Vienna gig.
22.10.77	Dornbirn, Stadthalle	Austria	Cancelled, replaced by the earlier Vienna gig.
22.10.77	Wiesbaden, Rhein-Main-Hallen	Germany	Originally scheduled for 17th Oct.
24.10.77	Colmar, Salle D'Exposition	France	Also seen listed as Marseille Salle Vallier.
25.10.77	Lyon, Palais Du Sport	France	
27.10.77	Paris, Porte De Pantin Pavillon	France	Originally scheduled for 26th Oct.
31.10.77	Newcastle, City Hall	UK	Support for the UK tour were Kingfish.
01.11.77	Newcastle, City Hall	UK	
03.11.77	Preston, Guildhall Lockley Grand Hall	UK	No encore.
04.11.77	Liverpool, Empire Theatre	UK	
05.11.77	Liverpool, Empire Theatre	UK	During encore, Ritchie appeared in one of the boxes, level with the balcony, playing guitar whilst dangling his legs over the edge, before demolishing guitar. Unimpressed, venue banned Rainbow after assessing damage.
07.11.77	Aberdeen, Capitol Theatre, Scotland	UK	
09.11.77	Glasgow, Apollo Theatre, Scotland	UK	
11.11.77	London, Finsbury Park Rainbow Theatre	UK	
12.11.77	London, Finsbury Park Rainbow Theatre	UK	
13.11.77	London, Finsbury Park Rainbow Theatre	UK	
14.11.77	London, Finsbury Park Rainbow Theatre	UK	
16.11.77	Oxford, New Theatre	UK	

Appendices

Date	Venue	Country	Notes
17.11.77	Leicester, Granby Halls	UK	A guitar went completely over the rainbow during encore!
18.11.77	Stafford, New Bingley Hall	UK	Encore with guitar demolition.
20.11.77	Manchester, Apollo Theatre	UK	No encore.
21.11.77	Manchester, Apollo Theatre	UK	Encore with guitar demolition.
22.11.77	Cardiff, Capitol Theatre, Wales	UK	
11.01.78	Nagoya, Shi Kokaido, Honshu	Japan	
12.01.78	Hiroshima, Kenritsu Taiikukan, Honshu	Japan	
13.01.78	Kumamoto (venue unknown), Kyushu	Japan	
14.01.78	Fukuoka, Kyuden-Kinen Taiikukan, Kyushu	Japan	
16.01.78	Osaka, Koseinenkin Kaikan (Festival Hall), Honshu	Japan	
17.01.78	Osaka, Koseinenkin Kaikan (Festival Hall), Honshu	Japan	
18.01.78	Kyoto, Kaikan Daiichi Hall, Honshu	Japan	
20.01.78	Osaka, Koseinenkin Kaikan (Festival Hall), Honshu	Japan	
21.01.78	Tokyo, Budokan, Honshu	Japan	
22.01.78	Tokyo, Budokan, Honshu	Japan	
24.01.78	Koriyama, Shimin Bunka Center, Honshu	Japan	A young female college student was killed and several others injured as crowd rushed the stage during encore.
27.01.78	Sapporo, Nakajima Sports Center, Hokkaido	Japan	Extra show, not on original itinerary.
28.01.78	Tokyo, Budokan, Honshu	Japan	
29.01.78	Akita, Kenmin Kaikan, Honshu	Japan	
31.01.78	Niigata, Kenmin Kaikan, Honshu	Japan	
01.02.78	Kanazawa, Shi Kanko Kaikan, Honshu	Japan	
03.02.78	Tokyo, Budokan, Honshu	Japan	

Early plans for the 1977/78 World Tour included Australia, New Zealand, Indonesia and Malaysia though no shows in these territories seem to have been played - or even booked then cancelled. After release of the *'Long Live Rock'n'Roll'* album, continued effort to break America seemed all-important.

1978 'LONG LIVE ROCK'N'ROLL' TOUR

Date	Venue	Country	Notes
05.78	Don Kirshner's 'Rock Concert'	USA	The band mimed this promo film (using backing tracks from original studio versions but with alternate vocals) including 'Long Live Rock'n'Roll', 'Gates Of Babylon' and

Date	Venue	Country	Notes
09.05.78	Memphis, Mid-South Coliseum, Tennessee	USA	'L.A. Connection'. Thought to have been recorded before North American leg of 'Long Live Rock'n'Roll' tour began.
11.05.78	St. Louis Arena ('The Checkerdome'), Missouri	USA	Supporting REO Speedwagon.
12.05.78	Kansas City, Kemper Arena, Missouri	USA	REO Speedwagon/Rainbow/No Dice.
13.05.78	Kansas City, Kemper Arena, Missouri	USA	REO Speedwagon/Rainbow/No Dice.
15.05.78	Parsons, Marvel Park Stadium, Kansas	USA	Cancelled. A surprisingly small community to host a concert. After Municipal Auditorium was closed in 1974, a teacher at local high school started to promote concerts including Styx in 1976. Agreement made with Rainbow's booking agent and posters printed but eventually the cost to put on concert made it prohibitive so it was cancelled.
18.05.78	Los Angeles, Shrine Auditorium, California	USA	REO Speedwagon/Rainbow/No Dice.
19.05.78	San Bernardino, Swing Auditorium, California	USA	
20.05.78	San Francisco, Winterland Ballroom, California	USA	
21.05.78	Fresno, Warnors Theatre, California	USA	
22.05.78	San Diego, Sports Arena, California	USA	REO Speedwagon/Rainbow/No Dice.
05.78	Cleveland, Richfield Coliseum, Ohio	USA	Black Oak Arkansas supporting. Short set, due to crowd throwing missiles.
26.05.78	Toledo, Sports Arena, Ohio	USA	Supported by Henry Gross and No Dice. A radio station promotion (WLRS 102) with admission pegged at $1.02.
27.05.78	Louisville Gardens, Kentucky	USA	
28.05.78	Allentown Fairgrounds, Pennsylvania	USA	Supporting Foghat. In case of cancellation, 30th May had been set aside as a 'rain date'.
29.05.78	Springfield, Civic Arena, Massachusetts	USA	Co-headliners with Foghat.
31.05.78	Dayton, Hara Arena, Ohio	USA	
01.06.78	Erie County Coliseum, Pennsylvania	USA	Cancelled due to illness.
02.06.78	Passaic, Capitol Theater, New Jersey	USA	Supported by Uriah Heep and No Dice. The set, no more than sixty minutes long, was played without the rainbow.
03.06.78	Albany Palace Theater, New York, USA		
04.06.78	Lynn Manning Bowl, Massachusetts, USA		
05/06.06.78	Boston Garden, Massachusetts	USA	
07.06.78	Poughkeepsie, Mid-Hudson Civic Center Arena, New York	USA	Exact date unconfirmed.

Date	Venue	Country	Notes
09.06.78	Rochester War Memorial Auditorium, New York	USA	Supporting REO Speedwagon.
10.06.78	Commack, Suffolk Forum, Long Island, New York	USA	Better known as the Long Island Arena, the venue was known as the Suffolk Forum for a while.
11.06.78	Largo Capitol Center, Maryland	USA	
16.06.78	Jacksonville (Civic Aud. or Vets.' Memorial Coliseum), Florida	USA	With Cheap Trick and Max Webster.
17.06.78	Lakeland Civic Center, Florida	USA	Listed as 18th June in the press.
19.06.78	Miami, Jai Alai Fronton, Florida	USA	Originally listed as Johnson City Tennessee in the press.
23.06.78	Greensboro Coliseum, North Carolina	USA	Supporting REO Speedwagon. This seems to have replaced gig at Fox Theatre originally scheduled 8th June. Recorded for BBC 'Rock Hour' radio show, though broadcast in States rather than UK. Two tracks included on 'Finyl Vinyl'.
24.06.78	Atlanta Omni, Georgia	USA	
25.06.78	Charlotte Coliseum, North Carolina	USA	
27.06.78	Knoxville, Civic Auditorium Coliseum, Tennessee	USA	
28.06.78	Nashville, Municipal Auditorium Arena, Tennessee	USA	
30.06.78	Little Rock, Barton Coliseum, Arkansas	USA	Listed as Jackson, Tennessee in the press.
01.07.78	Springfield Armory, Illinois	USA	Cheap Trick/Rainbow/Max Webster. Listed as Jackson, Missouri in the press.
02.07.78	Chicago, International Amphitheatre, Illinois	USA	Cheap Trick/Rainbow/Max Webster.
04.07.78	Cleves, Edgewater Speedway, Ohio	USA	The Outlaws/Rick Derringer/Rainbow/Rare Earth/Dixie Dregs. Rainbow played for about an hour. Ritchie smashed a guitar.
13.07.78	Houston, Sam Houston Coliseum, Texas	USA	Supporting REO Speedwagon.
07.78	San Antonio, Municipal Auditorium, Texas	USA	
21.07.78	Baton Rouge, Louisiana State Uni.Assembly Center, Louisiana	USA	
22.07.78	Beaumont, Fair Park Coliseum, Texas	USA	
23.07.78	Austin (University of Texas?), Texas	USA	
08.78	Bridgeport (venue unknown), Connecticut	USA	Festival cancelled.
01.08.78	Philadelphia Spectrum, Pennsylvania	USA	Cancelled. Possibly a planned co-headlining date with Cheap Trick. Tape exists purporting to be this show but is from 2nd Aug.
02.08.78	Philadelphia, Upper Darby Tower Theater, Pennsylvania	USA	Either with Cheap Trick or with REO Speedwagon and Nantucket.

08.78	Royal Oak Music Hall, Michigan	USA	Support The Cars.
17.08.78	Pittsburgh, Stanley Theater, Pennsylvania	USA	With Eddie Money. Near riot after Rainbow only played for 45 minutes.
18.08.78	Hempstead, Calderone Concerrt Hall, Long Island, New York	USA	With AC/DC supporting.
19.08.78	Wilkes-Barre Paramount Theater, Pennsylvania	USA	With AC/DC supporting.
08.78	Boston, Orpheum Theater, Massachusetts	USA	
24.08.78	New York Palladium, New York	USA	With AC/DC supporting. This performance abandoned after three numbers due to interference between the rainbow and PA. After a further 90 mins of efforts, Ronnie announced that ticket money would be refunded.
26.08.78	Asbury Park, Convention Hall, New Jersey	USA	Interference problems still persisting during soundcheck, show cancelled and ticket money refunded. Instead David Johansen (ex-New York Dolls) played a free show.
27.12.78	London, Soho, The Marquee Club	UK	Ritchie jams with Gillan.
01.79	Cozy played on a session for Gary Moore on BBC2's 'The Old Grey Whistle Test'.		

During Cheap Trick's 1979 UK tour, Cozy Powell sat in on the drums for a number of shows, including:

02.02.79	Bristol University	UK	Cozy played on last song of the evening, 'Goodnight Now'.
08.02.79	Oxford Polytechnic	UK	Cozy, with Dave Edmunds on guitar/vocals, performed 'Promised Land', 'Let It Rock' and 'Reeling And Rocking'.

1979-80 'DOWN TO EARTH' TOUR

The Blue Öyster Cult tour seemed to start without Rainbow whose first concert was in Rochester. Rainbow's tour was preceded by rehearsals in USA.

02.09.79	Lakeland, Civic Center, Florida	USA
04.09.79	Birmingham, Boutwell Auditorium, Alabama	USA
08.09.79	Fayetteville, Cumberland Cnty.Memorial Aud., North Carolina	USA
09.09.79	Greenville, Memorial Auditorium, South Carolina	USA

Appendices

Date	Venue	Country	Notes
09.79	Providence, Civic Center, Rhode Island	USA	Seems to have been cancelled and rescheduled.
14.09.79	Boston Garden, Massachusetts	USA	Supporting Blue Öyster Cult.
15.09.79	Presque Isle Forum, Maine	USA	Supporting Blue Öyster Cult.
16.09.79	Portland, Cumberland County Civic Center, Maine	USA	Supporting Blue Öyster Cult.
18.09.79	New Haven Coliseum, Connecticut	USA	Supporting Blue Öyster Cult.
19.09.79	Glens Falls, Civic Center, New York	USA	Supporting Blue Öyster Cult.
20.09.79	Rochester, War Memorial Auditorium, New York	USA	Supporting Blue Öyster Cult.
21.09.79	Detroit, Cobo Hall, Michigan	USA	Supporting Blue Öyster Cult.
22.09.79	Lansing, Civic Center, Michigan	USA	Supporting Blue Öyster Cult.
23.09.79	Marquette, Lakeview Arena, Michigan	USA	Supporting Blue Öyster Cult.
26.09.79	Binghamton, Broome County Vets.' Mem. Arena, New York	USA	Supporting Blue Öyster Cult.
27.09.79	Glens Falls, Civic Center, New York	USA	Supporting Blue Öyster Cult.
28.09.79	Utica, Memorial Auditorium, New York	USA	Supporting Blue Öyster Cult.
29.09.79	Philadelphia, Spectrum, Pennsylvania	USA	Supporting Blue Öyster Cult.
30.09.79	Baltimore, Civic Center, Maryland	USA	Supporting Blue Öyster Cult.
02.10.79	Columbus, Veterans' Memorial Auditorium, Ohio	USA	Supporting Blue Öyster Cult.
03.10.79	Saginaw, Wendler Arena, Michigan	USA	Supporting Blue Öyster Cult.
04.10.79	Buffalo, War Memorial, New York	USA	Supporting Blue Öyster Cult.
05.10.79	Pittsburgh, Civic Arena, Pennsylvania	USA	Supporting Blue Öyster Cult.
06.10.79	Dayton, Hara Arena, Ohio	USA	Supporting Blue Öyster Cult.
07.10.79	Cleveland, Richfield Coliseum, Ohio	USA	Supporting Blue Öyster Cult. This show was abandoned due to crowd trouble.
10.10.79	Madison, Dane County Coliseum, Wisconsin	USA	Supporting Blue Öyster Cult.
11.10.79	Green Bay, Brown County Vets.' Memorial Arena, Wisconsin	USA	Supporting Blue Öyster Cult.
12.10.79	Chicago, International Amphitheatre, Illinois	USA	Supporting Blue Öyster Cult. Recorded by radio station.
13.10.79	Omaha, Civic Auditorium, Nebraska	USA	Supporting Blue Öyster Cult.
16.10.79	Kalamazoo, Wings Stadium, Michigan	USA	Supporting Blue Öyster Cult. Rainbow didn't play. The Hounds were a last minute replacement.
18.10.79	Indianapolis, Market Square Arena, Indiana	USA	Supporting Blue Öyster Cult.
19.10.79	Johnson City, Freedom Hall Civic Centre, Tennessee	USA	Supporting Blue Öyster Cult.
21.10.79	Huntington, Civic Center, West Virginia	USA	Supporting Blue Öyster Cult.
24.10.79	Springfield, State Fairgrounds, Illinois	USA	Supporting Blue Öyster Cult.

Date	Venue	Country	Notes
26.10.79	Minneapolis, Met Center, Minnesota	USA	Supporting Blue Öyster Cult. Final date of this tour. Blue Öyster Cult then travelled to the UK.

European tour dates for Rainbow were cancelled in order to continue the assault on North America:

Date	Venue	Country	Notes
05.11.79	Offenbach, Stadthalle	Germany	Cancelled.
06.11.79	Hanover, Niedersachsenhalle	Germany	Cancelled.
07.11.79	Münster, Münsterlandhalle	Germany	Cancelled.
08.11.79	Brussels, Forest National	Belgium	Cancelled.
09.11.79	Rotterdam, Sportpaleis Ahoy	Holland	Cancelled.
11.11.79	Cologne, Sporthalle	Germany	Cancelled.
16.11.79	Heidelberg, Eppelheim Rhein-Neckarhalle	Germany	Cancelled.
17.11.79	Nuremberg, Neunkirchen Hemmerleinhalle	Germany	Cancelled.
19.11.79	Essen, Gruga-Halle	Germany	Cancelled.
20.11.79	Bremen, Stadthalle	Germany	Cancelled.
22.11.79	Munich, Circus Krone	Germany	Cancelled.
23.11.79	Ravensburg, Oberschwabenhalle	Germany	Cancelled.

UK dates had been planned for December. The band were then reported instead to be playing twenty shows in the USA as headliners:

Date	Venue	Country	Notes
06.11.79	Santa Cruz, Civic Auditorium, California	USA	Supported by Gamma.
07/08.11.79	Oakland, Civic Auditorium, California	USA	Exact date unconfirmed.
09.11.79	San Bernardino, Swing Auditorium, California	USA	With Randy Hansen's Machine Gun, John Cougar, The Zone.
10.11.79	San Diego, Fox Theater, California	USA	Now known as the Copley Symphony Hall.
11.11.79	Los Angeles, Long Beach Arena, California	USA	With Randy Hansen's Machine Gun, John Cougar, The Zone.
13.11.79	Fresno, Selland Arena, California	USA	
15.11.79	Worcester, War Memorial Auditorium, Massachusetts	USA	With Scorpions.
16.11.79	Denver, McNichols Arena, Colorado	USA	Recorded for radio.
11.79	Salt Lake City, Salt Palace, Utah	USA	
11.79	Toledo, Sports Arena, Ohio	USA	
20.11.79	Royal Oak Music Hall, Michigan	USA	Support Cub Coda. Show said to have been rescheduled after a cancellation twenty minutes prior to the doors opening earlier in the year. Tapes dated 14th Dec.

Date	Venue	Country	Notes
11.79	Detroit, Cobo Hall, Michigan	USA	
23.11.79	New York, Beacon Theater, New York	USA	Recorded for radio.
30.11.79	Hempstead, Calderone Concert Hall, Long Island, New York	USA	With Scorpions.
01.12.79	Passaic, Capitol Theater, New Jersey	USA	With Scorpions.
02.12.79	Allentown, Fairgrounds, Pennsylvania	USA	With Gamma.
04.12.79	Pittsburgh, Stanley Theater, Pennsylvania	USA	
05.12.79	Portland, Cumberland County Civic Center, Maine	USA	
06.12.79	Lynn Manning Bowl, Massachusetts	USA	With Scorpions.
07.12.79	Providence, Ocean State Perf. Arts Centre, Rhode Island	USA	With Gamma.
08.12.79	Syracuse, Onondaga Cnty.War Memorial Arena, New York	USA	Described as last of twenty headlining dates. However, it seems that two more dates had been added to the itinerary since the initial press release.
09.12.79	Albany Palace Theater, New York	USA	
01.80	Cozy Powell appeared on the BBC's 'Old Grey Whistle Test'. Plans for some solo shows by Cozy were cancelled.		
17.01.80	Gothenburg, Scandinavium	Sweden	With rehearsals the previous day. Support Reeperbahn.
18.01.80	Stockholm, Johanneshov Isstadion	Sweden	Support Reeperbahn. 'Weiss Heim', released as a b-side less than three weeks later, was recorded in Copenhagen on 19th Jan and later included on 'Finyl Vinyl'.
20.01.80	Copenhagen, Falkoner Teatret	Denmark	Support Reeperbahn.
22.01.80	Hanover, Eilenriederhalle, Germany	Germany	
23.01.80	Frankfurt, Festhalle	Germany	
25.01.80	Saarbrucken, Saarlandhalle	Germany	
26.01.80	Strasbourg, Le Rhenus Hall	France	
27.01.80	Cambrai, Palais Des Grottes	France	
29.01.80	Essen, Gruga-Halle	Germany	
30.01.80	Bremen, Stadthalle	Germany	
01.80	Dortmund (venue unknown)	Germany	Not thought to have even been scheduled let alone played, though a tape recording exists purporting to be from show.
01.02.80	Brussels, Forest National	Belgium	Support Katchis.
02.02.80	Rotterdam, Sportpaleis Ahoy	Holland	Support Katchis.
03.02.80	Kerkrade, Roda-hal	Holland	Support Katchis.

Rainbow RISING

Date	Venue	Country	Notes
05.02.80	Cologne, Sporthalle	Germany	Roger collapsed after the concert. No encore.
06.02.80	Nuremberg, Neunkirchen Hemmerleinhalle	Germany	Cancelled (Roger ill).
07.02.80	Stuttgart, Sindelfingen Messehalle, Germany		
09.02.80	Grenoble, Parc des Expositions Alexpo Hall	France	
10.02.80	Winterthur, Eulachhalle	Switzerland	
12.02.80	Paris, Porte De Pantin Pavillon	France	
14.02.80	Münster, Münsterlandhalle	Germany	Support Einstein.
15.02.80	Heidelberg, Eppelheim Rhein-Neckarhalle	Germany	Possibly originally scheduled for Munich Rudi-Sedlmayer-Halle. David Coverdale invited backstage at this show with disastrous results!
16.02.80	Munich, Olympiahalle	Germany	UK tour support started out as Samson.
19.02.80	Newcastle, City Hall	UK	
20.02.80	Newcastle, City Hall	UK	
22.02.80	Edinburgh, Ingliston Exhibition Hall, Scotland	UK	
23.02.80	Stafford, New Bingley Hall	UK	
24.02.80	Bristol Hippodrome	UK	Cancelled.
24.02.80	Stafford, New Bingley Hall	UK	
26.02.80	Manchester, Apollo Theatre	UK	
27.02.80	Chester, Deeside Leisure Centre	UK	
29.02.80	London, Wembley Arena	UK	No encore, fans rioted. Ian Gillan had been due to jam during encore, whilst music press had been full of stories that The Troggs were going to be special guests!
01.03.80	London, Wembley Arena	UK	Support Katchis; Samson only found out when they arrived!
03.03.80	Leicester, Granby Halls	UK	Tickets were dated 2nd March.
04.03.80	Brighton, Brighton Centre	UK	Jeff Beck watches show. Steve Gett of Melody Maker arranged for five fans - Dave, Graham, Nobby, Spike and Karen - to interview Ritchie after the show. This was published just before Castle Donington show in August.
05.03.80	Cardiff, Sophia Gardens, Wales	UK	
06.03.80	Manchester, Apollo Theatre	UK	
08.03.80	London, Finsbury Park Rainbow Theatre	UK	Tickets were dated 7th March.

Appendices

Date	Venue	Country	Notes
10.03.80	London, Finsbury Park Rainbow Theatre	UK	Not a Rainbow but a Gillan gig. Ritchie jams for the second time with Gillan. Roger Glover was also there.
08.05.80	Tokyo, Budokan, Honshu	Japan	
09.05.80	Tokyo, Budokan, Honshu	Japan	Cozy appears at a 'Special Rock Drum Seminar'.
10.05.80	Tokyo, Science Hall, Honshu	Japan	
12.05.80	Tokyo, Budokan, Honshu	Japan	
13.05.80	Osaka, Koseinenkin Kaikan (Festival Hall), Honshu	Japan	
14.05.80	Osaka, Koseinenkin Kaikan (Festival Hall), Honshu	Japan	
15.05.80	Osaka, Koseinenkin Kaikan (Festival Hall), Honshu	Japan	
19.05.80	Tokyo, Budokan, Honshu	Japan	Unconfirmed.
08.08.80	Aarhus, Vejlby-Risskov Hallen	Denmark	Support Touch.
09.08.80	Malmö, Folkets Park	Sweden	Support Touch.
10.08.80	Aalborg, Hallen	Denmark	Support Touch.
16.08.80	Castle Donington, Donington Park	UK	Last concert with Powell and Bonnet. First 'Monsters Of Rock Festival'. Rainbow/Judas Priest/Scorpions/April Wine/Saxon/Riot/Touch. Filmed for BBC. 'All Night Long' and 'Stargazer' included on 'Monsters Of Rock' compilation. 'Since You Been Gone' on 'Finyl Vinyl'. Rainbow's soundcheck from the day before is also in circulation.
18/20.08.80	London, Soho, The Marquee Club	UK	Exact date unconfirmed. Ritchie jams with the band Girl on 'Born To Be Wild' before hosting an informal party at the Holiday Inn in Swiss Cottage.

1981 'DIFFICULT TO CURE' TOUR

Date	Venue	Country	Notes
20.02.81	Virginia Beach, Peppermint Beach Club, Virginia	USA	Unconfirmed.
21.02.81	Richmond, Empire Theater, Virginia	USA	Rare performance of 'No Release'.
22.02.81	Alexandria, Louis Rock City, Virginia	USA	Supporting Pat Travers.
02.81	Albany (venue unknown), New York	USA	Described in Rolling Stone as one of several club dates.
10.03.81	Banff, Max Bell Arena, Alberta	Canada	Described in the press as the first of 45 dates in 63 days.
14.03.81	Edmonton, Concert Bowl, Alberta	Canada	

Date	Venue	Country	Notes
16.03.81	Vancouver, Pacific Coliseum, British Columbia	Canada	
18.03.81	Seattle, Arena, Washington	USA	
19.03.81	Portland, Coliseum, Oregon	USA	
21.03.81	San Francisco, Cow Palace, California	USA	
22.03.81	Los Angeles, Forum, California	USA	With Pat Travers.
23.03.81	San Diego, Sports Arena, California	USA	With Pat Travers.
24.03.81	Phoenix, Coliseum, Arizona	USA	
25.03.81	San Bernardino, Swing Auditorium, California	USA	With Pat Travers.
26.03.81	Fresno, Selland Arena, California	USA	
29.03.81	Salt Lake City, Salt Palace Expo Hall, Utah	USA	
30.03.81	Denver, Regis College Fieldhouse, Ohio	USA	
02.04.81	San Antonio, Convention Center, Texas	USA	
03.04.81	Dallas, Moody Coliseum, Texas	USA	Pat Travers/Rainbow/Lightning.
04.04.81	Beaumont, Fair Park Coliseum, Texas	USA	
05.04.81	Houston, Sam Houston Coliseum, Texas	USA	Supporting Pat Travers.
07.04.81	Lubbock, Municipal Coliseum, Texas	USA	
08.04.81	Tulsa, Brady Theater, Oklahoma	USA	
09.04.81	Norman, Uni.of Oklahoma, Lloyd Noble Arena, Oklahoma	USA	
10.04.81	St. Louis, Granite City, Missouri	USA	Co-headliners with Pat Travers, special guests Krokus.
11.04.81	Memphis, Dixon-Myers Hall (Auditorium North), Tennessee	USA	Rainbow opened for Pat Travers.
12.04.81	Nashville, Municipal Auditorium Arena, Tennessee	USA	
15.04.81	St. Paul/Minneapolis, Civic Center, Minnesota	USA	With Pat Travers/Krokus.
16.04.81	Chicago, International Amphitheatre, Illinois	USA	With The Pat Travers Band billed as special guests.
17.04.81	Detroit, Cobo Hall, Michigan	USA	With Pat Travers/Krokus.
18.04.81	Indianapolis, Convention Center, Indiana	USA	Pat Travers' band opened though Pat was ill, so rest of band went on without him.
19.04.81	Louisville, Gardens Memorial Auditorium, Kentucky	USA	With Pat Travers/Krokus.
21.04.81	Davenport, Palmer College Alumni Auditorium, Iowa	USA	Co-headliners with Pat Travers, special guests Krokus.
22.04.81	Springfield, Prairie Capital Convention Center, Illinois	USA	With Pat Travers/Krokus.
24.04.81	Madison, Dane County Coliseum, Wisconsin	USA	
25.04.81	Milwaukee, Auditorium, Wisconsin	USA	
26.04.81	Toledo, Sports Arena, Ohio	USA	

Appendices

Date	Venue	Country	Notes
27.04.81	Cleveland, Music Hall, Ohio	USA	With Pat Travers.
28.04.81	Kalamazoo, Wings Stadium, Michigan	USA	With Pat Travers.
30.04.81	Pittsburgh, Stanley Theater, Pennsylvania	USA	With Pat Travers. Recorded. 'Can't Happen Here' included on *'Finyl Vinyl'*.
02.05.81	Nassau, Coliseum, Long Island, New York	USA	
03.05.81	Waterbury, Palace Theater, Connecticut	USA	With Pat Travers and The Jon Butcher Axis. Extra show.
06.05.81	Boston, Orpheum Theater, Massachusetts	USA	With Pat Travers and The Jon Butcher Axis.
07.05.81	Boston, Orpheum Theater, Massachusetts	USA	Originally scheduled 9th May. Recorded for the King Biscuit Flower Hour radio show.
08.05.81	Passaic, Capitol Theater, New Jersey	USA	Supported by Pat Travers.
09.05.81	Philadelphia, Upper Darby Tower Theater, Pennsylvania	USA	Billed as Pat Travers headlining on the first night. As it was, Travers opened the show.
10.05.81	Philadelphia, Upper Darby Tower Theater, Pennsylvania	USA	With Pat Travers.
12.05.81	Albany Palace Theater, New York	USA	Said to have been the final date of tour.
13.05.81	Springfield, Civic Arena, Massachusetts	USA	Unconfirmed and unlikely to have happened given that the band had played two nights in Boston previous week.
03.06.81	Gothenburg, Scandinavium	Sweden	Supported by Def Leppard.
04.06.81	Stockholm, Johanneshov Isstadion	Sweden	Supported by Def Leppard.
05.06.81	Copenhagen, Brøndby-Hallen	Denmark	Supported by Def Leppard.
07.06.81	Helsinki, UKK Halli	Finland	Supported by Def Leppard.
10.06.81	Essen, Gruga-Halle	Germany	Supported by Def Leppard.
11.06.81	Paris, Patinoire de Boulogne	France	Supported by Def Leppard.
12.06.81	Lille, Palais Saint-Saveur	France	Supported by Def Leppard.
13.06.81	Rotterdam, Sportpaleis Ahoy	Holland	Supported by Def Leppard.
14.06.81	Hanover, Niedersachsenhalle	Germany	Supported by Def Leppard.
16.06.81	Würzburg, Carl-Diem-Halle	Germany	Supported by Def Leppard.
17.06.81	Kockelscheuer, Eissporthalle	Luxembourg	Supported by Def Leppard.
18.06.81	Cologne, Sporthalle	Germany	Supported by Def Leppard.
19.06.81	Brussels, Forest National	Belgium	Supported by Def Leppard. Some UK fans took advantage of well-organised coach trip, many of whom were rewarded by being invited backstage afterwards.

Date	Venue	Country	Notes
21.06.81	Berlin, Waldbühne	Germany	Supported by Def Leppard.
23.06.81	Stuttgart, Sindelfingen Messehalle	Germany	Supported by Def Leppard.
25.06.81	Hamburg, Ernst-Merck Halle	Germany	Supported by Def Leppard.
26.06.81	Frankfurt, Festhalle	Germany	Supported by Def Leppard.
27.06.81	Munich, Rudi-Sedlmayer-Halle	Germany	Supported by Def Leppard.
29.06.81	Heidelberg, Eppelheim Rhein-Neckar Halle	Germany	Supported by Def Leppard.
30.06.81	Lausanne, Palais Du Beaulieu	Switzerland	Supported by Def Leppard.
01.07.81	Grenoble, Parc des Expositions Alexpo Hall	France	Supported by Scorpions and Def Leppard.
03.07.81	Barcelona, Plaza de Toros	Spain	Supported by UFO and Def Leppard. With Spanish promoters refusing to start gig in daylight and Ritchie not wanting to be on stage after midnight, running order was changed - UFO opened followed by Rainbow. Def Leppard went on last but, by then, most of crowd had gone home.
04.07.81	Madrid, Estadio Roman Valero	Spain	
05.07.81	San Sebastian, Velodromo de Anoeta	Spain	Supported by Def Leppard.
07.07.81	Nantes, La Beaujoire	France	Cancelled.
08.07.81	Brest, Parc d'Exposition	France	Cancelled.
08.07.81	London, Finsbury Park Rainbow Theatre	UK	Support for UK were Rose Tattoo. Recording from lengthy soundcheck includes 'Spotlight Kid', 'Love's No Friend', 'Catch The Rainbow' and a number of goes at 'Since You Been Gone'.
09.07.81	London, Finsbury Park Rainbow Theatre	UK	
10.07.81	Edinburgh, Ingliston Exhibition Hall, Scotland	UK	
11.07.81	Edinburgh, Ingliston Exhibition Hall, Scotland	UK	
13.07.81	Leeds, Queens Hall	UK	
14.07.81	Leeds, Queens Hall	UK	
15.07.81	Leicester, Granby Halls	UK	
16.07.81	Leicester, Granby Halls	UK	
18.07.81	Stafford, Bingley Hall	UK	
19.07.81	Stafford, Bingley Hall	UK	Show was filmed and Cozy Powell saw this one as did many who had been coached down from Manchester after Belle Vue gig was cancelled late on (supposedly poor acoustics).

Appendices

Date	Venue	Country	Notes
20.07.81	St. Austell, Coliseum	UK	Originally planned for Belle Vue.
22.07.81	Manchester, Apollo Theatre	UK	
23.07.81	Newcastle, City Hall	UK	Backing vocalists added for first time. Lin Robinson and Dee Beale previously recorded with band Reflections for Purple Records in 1974 and 1975.
24.07.81	Newcastle, City Hall	UK	
26.07.81	London, Hammersmith Odeon	UK	
27.07.81	London, Hammersmith Odeon	UK	
07.81	Cardiff, Sophia Gardens Wales	UK	Unconfirmed. Though mooted in the UK press before the tour, this gig doesn't seem to have happened.
18.08.81	Fukuoka, Kyuden-Kinen Taiikukan, Kyushu	Japan	
20.08.81	Osaka, Koseinenkin Kaikan (Festival Hall), Honshu	Japan	
21.08.81	Osaka, Koseinenkin Kaikan (Festival Hall), Honshu	Japan	
22.08.81	Fukuoka, Kyuden-Kinen Taiikukan, Kyushu	Japan	
23.08.81	Nagoya, Shi Kokaido, Honshu	Japan	
24.08.81	Kyoto, Kaikan Daiichi Hall, Honshu	Japan	
26.08.81	Tokyo, Budokan, Honshu	Japan	
27.08.81	Tokyo, Budokan, Honshu	Japan	
28.08.81	Tokyo, Budokan, Honshu	Japan	
08.81	Honolulu (venue unknown), Hawaii	USA	Possibly played early in September.

1982 'STRAIGHT BETWEEN THE EYES' TOUR

Date	Venue	Country	Notes
10.05.82	London, Gardens Arena, Ontario	Canada	Rescheduled for 7th June.
11.05.82	Toronto, Coliseum, Ontario	Canada	Rescheduled for 9th June.
11.05.82	Flint, IMA Auditorium, Michigan	USA	Supported by Iron Maiden.
13.05.82	Grand Rapids, Welsh Auditorium, Michigan	USA	Supported by Iron Maiden. Listed as Lansing, Michigan.
14.05.82	Detroit, Cobo Hall, Michigan	USA	Supported by Iron Maiden with .38 Special.
15.05.82	Kalamazoo, Wings Stadium, Michigan	USA	Supported by Iron Maiden.
16.05.82	Fort Wayne, Coliseum, Indiana	USA	Supported by Iron Maiden.
18.05.82	Toledo, Sports Arena, Ohio	USA	Supported by Iron Maiden with .38 Special.

Date	Venue	Country	Notes
20.05.82	Cincinnati, Gardens, Ohio	USA	Supported by Iron Maiden.
21.05.82	Louisville, Gardens Memorial Auditorium, Kentucky	USA	Supported by Iron Maiden.
22.05.82	Cleveland, Richfield Coliseum, Ohio	USA	Supported by Iron Maiden.
23.05.82	Indianapolis, Convention Center, Indiana	USA	Supported by Iron Maiden.
25.05.82	Merrillville, Holiday Star Theater, Indiana	USA	Supported by Iron Maiden.
26.05.82	Davenport, Palmer College Alumni Auditorium, Iowa	USA	Supported by Iron Maiden.
28.05.82	Dortmund, Westfalenhalle	Germany	Rainbow pulled out of this festival after two other groups had cancelled.
29.05.82	Würzburg (venue unknown)	Germany	Cancelled.
29.05.82	Des Moines, Iowa State Fairgrounds, Iowa	USA	Supported by Iron Maiden.
02.06.82	Minneapolis, Met Center, Minnesota	USA	Supported by UFO and Riot.
04.06.82	Green Bay, Brown County Vets.' Memorial Arena, Wisconsin	USA	Supported by UFO and Riot.
05.06.82	Milwaukee, Alpine Valley Music Theatre, Wisconsin	USA	Supported by UFO and Riot. Adverts mentioned special guests Iron Maiden but, at the start of June, they joined .38 Special's tour. An outdoor venue and a cold evening - Ritchie walked off stage after half an hour.
06.06.82	St. Louis (venue unknown), Missouri	USA	Cancelled.
07.06.82	London, Gardens Arena, Ontario	Canada	Supported by Scorpions.
08.06.82	Kitchener, Memorial Auditorium, Ontario	Canada	Supported by Scorpions. Tulsa Oklahoma, listed in Circus, cancelled.
09.06.82	Toronto, Coliseum, Ontario	Canada	Supported by Scorpions. Norman Oklahoma, listed in Circus, cancelled.
10.06.82	Québec, City Le Colisée	Canada	Supported by Scorpions.
12.06.82	Montréal, Verdun Auditorium, Québe	Canada	Supported by Scorpions.
13.06.82	Glens Falls, Civic Center, New York	USA	
15.06.82	Allentown, Fairgrounds, Pennsylvania	USA	Supported by Scorpions and Riot.
16.06.82	Rochester, War Memorial Auditorium, New York	USA	
17.06.82	Utica, Memorial Auditorium, New York	USA	
18.06.82	New Haven, Coliseum, Connecticut	USA	
19.06.82	New York, Madison Square Garden, New York	USA	
21.06.82	Harrisburg, City Island, Pennsylvania	USA	
22.06.82	Buffalo, War Memorial, New York	USA	

Appendices

Date	Venue	Country	Notes
23.06.82	Binghamton, Broome Cnty.Vets.' Memorial Arena, New York	USA	With Scorpions and Riot.
25.06.82	Providence, Civic Center, Rhode Island	USA	Supported by Scorpions.
26.06.82	South Yarmouth, Cape Cod Coliseum, Massachusetts	USA	
27.06.82	Philadelphia, Spectrum, Pennsylvania	USA	
09.07.82	Los Angeles, Forum, California	USA	
10.07.82	San Bernardino, Swing Auditorium, California	USA	
11.07.82	San Diego, Sports Arena, California	USA	
12.07.82	Fresno, Selland Arena, California	USA	
14.07.82	Bakersfield, Civic Auditorium, California	USA	
16.07.82	Sacramento, Memorial Auditorium, California	USA	
17.07.82	San Francisco, Cow Palace, California	USA	
18.07.82	Reno, Centennial Coliseum, Nevada	USA	
20.07.82	Largo, Capitol Center, Maryland	USA	Support Krokus/Rods. One-off east coast gig amongst three weeks of west coast dates, replacing a gig in Boise, Idaho which had been advertised in May.
22.07.82	Seattle, Arena, Washington	USA	
23.07.82	Portland, Coliseum, Oregon	USA	
24.07.82	Portland, Coliseum, Oregon	USA	
25.07.82	Spokane, Coliseum, Washington	USA	
27.07.82	Vancouver, Pacific Coliseum, British Columbia	Canada	
31.07.82	Springfield, Prairie Capital Convention Center, Illinois	USA	Supported by Scorpions.
07.08.82	Lubbock, Municipal Coliseum, Texas	USA	
09.08.82	El Paso, Ector County Coliseum, Texas	USA	
10.08.82	Midland (venue unknown), Texas	USA	
11.08.82	Amarillo, Civic Center, Texas	USA	
13.08.82	St. Louis, Busch Memorial Stadium, Missouri	USA	REO Speedwagon/Ted Nugent/John Cougar Mellencamp/Rainbow/707.
15.08.82	Kansas City, Arrowhead Stadium, Missouri	USA	REO Speedwagon/Ted Nugent/John Cougar Mellencamp/Rainbow/707.
08.82	Boulder (venue unknown), Colorado	USA	REO Speedwagon/Ted Nugent/Scorpions/Rainbow/707.
17.08.82	Houston, Sam Houston Coliseum, Texas	USA	Supported by Saxon. Filmed. Released as 'Live Between The Eyes'. Three tracks included on 'Finyl Vinyl'.
18.08.82	San Antonio, Convention Center, Texas	USA	

Rainbow RISING

Date	Venue	Country	Notes
19.08.82	Dallas, Wintergarden Ballroom, Texas	USA	Supported by Saxon/Riot. Originally scheduled for the Dallas County Convention Center but switched a few days before the show to this smaller venue.
08.82	Lakeland, Civic Center, Florida	USA	Supported by Krokus replacing The Outlaws who had cancelled. Tickets dated 25th July but show rescheduled.
23.08.82	New York (location/venue unknown)	USA	Supported by Saxon. Unconfirmed.
12.10.82	Osaka, Koseinenkin Kaikan (Festival Hall), Honshu	Japan	
13.10.82	Osaka, Koseinenkin Kaikan (Festival Hall), Honshu	Japan	
14.10.82	Osaka, Koseinenkin Kaikan (Festival Hall), Honshu	Japan	
16.10.82	Kyoto, Kaikan Daiichi Hall, Honshu	Japan	
17.10.82	Fukuoka, Sun Palace, Kyushu	Japan	
18.10.82	Nagoya, Shi Kokaido, Honshu	Japan	
19.10.82	Nagoya, Shi Kokaido, Honshu	Japan	
21.10.82	Tokyo, Budokan, Honshu	Japan	
22.10.82	Tokyo, Budokan, Honshu	Japan	
29.10.82	Oslo, Drammenshallen	Norway	Support Girlschool who did most of the European dates.
30.10.82	Aarhus, Vejlby-Risskov Hallen	Denmark	
02.11.82	Oulu, Jäähalli Ice Hall	Finland	
03.11.82	Helsinki, Isshallen	Finland	
05.11.82	Copenhagen, Brøndby-Hallen	Denmark	
06.11.82	Stockholm, Johanneshov Isstadion	Sweden	
08.11.82	Hamburg, Ernst-Merck Halle	Germany	Support Girlschool.
09.11.82	Berlin, Deutschlandhalle	Germany	Support Girlschool.
11.11.82	Essen, Gruga-Halle	Germany	
12.11.82	Heidelberg, Eppelheim Rhein-Neckarhalle	Germany	Support Girlschool.
13.11.82	Nuremberg, Neunkirchen Hemmerleinhalle	Germany	
15.11.82	Frankfurt, Russelheim Walter-Köbel-Halle	Germany	Possibly originally scheduled for Frankfurt Festhalle.
16.11.82	Rotterdam, Sportpaleis Ahoy	Holland	
18.11.82	Freiburg, Stadthalle	Germany	
19.11.82	Munich, Rudi-Sedlmayer-Halle	Germany	
21.11.82	Geneva, Patinoire des Vernets	Switzerland	
24.11.82	Stuttgart, Böblingen Sporthalle	Germany	Possibly rescheduled from 20th Nov.
25.11.82	Hanover, Eilenriederhalle	Germany	

Date	Venue	Country	Notes
26.11.82	Hamburg, Alsterdorfer Sporthalle	Germany	
27.11.82	Brussels, Forest National	Belgium	
28.11.82	Paris, Hippodrome De Pantin	France	
30.11.82	Barcelona, Plaza de Toros Monumental	Spain	Support UFO.
01.12.82	Madrid, Pabellon de Deportes	Spain	Support UFO.

1983-84 'BENT OUT OF SHAPE' TOUR

Date	Venue	Country	Notes
09.83	London, Fulham New Golden Lion	UK	Ritchie jams with the Jackie Lynton Band. Lynton had recorded a live album at this pub, in August, 1980. Ritchie is not on that as he was in Sweden at the time.
06.09.83	Liverpool, Royal Court Theatre	UK	Support for the UK and Scandinavian tours was Lita Ford. Rainbow did a full rehearsal during the day.
07.09.83	Liverpool, Royal Court Theatre	UK	
08.09.83	Whitley Bay, Ice Rink	UK	
10.09.83	Stafford, New Bingley Hall	UK	Regaining it's 'new' tag.
11.09.83	Bristol Hippodrome, UK		
12.09.83	Nottingham, Royal Concert Hall	UK	Rescheduled from 5th Sep.
14.09.83	Cardiff, St. David's Hall, Wales	UK	Recorded by RKO. Two tracks on b-side of 'Can't Let You Go'.
15.09.83	Cardiff, St. David's Hall, Wales	UK	
17.09.83	London, Finsbury Park, Michael Sobell Sports Centre	UK	
18.09.83	London, Finsbury Park, Michael Sobell Sports Centre	UK	
19.09.83	St. Austell, Coliseum	UK	
22.09.83	Edinburgh, Playhouse, Scotland	UK	Originally scheduled for 20th Sep.
23.09.83	Edinburgh, Playhouse, Scotland	UK	
29.09.83	Odense (venue unknown)	Denmark	Cancelled.
30.09.83	Gothenburg, Scandinavium	Sweden	
01.10.83	Stockholm, Johanneshov Isstadion	Sweden	
02.10.83	Lund, Olympen	Sweden	Cancelled. Ads mention The Lita Ford Band as special guest.
03.10.83	Helsinki (venue unknown)	Finland	Cancelled.
04.10.83	Aarhus (venue unknown)	Denmark	Cancelled.

Date	Venue	Country	Notes
05.10.83	Copenhagen, Falkoner Teatret	Denmark	
07.10.83	Helsinki, Isshallen	Finland	
28.10.83	Worcester, Centrum, Massachusetts	USA	
29.10.83	New Haven, Veterans' Memorial Coliseum, Connecticut	USA	
31.10.83	Philadelphia, Spectrum, Pennsylvania	USA	Postponed, rescheduled 2nd Nov. This seems to have been due to one of the band, possibly Ritchie, sustaining a back injury whilst playing soccer.
01.11.83	Pittsburgh, Stanley Theater, Pennsylvania	USA	
02.11.83	Philadelphia, Spectrum, Pennsylvania	USA	
04.11.83	Rochester, War Memorial, Auditorium New York	USA	Support Aldo Nova.
05.11.83	Buffalo, War Memorial, New York	USA	
07.11.83	Bethlehem, Stabler Arena, Pennsylvania	USA	
08.11.83	Baltimore, Civic Center, Maryland	USA	
09.11.83	Syracuse, Onondaga Cnty. War Memorial Arena, New York	USA	Supported by Aldo Nova.
11.11.83	Providence, Civic Center Rhode Island	USA	
12.11.83	Poughkeepsie, Mid-Hudson Civic Center Arena, New York	USA	
13.11.83	Glens Falls, Civic Center, New York	USA	

Further US dates are believed to have been cancelled due to poor ticket sales. The band then joined up with Blue Öyster Cult though it is not clear if Rainbow played at the first two shows in Iowa.

Date	Venue	Country	Notes
16.11.83	Cedar Rapids, Five Seasons Center, Iowa	USA	Unconfirmed.
17.11.83	Sioux City, Auditorium, Iowa	USA	Unconfirmed.
18.11.83	Wichita, Coliseum, Kansas	USA	Supporting Blue Öyster Cult.
20.11.83	Albuquerque, Tingley Coliseum, New Mexico	USA	Supporting Blue Öyster Cult.
21.11.83	Phoenix, Coliseum, Arizona	USA	Supporting Blue Öyster Cult.
23.11.83	San Diego, Sports Arena, California	USA	Supporting Blue Öyster Cult.
25.11.83	San Francisco, Cow Palace, California	USA	Supporting Blue Öyster Cult.
27.11.83	Fresno, Selland Arena, California	USA	Supporting Blue Öyster Cult.
29.11.83	San Bernardino, Orange Pavilion, California	USA	Supporting Blue Öyster Cult.
30.11.83	Los Angeles, Long Beach Arena, California	USA	Supporting Blue Öyster Cult.
01.12.83	Sacramento, Memorial Auditorium, California	USA	Supporting Blue Öyster Cult.

02.12.83	Reno, Lawlor Events Center, Nevada	USA	Supporting Blue Öyster Cult.
04.12.83	Denver, McNichols Arena, Colorado	USA	Supporting Blue Öyster Cult.

The Blue Öyster Cult tour continued on through Texas, Oklahoma, Missouri, Illinois, Michigan and Oregon through to and beyond Christmas but without Rainbow. Plans for a tour of mainland Europe in February were never confirmed.

11.03.84	Osaka, Jo Hall (Castle Hall), Honshu	Japan	
13.03.84	Tokyo, Budokan, Honshu	Japan	
14.03.84	Tokyo, Budokan, Honshu	Japan	Support band Action. Filmed. 'Difficult To Cure' performed with an orchestra. Released on video in Japan as *'Japan Tour '84'*. Four tracks included on *'Finyl Vinyl'*. When the CD was remastered in 1999, a fifth track, 'Street Of Dreams' (previously only available on cassette version), was included.

1995-97 'STRANGER IN US ALL' TOUR

30.09.95	Helsinki, Kultuuritalo (House of Culture)	Finland	Support for European tour was to be Thunder but they pulled out and were replaced by Scandinavian band, Milky. This debut show preceded by four days of rehearsals at Copenhagen K.B. Hallen, Denmark. Russian dates planned.
02.10.95	Stockholm, Circus	Sweden	Recorded for radio.
03.10.95	Oslo, Sentrum Scene, Norway		
06.10.95	Copenhagen, K.B. Hallen	Denmark	Support Milky.
08.10.95	Hanover, Musikhalle	Germany	English 'Music Hall' spelling (not 'Musikhalle') on tickets.
09.10.95	Düsseldorf, Philipshalle	Germany	Filmed by WDR.
10.10.95	Berlin, Huxley's Neue Welt	Germany	
12.10.95	Appenweier, Schwarzwaldhalle	Germany	
13.10.95	Ludwigshafen, Friedrich-Ebert-Halle	Germany	
14.10.95	Stuttgart, Kongresszentrum	Germany	
16.10.95	Osnabrück, Stadthalle	Germany	

Date	Venue	Country	Notes
17.10.95	Rotterdam, Sportpaleis Ahoy	Holland	
18.10.95	Hamburg, Alsterdorfer Sporthalle	Germany	Support Milky.
20.10.95	Erlangen, Stadthalle	Germany	
21.10.95	Munich, Terminal 1	Germany	
22.10.95	Leipzig, Easy Auensee	Germany	
24.10.95	Offenbach, Stadthalle	Germany	
25.10.95	Hof, Freiheitshalle	Germany	
26.10.95	Zürich, Volkshaus	Switzerland	
28.10.95	Milan, Palalido	Italy	
30.10.95	Lyon, Le Transbordeur	France	
31.10.95	Paris, Elysée Montmartre	France	
01.11.95	Brussels, Forest National	Belgium	
03.11.95	London, Hammersmith Apollo	UK	Support Milky.
04.11.95	London, Hammersmith Apollo	UK	Support group The Jackie Lynton Band.
11.11.95	Tokyo, Yoyogi Olympic Pool, Honshu	Japan	Support group The Jackie Lynton Band.
12.11.95	Tokyo, Yoyogi Olympic Pool, Honshu	Japan	Support for Tokyo, and possibly other Japanese dates, were DC Valentine. Doogie White fined for jumping off stage!
14.11.95	Kyoto, Kaikan Daiichi Hall, Honshu	Japan	
16.11.95	Osaka, Kaikan (Furitsu Gym), Honshu	Japan	
17.11.95	Nagoya, Century Hall, Honshu	Japan	
19.11.95	Osaka, Koseinenkin Kaikan (Festival Hall), Honshu	Japan	
20.11.95	Fukuoka, Koseinenkin Kaikan, Kyushu	Japan	
22.11.95	Yokohama, Bunka Taiikukan, Honshu	Japan	
23.11.95	Tokyo, Bay Chiba NHK Hall, Honshu	Japan	
27.06.96	Santiago, Teatro Monumental	Chile	No support band. Originally scheduled for May.
29.06.96	Buenos Aires, Teatro Opera	Argentina	Part-filmed for MTV. Originally scheduled for May.
30.06.96	Buenos Aires, Teatro Opera	Argentina	Originally scheduled for May.
02.07.96	Porto Alegre Bar, Opiniao	Brazil	Originally scheduled for May.
04.07.96	Curitiba, Aeroanta	Brazil	Originally scheduled for May.
05.07.96	São Paulo, Olympia	Brazil	Originally scheduled for May.
06.07.96	São Paulo, Olympia	Brazil	Originally scheduled for May.
07.07.96	São Paulo, Olympia	Brazil	Originally scheduled for May.

Appendices

Date	Venue	Country	Notes
09.07.96	Rio De Janeiro, Barra Metropolitan	Brazil	Cancelled. Originally scheduled for May.
07.96	Bogota	Columbia	Cancelled. Originally scheduled for May.
07.96	La Paz	Bolivia	Cancelled. Originally scheduled for May.
21.07.96	Balingen, Messegelände	Germany	'Radio SWF3 Festival' - ZZ Top headlining.
24.07.96	Vienna, Sommerarena	Austria	
26.07.96	Passau, Nibelungenhalle	Germany	
28.07.96	Vosselaar, Gemeentehal	Belgium	
30.07.96	Nuremberg, Serenadenhof	Germany	
01.08.96	Schmallenberg, Stadthalle	Germany	
02.08.96	Bremen, Pier 2	Germany	
03.08.96	Bad Wörishofen, Eissporthalle	Germany	
06.08.96	Oslo, Sentrum Scene	Norway	
07.08.96	Gothenburg, Rondo	Sweden	Support Freak Kitchen.
09.08.96	Lidköping, Folkets Park, Sweden	Denmark	'Smukkeste Festival' - filmed.
10.08.96	Skanderborg, Dyrehaven	Denmark	'Giants Of Rock' festival - Rainbow/Mercyful Fate/Pretty
11.08.96	Copenhagen, 5-øren Amager, Strandpark	Denmark	Maids/Led Zeppelin Jam (not THE Led Zeppelin but a cover band). Babylon Zoo cancelled. Paul Morris played show with patch over his right eye. Doogie fired after gig but later reinstated.
20.02.97	Old Bridge, Birch Hill Nite Club, New Jersey	USA	
21.02.97	Providence, The Strand Theater, Rhode Island	USA	Support Great White.
22.02.97	West Springfield Jaxx, Virginia	USA	
26.02.97	Toronto, Warehouse, Ontario	Canada	Support band were ??? Dolls.
27.02.97	Massillon, The Machine, Ohio	USA	
28.02.97	Columbus, Alrosa Villa, Ohio	USA	
01.03.97	Detroit, Harpo's Concert Theater, Michigan	USA	
02.03.97	Schaumburg, Jack Hammers, Illinois	USA	
06.03.97	Milwaukee, Rave, Wisconsin	USA	
07.03.97	Minneapolis, Medina Entertainment Center, Minnesota	USA	Supported by Big 'Stache And His Texans. Doogie, for his birthday, was 'custard-pied' on stage.
08.03.97	Omaha, Ranch Bowl Entertainment Center, Nebraska	USA	

Rainbow RISING

09.03.97	Kansas City, Beaumont Club, Missouri	USA
13.03.97	Tempe, Electric Ballroom, Arizona	USA
14.03.97	Las Vegas, Huntridge Performing Arts Theater, Nevada	USA
16.03.97	Santa Ana, Galaxy Theatre, California	USA
17.03.97	West Hollywood, Billboard Live, California	USA
18.03.97	West Hollywood, Billboard Live, California	USA
19.03.97	Palo Alto Edge, California	USA
20.03.97	Ventura Theatre, California	USA	Cancelled.

Dates were planned for Poland, Russia, Hungary, Spain, Italy and Greece.

10.05.97	Poznan Arena	Poland	Cancelled.
11.05.97	Katowice Spodek	Poland	Cancelled.
31.05.97	Esbjerg, Festpladsen Gl. Vardevej	Denmark	Legend has it that Cozy Powell had been scheduled to join the band for the encores.

Gig list © 2002 Nigel Young and the DPAS/Deep Purple Archives. Not to be replicated, reproduced, stored and/or distributed in any way without their express prior written permission. Thank you to the following people who have directly assisted in this work: Mark Cantin, Jim Collins, Jim Corrigan, Roy Davies, Herbert Feldhaus, Mike Fred, Bobby Gervais, Ron Harper, Jacob Hastedt, Matthew Hosington, Benny Holmstrom, John Hopkins, Phil Jilka, Fedor de Lange, Patrick McDonald, Ian Nichols, Thierry Pierron, Steve Phillips, Michael Richards, Garry Smith, Brian Stephen, Bobby Tanzilo, John Tramontanis, David Weickel and Dougie White. Thanks also to the many people who have contributed details to Stargazer and Darker Than Blue over the years and Jerry Bloom for the Hawaii gig mentioned by Don Airey. This listing will soon be available online at www.deep-purple.net where set lists, reviews and memorabilia will be added. If anyone is aware of errors and omissions, it would be appreciated if they would get in touch via the website.

Appendices

SONGS RAINBOW PERFORMED LIVE

DIO-FRONTED LINE-UPS 1975-78:

A Light In The Black, Catch The Rainbow, Do You Close Your Eyes, If You Don't Like Rock'n'Roll, Kill The King, Long Live Rock'n'Roll, Man On The Silver Mountain, Mistreated, Self Portrait, 16th Century Greensleeves, Stargazer, Still I'm Sad, Temple Of The King

EXTRACTS/REPRISES: Apache, Blues, Deutschland Über Alles, Hall Of The Mountain King, Jingle Bells, Lazy, Night People, Ode To Joy - Beethoven's 9th, Over The Rainbow, Peter Gunn, Purple Haze, Smoke On The Water, Starstruck, White Christmas, 1812 Overture

BONNET-FRONTED LINE-UP 1979-80:

All Night Long, Catch The Rainbow, Eyes Of The World, Kill The King, Long Live Rock'n'Roll, Lost In Hollywood, Love's No Friend, Makin' Love, Man On The Silver Mountain, Stargazer, Since You Been Gone, Will You Still Love Me Tomorrow

EXTRACTS/REPRISES: Blues, Greensleeves, Land Of Hope And Glory, Kill The King, Lazy, Ode To Joy - Beethoven's 9th, Over The Rainbow, Weiss Heim, 1812 Overture

TURNER-FRONTED LINE-UP 1981-84:

All Night Long, Can't Happen Here, Catch The Rainbow, Death Alley Driver, Difficult To Cure, Drinking With The Devil, Fire Dance, Fool For The Night, I Surrender, Jealous Lover, Kill The King, Long Live Rock'n'Roll, Lost In Hollywood, Love's No Friend, Man On The Silver Mountain, Maybe Next Time, Miss Mistreated, No Release, Power, Rock Fever, Since You Been Gone, Smoke On The Water, Spotlight Kid, Stranded, Stone Cold, Street Of Dreams, Tearin'Out My Heart

EXTRACTS/REPRISES: Blues, 'Call Me Cab' Medley, Child In Time, Fire, Hey Joe, I Got A Warm Desire, Land Of Hope And Glory, Lazy, Over The Rainbow, Rule Britannia, Stargazer, Weiss Heim, Woman From Tokyo

WHITE-FRONTED LINE-UP 1995-97:

Ariel, Black Masquerade, Burn, Difficult To Cure, Hall Of The Mountain King, Hunting Humans (Insatiable), Long Live Rock'n'Roll, Man On The Silver Mountain, Maybe Next Time, Miss Mistreated, Perfect Strangers, Smoke On The Water, Spotlight Kid, Stand And Fight, Still I'm Sad, Stone Cold, Street Of Dreams, Temple Of The King, Too Late For Tears, Wolf To The Moon

EXTRACTS/REPRISES: Blues, Black Night, Catch The Rainbow, The Happy Wanderer, Greensleeves, Hey Joe, O.J., I Belong To Glasgow, Lazy, Love Hurts, The Northern Lights Of Old Aberdeen, Over The Rainbow, Rainbow Eyes, Since You Been Gone, Steamroller Blues, Waltzing Matilda, Woman From Tokyo

RAINBOW BOOTLEGS

The whole subject of 'bootleg' recordings remains a complex, not to say controversial, issue.

'Bootlegs' should be defined as commercially available (usually live, occasionally studio) recordings, independently produced and authorised by neither artist nor record company. Such product has been around since the advent of affordable recording equipment and initially became popular in the early seventies using reel-to-reel tape machines and/or sourced direct from soundboard, then pressed up in Europe and sold on vinyl.

The cassette tape revolution of the mid-seventies further broadened the appeal of such recordings, with many committed fans swapping or trading a range of their favourite band's 'boots'. The more recent advances in technology meant vinyl had all but disappeared by the early nineties - as did attempts at any sort of quality control. Recordings could now easily be copied *ad infinitum*, and this has meant many seventies concerts released on vinyl are now available in a range of formats, often from multiple-generation sources of ever worsening quality. The advent of small portable MP3 players, CD-R, DAT and the ease with which contemporary concerts can be captured for posterity means we now find whole tours recorded and commercially available. Despite recent record industry pressure and regulatory clampdowns, the popularity of such releases remains high, particularly now the internet enables more and more fans to become aware of what is available and gain access to such items should they wish.

Indeed, the future of the bootleg recording as a (dodgy) commercial product seems unsure, with many fans now ironically 'booting' the bootlegs, by getting together and taking CDR copies of the best bootlegs as required rather than investing in the packaged releases. Many bands are also now taking advantage by recording their concerts at their own expense and releasing whole series of superb quality live sets themselves as limited edition or mail order-only releases.

Ritchie Blackmore's formidable improvisational talents and his often blistering live performances have seen the guitarist become a firm favourite for bootleggers, his career well documented by many such unauthorised releases. The following list concentrates on the Rainbow era.

The information is presented in a quick reference format. The items are sorted by concert date, place, then by bootleg title. Other information on label and catalogue number is given where known. Format gives some idea as to the availability of vinyl versions or not - most of what is listed is on CD, though many still prefer vinyl. The quality of sound is rated 1-5: 1 is unlistenable, whereas 5 is soundboard or radio broadcast quality. After trawling through numerous 'boots' and cross-referencing with concert reviews information is also supplied on the band performance and the gig itself.

The potential bootleg purchaser should, however, always bear in mind certain points when using this listing. The attached data is extensive but by no means exhaustive, and many other variations of those listed can and do exist, sometimes many generations of recording removed from the original masters. Reproductions of album covers have not been included due to space constraints and the fact that (again) many versions exist, over-complicating what is already a difficult enough task. Similarly, set lists have been omitted for simplicity and to avoid repetition, as Rainbow running orders remained often fairly static from tour to tour.

For those who require more detailed information, I can recommend Ingo Fengler's excellent series of bootleg guides, and of course the relevant sections of the More Black Than Purple magazine. The list is intended as a handy companion for both the casual and serious bootleg collector, hopefully guiding the discerning Rainbow fan towards the more cost-effective and interesting items, and giving warning when quality or content is deemed 'doubtful'.

But, as with all such items, let the buyer beware! Ultimately it is up to you whether or not you part with your cash.

Date	Venue	Title	Label/Catalogue No.	Format	Sound	Performance	Notes
12.11.75	New York	'First gig in N.Y.'	My Phoenix Co BS2/3	CD	?	Solid	Beacon Theatre. Complete gig.
12.11.75	New York	'Martian Rainbow'	RB01	CD	?	Solid	Beacon Theatre. Some incorrectly dated as 9.22.75. Incomplete gig. CD runs fast.
14.11.75	New York	?	?	CD	?	Good	Calderone Hall.
15.11.75	Philadelphia	'Shut Up'	?	2CD	?	?	Tower Theatre.
18.11.75	Pittsburgh	'Perfect Night'	?	2CD	2	Fairly Good	Not complete set. 'SP' very good.
18.11.75	Pittsburgh	'Pittsburgh 11.18.75'	DP-020	CD	2	Fairly Good	The 18.11.75 date not validated; could be 18.12.75.
18.11.75	Pittsburgh	'Ritchie Blackmore's Rainbow 1975'	Starquake SQ02	CD	2	Fairly Good	Also seen listed as '1975' from

Date	City	Title	Label/Ref	Discs	Format	Rating	Sound	Notes
20.11.75	Detroit	'1975'	SQ02	CD	2	Fairly Good		'Detroit 18.11.75'. 74 mins. 'SP' heavier than studio. 'CTR' fades after 10 mins. 'MOSM' punchy. Breaks in 'Stargazer' and 'LITB'. Limited edition of 1000.
20.11.75	Detroit	'1975 Final Edition'	Demons Eye 014/015	2CD	2	Fairly Good		Incomplete set, edited version of '1975 Final Edition'.
5.76	?	'Tower of Babel'	Supersonic 2000	3CD	4	Very Good		Best example early show, though sound varies. Excellent 'SIS', 'LITB'. Rehearsals for first world tour. Different and interesting 'KTK', 'Mistreated', 'Stargazer' and 'LITB'. 3rd CD is Aussie RB/RJD interview (from 'On Stage' radio promo).
17.6.76	New York	'Beaconfire 1976'	?	2CD	?	?		Beacon Theatre. 2 hour show, Ends with guitar trash.
22.6.76	Dayton	'A Day at Dayton'	?	2CD	?	?		
25.6.76	Chicago	'Captured a Legend'	Bondage BON080/081	2CD	3	Excellent		Great 'KTK'. No quiet bit in 'CTR' nor 'Blues' in 'MOSM'. Back-to-back 'Stargazer'/'LITB'! Awesome show all-round, especially RB and RJD. Speed and background noise can vary slightly.
15.7.76	Miami	'Miami 15.7.76'	DP021-1/2	2CD	3	Excellent		Jai Alai Fronton, Miami. Good 'Mistreated' and 'LITB'. 'MOSM' edited 'SIS' fades after drum solo. One of best 1976 gigs.
15.7.76	Miami	'Miami Vice'	?	2CD	?	Excellent		Jai Alai Fronton, Miami. Good 'Mistreated' and 'LITB'.
3.8.76	Burbank	'A Light in Your Eyes'	Demons Eye 006/007	2CD	2	Fair		CD runs a little fast. Supposed limited edition of 300.
31.8.76	Bristol	'Very First Night'	?	CD	2	Good		Historic debut UK concert. Dio in good form, rest of band nervous. Great 'CTR'.
1.9.76	Leicester	'Leicester Rising'	Demon's Eye 017/018	2CD	2	Very Good		No edits. Great 'Mistreated',

Appendices

Date	City	Title	Label/Cat#	Format	Rating	Quality	Notes
5.9.76	Manchester	'Insanity Party'	Wyvern WLG-136R1/2	2CD	3	Very Good	'Stargazer' and 'CTR' is magical. Dio vocals mixed too low. Extended 'Greensleeves' preamble. Part of 'Insanity Party' box set.
5.9.76	Manchester	'Manchester '76'	Wyvern WLG-136R1/2	2CD	3	Very Good	One of the best of '76 UK gigs. Good all-round perf. Vocals well up in mix. Part of 'Insanity Party' 6 CD set.
7.9.76	London	'Audition Night'	Concrete God CGR001/2	2CD	3	Average	One of the best '76 UK gigs. Good all-round performance. Brilliant intro to 'MOSM'. Vocals well up in mix though a little hiss in places. Direct lift and re-issue of part of 'Insanity Party' 6 CD set.
8.9.76	London	'Ronnie's Night'	?	2CD	2	Good	Incomplete show. Poor crowd response, band seems to quickly lose interest. Distorted 'Stargazer', no encore. 'SIS' edited by 1 min. Nice RB solo in 'CTR'. CD2 includes RB/RJD 1975 radio interview. Hammersmith Odeon - 2nd night. Date error on some sleeves as '08.07.76'. Powerful - much better than first night, RB better mood.
11.9.76	Birmingham	'Victory Night'	?	2CD	1	Fairly Good	Brum Odeon. Weedy distant sound but superb 'Mistreated' and great 'CTR'. Dio on great form!
20.9.76	Stockholm	'First Hit On The Old Continent'	?	2CD	1	Good	Not brilliant sound or recording. Great RB intro to '16CGS'. Slagged by Swedish press!
22.9.76	Copenhagen	'Songs For Gefion'	Demons Eye 028/029	2CD	3	Okay	Incomplete set. Solid performance, keys clear in the mix for once. No encore from the night, instead get

Date	Location	Title	Label/Cat #	Format	Rating	Quality	Notes
27.9.76	Dusseldorf	'Crossbows In The Firelight'	?	Tape	?	?	'DYCYE' from Stockholm 20.9.76. Limited edition of 300 pressings.
13.10.76	Amsterdam	?	?	Tape	3	?	
18.10.76	The Hague	'A Hymn'	?	2CD	?	?	
9.11.76	Melbourne	'Dragon's Mural'	GAEA693-1/2	2CD	2	Very Good	Edem Hall. Date incorrect. Full set. Heavy 'KTK', superb 'MOSM'. Muffled sound, 2 extra tracks from Munich 20.10.77 much clearer.
9.11.76	Melbourne	'Over Melbourne'	Red Hot RH010/1	2CD	3	Very Good	Complete set. Heavy 'KTK', superb 'MOSM'. 50 min. Interview with RB from Melbourne included. Original edition limited to 500 copies.
11.11.76	Sydney	'On Stage Down Under'	MN52-9321/2	2CD	3	Very Good	Complete set. Bonus tracks 'LLR&R', 'LAC', 'GOB' from promos shot in 1978.
22.11.76	Melbourne	'Live In Australia'	Kornyfone TAKRL24904	2LP	2	Good	Edit in 'MOSM'. Speed varies on Side 4. Great 'CTR'. Sound suffers in 'DYCYE'.
2.12.76	Tokyo	'Blackmore the Raider'	IMP-1202	LP	2	Good	First Japanese gig. Group leaves the stage after 'KTK' for crowd to calm down. 'KTK' wrongly listed as 'LITB'. Great 'MOSM'. Edit in 'CTR'.
2.12.76	Tokyo	'Blackmore the Raider'	IMP-1202CD	CD	2	Good	Straight copy of vinyl original.
2.12.76	Tokyo	'First Rising Sun'	?	2CD	2	Good	First Japanese gig. Group leaves the stage after 'KTK' for crowd to calm down.
5.12.76	Osaka	'Nippon Eyes'	LP RB	2LP	2	Okay	Bits of hiss and crackle, re-issued 1984. No real highlights, solid all-round performance. Part show (encore omitted).
5.12.76	Osaka	'Nippon Eyes'	Black Suede	CD	2	Okay	Directly copied from vinyl version with all the hiss and crackle left on. No real highlights, just solid

Appendices

Date	City	Title	Catalog	Format	Rating	Quality	Notes
5.12.76	Osaka	'Raged in the Backstage'	Gryphon 009/10	2CD	3	Okay	all-round performance. 'MOSM' starts in 'Blues' bit. Running order altered on the CD.
5.12.76	Osaka	'Rainbow on Tour 1976'	Stargazer OMR76125	2CD	5	Okay	Complete show. No real highlights, just solid all-round performance. Complete set. Includes 'LITB' from Kyoto. Superb sound. No highlights, just solid all-round perf. Reissued 1998 with new artwork.
5.12.76	Osaka	'Stargazer'	R76121/2	2CD	2	Okay	Complete show. No real highlights, just solid all-round performance.
5.12.76	Osaka	'War of Nerves in 1976'	H400/500	2LP	2	Okay	Extra tracks from Kyoto 10.12.76. No highlights, solid all-round perf.
5.12.76	Osaka	'War of Nerves in 1976'	Black Suede	CD	2	Okay	Part show (encore omitted). No highlights, just solid all-round perf. Directly copied from vinyl version.
7.12.76	Nagoya	'Catch the Niji'	Niji N001/2	2CD	3	Good	Complete set. Dio dedicates 'Mistreated' to Tommy Bolin. Great Carey intro to 'Stargazer'.
8.12.76	Osaka	'Seven Bridge'	?	LP	2	Okay	Incomplete set of 45 mins. 'SIS', 'Stargazer' and 'DYCYE'.
8.12.76	Osaka	'Seven Bridge'	BR-726CD	CD	2	Okay	Direct copy of vinyl version.
8.12.76	Osaka	'Heroic Verse'	?	CD	?	Okay	
9.12.76	Osaka	'Chase the Rainbow'	BR1214	LP	2	Very Good	Lots of surface noise. Extra tracks from Osaka 5.12.76, Donington '80 San Antonio '82 and Cardiff '83.
9.12.76	Osaka	'Chase the Rainbow'	TNT930135/6	2CD	2	Very Good	Retains the surface noise as on vinyl. Extra tracks from Osaka 5.12.76, Donington '80, San Antonio '82 and Cardiff '83.
9.12.76	Osaka	'Kill The King'	Pandora 001/2	CD	3	Very Good	Complete show. RB very good. Bonus tracks from Fukuoka 13.12.76 but sound not as good.
9.12.76	Osaka	'Time Standing Still'	Dynamite Studio DSA025	CD	4	Very Good	Incomplete. Radio recording so

Date	City	Title	Label/Cat#	Format	#	Quality	Notes
9.12.76	Osaka	'Guitar Vanguard'	MBP 992	LP	2	Very Good	great quality. RB very good. 'Stargazer' fades in RB solo, 'SIS' and 'MOSM' both edited. Beware as some CDs are badly pressed/lacquered and play awful!
9.12.76	Osaka	'Guitar Vanguard'	C1977	LP	2	Very Good	Date not specified but is Osaka. 'CTR' edited. 'Kill the King' listed as 'Light In The Black'!
9.12.76	Japan	'On Stage Outtakes'	MN54-8905	CD	5	Good	1983 re-issue of original. Different cover, otherwise the same. Probably from official tapes. 3 tracks from Osaka 9.12.76 and 1 each from Cologne 25.9.76 and Munich 29.9.76.
10.12.76	Kyoto	'Incubus '76'	Wyvern WLG-121 R1/2	2CD	3	Good	Complete set. Part of 'Incubus Party 76-84' box set. Nice Hank Marvin/Shadows impersonation by RB! Limited edition of 777 copies.
10.12.76	Kyoto	'Just a Crazy Dream'	H-Bomb HBM9505/6	2CD	4	Good	Complete set. Good all-round show. RB good, Dio low in mix.
13.12.76	Fukuoka	'Clashed in Fukuoka'	Gryphon 015/6	2CD	3	Okay	Complete set. Noisy recording with audience and tape hiss.
13.12.76	Fukuoka	'Do You See the Light'	?	?	?	Okay	Complete set. Blackmore in less playful mood - less improvs than prev. 'Stargazer' keys intro edited.
14.12.76	Hiroshima	'A Light in The Black'	Sonic Zoom SZ2003/4	2CD	3	Okay	
14.12.76	Hiroshima	'Chase the Rainbow'	?	2CD	?	Okay	Covers the 2 complete evening and night shows. Early show - 'MOSM' best. Shorter intros, 'LITB' done well, no encores. Late show - 'MOSM' again best, 'Stargazer' links into 'SIS' instead of doing 'LITB'. Limited edition of 300.
16.12.76	Tokyo	'Aurora'	Aurora 4-1	4CD	2	Good	
16.12.76	Tokyo	'Definitive Last Night'	?	2CD	?	Good	Complete. Evening show, last date.

Date	Location	Title	Label/Cat. No.	Format	Discs	Quality	Notes
16.12.76	Tokyo	'The Two Acts Through the Day'	Gryphon 004/5/6	3CD	3	Good	Covers the 2 complete evenings and night shows - no edits. Early show, 'MOSM' best. Shorter intros, 'LITB' done well, no encores. Late show - 'MOSM' again best, 'Stargazer' links into 'SIS' instead of doing 'LITB'. Volume low.
16.12.76	Tokyo	'The Complete 2 Acts Through the Day'	Demons Eye DE-020-1/2	3CD	3	Good	Limited edition of 300.
25.9.77	Stockholm	'Long Live Triumvirate'	Demons Eye DE012/013	2CD	3	Good	Incomplete show. Epic 'SIS' with start edited. Drum solo edited. Fascinating 3 min '16CGS' RB intro.
26.9.77	Gothenborg	'Scandinavian Scamps'	?	?	?	?	Lo-fi, otherwise good all-round. Copied from vinyl version.
27.9.77	Oslo	'Catch The Rainbow'	Mini Music BF94052	2LP	1	Good	
27.9.77	Oslo	'Catch The Rainbow'	?	2CD	1	Good	
27.9.77	Oslo	'Grandmother's Dread'	?	2CD	3	Good	
4.10.77	The Hague	'Kill the King'	Phonedool 4010	LP	3	Good	Japanese origin-rare. Part gig, no encore (not played/not recorded?) Dio is brilliant!
4.10.77	The Hague	'Kill the King'	Black Suede	2CD	3	Good	Part of 'Ritchie's Box' set. Lifted from vinyl boot of same name. Japanese origin-rare. Part gig, no encore (not played/recorded?).
18.10.77	Vienna	'Kicks'	Heritage 016/17	2CD	3	Okay	Complete gig. RB gets arrested for kicking bouncer! Nice 'CTR' and 'MOSM', rest of set a bit frantic. Decent sound overall, but breaks up at times.
20.10.77	Munich	'Catch The Rainbow'	Metal Memory 90022-2	2CD	2	Very Good	Complete set from Rockpalast TV broadcast. Poorer copy with edits. CD2 includes 3 Donington tracks.
20.10.77	Munich	'Germany 1977'	?	2CD	4	Very Good	Complete. Better sound - taken from recent Rockpalast TV repeat.

Rainbow RISING

Date	City	Title	Ref	Format	Rating	Quality	Notes
20.10.77	Munich	'Live at Olympiahalle, Munich, Germany'	?	2CD	4	Very Good	Complete. Better sound - taken from recent Rockpalast TV repeat.
20.10.77	Munich	'Over the Olympia'	GAEA776-1/2	2CD	4	Very Good	From Rockpalast TV broadcast.
20.10.77	Munich	'Sort of F**king Boring Old Fart'	HE9314 A/B	2LP	3	Very Good	Includes audience tape of 'Stargazer' from un-named gig and 2 Cozy Powell singles!
20.10.77	Munich	'Still I'm Sad'	Fire Power 0049 - A/B	2CD	4	Very Good	From Rockpalast TV broadcast.
27.10.77	Paris	'Parisien Night'	Bondage Music BON 028/29	2CD	4	Good	Great example of '77 tour. Good all-round performance. Full show. Great 'MOSM'. Incl. 'Night People'.
31.10.77	Newcastle	'You Make Us Feel At Home'	?	2CD	2	Good	Full show.
1.11.77	Newcastle	'Night People'	Concrete God CGR0015/16	2CD	1	Good	Noisy - avoid! Includes 3 promos from 'LLR&R' Don Kirshner Show.
1.11.77	Newcastle	'Second Night'	?	2CD	?	Good	Complete gig. Sometimes noisy audience recording. Some great RB doodles in 'CTR'.
4.11.77	Liverpool	'Mark 2'	R77	2LP	3	Good	
4.11.77	Liverpool	'Mark 2'	Black Suede	2CD	3	Good	Part of 'Ritchie's Box' set. Lifted from vinyl boot. 'SIS' listed as 'Beethoven's 9th'.
5.11.77	Liverpool	'The Night People'	?	2CD	?	Good	Workmanlike. 'Stone' mixed down and was difficult to hear on stage.
18.11.77	Stafford	'Long Live Rock'n'Roll'	?	2CD	2	Fair	
18.11.77	Stafford	'Stafford '77'	?	2CD	2	Fair	Ritchie well on form, superb improvs, great all-round perfs.
21.11.77	Manchester	'Manchester '77'	?	CD	3	Excellent	
11.1.78	Nagoya	'Brain Dies Slowly'	Independence RA78111-1/2	2CD	4	Excellent	Complete show. First gig Japanese tour. Extended 'Stargazer'. Great

Date	City	Title	Label/Ref	Format	Rating	Quality	Notes
11.1.78	Nagoya	'Full Moon'	Crystal Sound CS23/24	2CD	4	Excellent	all-round perf., more improv. from RB than in Europe. Short 'MOSM', 'Beethoven's 9th' in 'SIS'.
12.1.78	Hiroshima	'Paranoia'	GAEA692-1/2	2CD	3	Okay	Complete show. First gig Japanese tour. Extended 'Stargazer'. Great all-round perf. More improv. from RB than in Europe. Short 'MOSM', 'Beethoven's 9th' in 'SIS'.
12.1.78	Hiroshima	'The Ship From Hiroshima'	Aurora Records 2-1	2CD	2	Okay	Straightforward solid gig, clipped intros, little humour or improvisational interplay.
14.1.78	Fukuoka	'Sadistic Rainbow'	GAEA69-1/2	2CD	3	Okay	Complete show. Straightforward gig, clipped intros, little humour or improv. interplay. Limited 300. Ronnie sings through part of 'Blues', great vocals on 'CTR' too. CD1 speed varies slightly.
16.1.78	Osaka	'I See a Glow'	Shelter	2CD	3	Good	Edit in 'CTR' and 'SIS'. 'HOTMK' incl. in 'SIS'! 26 minute 'SIS', no encore. Part of 'Ritchie's Box' set. Very rare.
16.1.78	Osaka	'Satisfaction'	?	LP	3	Good	Part show. 'HOTMK' included in 'SIS'! 26 minute 'SIS', no encore.
16.1.78	Osaka	'Satisfaction'	Black Suede	CD	3	Good	Part show. Lifted for vinyl boot of same name.
17.1.78	Osaka	'Rainbow on Tour 1978'	Starstruck OMR78117	2CD	5	Inspired!	Superb mix - soundboard? RB and RJD well on form, great solos. Blistering 'KTK', great 'Stone' intro to 'SIS', 'CTR', 'MOSM' superb. No edits, full show. Best of '78 shows!
17.1.78	Osaka	'Starstruck'	R78011/2	2CD	3	Inspired!	Not as good as OMR boot, but more commonly available.
17.1.78	Osaka	'Succubus '78'	Wyvern WLG-121 R3/4	2CD	3	Inspired!	Part of 'Incubus's Party '76-'84' box set. Almost as good as OMR boot.

Date	City	Title	Label	Format	Rating	Quality	Notes
18.1.78	Kyoto	'Dark and Light'	Shelter	2CD	4	Good	Incomplete set. Great bluesy 'Mistreated'. 'Blues' has bass solo. CD2 'Lazy' is 'MOSM'.
20.1.78	Osaka	'Long Live Rainbow'	Wyvern WLG-82281/2	2CD	3	Very Good	Complete set. Too bassy soundwise. 'Mistreated' and 'CTR' very good, great 'MOSM' mess-about. BD bass solo on 'Blues'. 'Love in Blue' is RB's take on the German national anthem.
20.1.78	Osaka	'Walk On The Rainbow'	Independence RA78120-1/2	2CD	4	Very Good	Complete show. 'Mistreated' and 'CTR' very good, great mess-about in 'MOSM'. BD bass solo on 'Blues'. 'Love In Blue' is RB's take on the German national anthem.
21.1.78	Tokyo	'Chaos At Concert'	?	2CD	?	Average	Short, rather hurried and throwaway performance, no encore.
22.1.78	Tokyo	'Perfect On Stage'	Shelter	2CD	4	Good	Keys buried in mix, though guitar well to the fore. Emotional 'Mistreated', '16CGS' starts a few seconds into song. 'LLR&R' fades out at end of CD1 - a minute or so missing by CD2. Good show with lots of RJD/RB interplay.
27.1.78	Sapporo	'An Act of God'	Shelter	2CD	2	Okay	(given circumstances) Full set though 'Starstruck' fades after a minute. 'Blues' interrupted for 2 minutes by Japanese announcer after young girl was crushed to death. 'Starstruck' edit featured as separate track.
27.1.78	Sapporo	'Misconduct'	Good Believe 004/5	2CD	2	Okay	(given circumstances) Incomplete set - missing 'DYCYE'. Poor sound - lots of hiss. CD2 runs slow. 'Blues' interrupted for 2 mins by after

Date	City	Title	Label	Format	#	Quality	Notes
31.1.78	Niigata	'After Four Days'	?	CD	3	Fair	girl crushed to death. 'Starstruck' edit as separate track. Audience noise fades in and out on CD1.
3.2.78	Tokyo	'Another Last Day'	Shelter	2CD	3	Fair	Complete. No bass at all, 'Blues' cut in two. Not many extended intros, except 'Mistreated'. Not really inspiring, just a good gig.
3.2.78	Tokyo	'Kerr-aannngg!!'	RB1528	LP	4	Fair	Nicely balanced sound for 1978 - guitar well mixed, as are vocals.
3.2.78	Tokyo	'The Last Day'	Pandora 003/4	2CD	2	Fair	Complete. Extra tracks from Fukuoka 14.1.78.
23.6.78	Atlanta	'Act 2 '77-78'	?	CD	?	Good	Part of 'Monster Party 76-95' box.
23.6.78	Atlanta	'Hit The Rainbow'	RTW211	CD	3	Good	Poorer sound than 'I'm Losing Control'. No edits. Includes Don Kirshner tracks with poorer sound.
23.6.78	Atlanta	'I'm Losing Control'	Magnitude G910102	CD	4	Good	50 minutes edited radio broadcast. Clear sound, especially drums. Mega 21 min 'SIS'!
23.6.78	Atlanta	'Mixed Emotions'	Baby Capone 021/2	2CD	?	Good	Including tracks off 'LBTE' video, Tokyo '84, Donington '80, Boston '81, Bad Girl.
23.6.78	Atlanta	'Somewhere Over...'	Taurus 002.9103	CD	3	Good	'SIS' fades out after 15 mins.
23.6.78	Atlanta	'The Third Eye'	Dr. GIG DGCD051	CD	?	Good	50 minutes edited radio broadcast. Clear sound, especially drums. 'Stargazer' from Chicago 12.10.79, 'EOTW' is from Donington '80.
2.7.78	Chicago	'Short Time Gig'	Gypsy Eye GE058	CD	3	Heavy	Short sharp 60 min. Support set (to Cheap Trick). No messing, shorter (but interesting) versions of 'Mistreated' and 'CTR' though 'SIS' nearly 40 mins! Little cut in 'Blues'.
1.8.78	Philadelphia	'At The End of a Dream'	?	CD	3	?	
29.9.79	Philadelphia	'Two Shows In 79'	?	?	3	Average	
30.9.79	Baltimore	'Maryland Go Round'	?	CD	?	?	Part of set with 23.11.79 NY show.

Rainbow RISING

Date	City	Title	Label/Cat#	Format	Rating	Quality	Notes
12.10.79	Chicago	'Rise over Chicago'	Bondage BON027	CD	4	Good	Complete (hour long). Sounds like sound-desk rec. Extra tracks 9.2.80.
11.11.79	Long Beach	'#9'	RACD-111179	CD	4	Average	Complete set of 75 mins - a bit nervy and cautious, GB feeling his way, few highlights.
13.11.79	Fresno	'Fresno '79'	Bondage BON155	CD	4	Average	Complete, though a few edits between songs. Great 28 mins 'LIH'. RB features a lot of improv. especially between songs. Bonnet sometimes overdoes vocals.
16.11.79	Denver	'Plugged Into Denver 1979'	SS 99002	CD	4	?	FM broadcast.
23.11.79	New York	'Two Shows In 79'	?	?	?	?	Part set with 29.9.79 Philly show.
30.11.79	New York	'All Night Long '79'	Borebeat BB12	2CD	3	Very Good	Calderone Hall. Radio broadcast of part show. Good performance, especially 'LNF' and 'ANL'. 'LIH' fades after RB solo. Essentially a copy of 'Roger's Birthday Party'.
30.11.79	New York	'Live at Calderone Hall'	IPN047	CD	3	Very Good	Radio broadcast but not lifted from vinyl version.
30.11.79	New York	'Roger's Birthday Party'	Haro Records RA2100	2LP	4	Very Good	
30.11.79	New York	'Roger's Birthday Party'	Bondage BON010	CD	4	Very Good	
30.11.79	New York	'Perfect Roger's Birthday Party'	Bondage BON068	CD	4	Very Good	Radio broadcast complete. Not copy of 'Roger's Birthday Party' - better source recording.
30.11.79	New York	'Roger's Birthday Party Final Cut'	Gryphon 011	CD	4	Very Good	Copy of 'Perfect Roger's Birthday Party'. Limited edition.
17.1.80	Gothenborg	'Mars'	?	CD	3	?	Full show, soundcheck available as bonus or separate item.
18.1.80	Stockholm	'Dangerous Express'	Crystal sound CS10	2CD	3	Good	Full show. Another solid and aggressive no-nonsense performance, less improvs.

Appendices

Date	City	Title	Label/Cat	Format	#	Rating	Notes
20.1.80	Copenhagen	'Over Europe'	Bondage 045/6/7	3CD	4	Very Good	Complete shows from Copenhagen and Hannover. Some good solos, Bonnet sounding much better. Copenhagen slightly better sound. Great 'LNF', epic 'EOTW' versions.
20.1.80	Copenhagen	'White Night'	?	CD	?	Very Good	Some good solos, Bonnet sounding much better. Copenhagen slightly better sound. Great 'LNF' and epic versions of 'EOTW'.
22.1.80	Hannover	'Over Europe'	Bondage 045/6/7	3CD	3	Very Good	Complete shows from Copenhagen and Hannover. Some good solos, Bonnet sounding much better. Great 'LNF', epic 'EOTW' versions.
29.1.80	Essen	'Eyes of Essen'	?	?	3	Average	Full show.
30.1.80	Bremen	'Tour Over Europe'	?	2CD	3	?	
3.2.80	Rotterdam	'Netherland Night '80'	Platinum and Gold PG800202	2CD	4	Okay	'CTR' split over 2 CDs! Good humorous show, neat guitar improvisations.
5.2.80	Koln	?	?	?	3	?	Full show recording exists.
9.2.80	Grenoble	'Grenoble '80'	Wyvern WLG136R3/4	2CD	?	Good	Complete show. Part of 'Insanity Party' box. Great 13 minute 'CTR' from 'TMIB' that fades just before end. Rare 'Makin' Love' featured but not listed. Limited edition 333.
16.2.80	Munich	'Bayern Night'	?	?	3	?	
26.2.80	Manchester	'Shelter From the Rain'	?	?	3	?	
29.2.80	London	'London Riot Gig'	?	2CD	2	Average	Wembley show.
4.3.80	Brighton	'Long Night Brighton '80'	Platinum and Gold PG800304	2CD	3	Just Okay	Great 'EOTW', a far too brief 'CTR', boring keys solo! Untogether at times. No edits.
4.3.80	Brighton	'Bright Lights'	?	2CD	4	Just Okay	Great 'EOTW', a far too brief 'CTR', boring keys solo! Bit untogether.
8.3.80	London	'Come Back To'	?	?	3	?	

Rainbow RISING

Date	City	Title	Label/Cat No.	Format	Rating	Quality	Notes
8.5.80	Tokyo	'Broken Dreams'	AMSterdam AMS1996-01-2-1/2	2CD	4	Fair	Complete set. Audience noise spoils some quieter bits. 30 minute 'LIH' incl. solos and 'Ode to Joy'. Mix sometimes loses GB or RB.
9.5.80	Tokyo	'London: March '80'	R212	2LP	3	Improves	Misleading title! Could also be 8.5.80 show. Airey solo cut out. Includes Cozy interview from BBC 'Old Grey Whistle Test'.
9.5.80	Tokyo	'Since You Been Gone'	R80051/2	2CD	3	Improves	Full show, 96 mins. Starts hesitantly but brilliant 32 min 'LIH' and encore! 'LLR&R' fades in late.
9.5.80	Tokyo	'Since You Been Gone'	OMR 80059-1/2	2CD	3	Improves	Re-issue of above set.
9.5.80	Tokyo	'Walkure'	Amsterdam AMS9606-2-1/2	2CD	4	Improves	Starts hesitantly but brilliant 32 min 'LIH' and encore! 'LLR&R' fades in late. Better sound than other boots.
12.5.80	Tokyo	'Down To Graham'	Bad Girl Songs CDJG	CD	3	Good	Incomplete. Most of 'LIH' missing, excl. CP's solo! Great RB run in 'LNF'. GB strains at times. Limited edition of 1000.
12.5.80	Tokyo	'Innocent Victims'	Meteorite MR07	CD	3	Good	Part show, edited in parts. Most of 'LIH' missing excl. CP's solo! Great RB run in 'LNF', GB strains at times.
12.5.80	Tokyo	'Solitary Traveller'	R527	2LP	3	Good	Full set. Guitar well mixed up. Great RB run in 'LNF', GB straining at times.
12.5.80	Tokyo	'All Night Long'	R80053/4	2CD	2	Good	Full show, lifted from 'Solitary Traveller'. Guitar well mixed up.
12.5.80	Tokyo	'All Night Long'	OMR 80055-1/2	2CD	3	Good	Full show, re-issue of above 2CD set but better sound.
13.5.80	Osaka	'The Colour of the Rainbow'	Independence RAIN 51380-1/2	2CD	3	Fair	Full set. Great RB. Mix just right. Break in keys solo.

230

Date	Location	Title	Source	Format	Rating	Average	Notes
14.5.80	Osaka	'Nightmare '80'	Wyvern WLG 121/R5/6	2CD	3	Average	Solid workmanlike performance - no real highlights. Limited to 777.
15.5.80	Osaka	'Chase After The Rainbow'	Independence Music RA80515-1	2CD	3	Very Good	Complete set. Nice all-round performance, great 'WYLMT'.
15.5.80	Osaka	'Over the Edge'	Bang 0212	2CD	4	Very Good	Complete set. Re-issue of above.
15.5.80	Osaka	'Cozy We Miss You'	?	2CD	4	Very Good	Complete set. Re-issue of above.
8.8.80	Aarhus	'Another On Line'	Nightlife N028/029	2CD	4	Okay	Complete show, not from soundboard as on the CD. Warm up for Donington. Good 'LNF'. 'KTK' features a guitar trash, includes reinstated 'Stargazer'.
9.8.80	Malmo	'On Line'	Nightlife N021	CD	4	Good	Only a 67 minute show so all on 1CD. Sound problems on first couple of songs (poor mastering?) An open-air gig, it started raining so the band left during Airey solo and didn't come back! Best perf. of Donington warm-ups.
10.8.80	Aalborg	'Perfect On Line'	Nightlife N038/039	2CD	3	Good	No edits. Great 'Stargazer' and extended solo in 'CTR'. Last of the Donington warm-ups.
15.8.80	Donington	'Monster Castle'	Crystal sound CS19	CD	3	Good	70 minute sound-check. Break in 'LNF', 'Weiss Heim' ends early.
16.8.80	Donington	'Donington Park 1980'	?	LP	0	Fair	Taped off TV highlights - 25 mins long! Flip side is blank! Barely listenable. Rip-off!
16.8.80	Donington	'Rockin' The Castle Donington (End Of A Rainbow)'	CP816	2LP	2	Fair	Full show. Bonnet nervous - forgets words to 'Stargazer'. Sing-along 'ANL' very cheesy! Set sounds rather rushed. Noisy crowd recording. Edit in promising 'CTR'.
16.8.80	Donington	'End Of A Rainbow'	R80081/2	2CD	2	Fair	Full set from 'Rockin' The Castle'.

Date	Location	Title	Label/Cat. No.	Format	Rating	Quality	Notes
16.8.80	Donington	'End Of A Rainbow'	Niji 001/2	2CD	2	Fair	Full show from audience source, varies from bass overload to noisy audience.
16.8.80	Donington	'End Of A Rainbow'	Wyvern 8880-1/2	2CD	2	Fair	Includes 5 sound-check tracks, as on 'Monster Castle', added to CD2.
21.2.81	Richmond	'No Release'	?	?	?	?	
22.2.81	Fairfax	'Do You Like Earache'	?	?	3	?	
16.4.81	Chicago	'Never Surrender '81'	RHEA 816-1/2	2CD	3	Very Good	Complete. Good all-round band performances, great solos and improvs. Great keys solo in 'DTC'. 47 minute CD features 'Space Trucking' from Paris Theatre 1972, rest from Boston.
7.5.81	Boston	'Ritchie Blackmore Solo'	Lobster Recs. CD030	CD	3	Very Good	Lifted from FM broadcast (with jingles). Best of JLT/81 boots. Great guitar and keyboards. Brilliant solo in 'LNF'. JLT is an immediate improvement vocally.
7.5.81	Boston	'Electrified'	AchCMV47919	2LP	5	Very Good	Lifted from vinyl boot of same name, sound not as good. Best JLT/81 boot. Part of the 'Ritchie's Box' series.
7.5.81	Boston	'Electrified'	Black Suede	2CD	4	Very Good	Complete set. Lifted from FM broadcast. CD 1 features Boston. Great 'DTC'. CD2 the 6.11.82 'Brainstorm' set.
7.5.81	Boston	'Coloured Rainbow'	Bondage BON 023/4	2CD	4	Very Good	Complete. Lifted FM broadcast.
7.5.81	Boston	'More Coloured Rainbow'	Bondage BON 069	CD	5	Very Good	Complete set. Break in 'CTR'. Not much treble but mix is good. Good all-round perf., especially JLT. Good 'IS', 'CTR'.
9.5.81	Philadelphia	'Ultimate Witchie's Night'	Demon's Eye DE-001/2	2CD	3	Good	
3.6.81	Gothenborg	'Fire!'	Demon's Eye DE-008/9	2CD	3	Good	Complete set. Blistering 'LNF' with long solo, 2 minute cover of 'Fire' -

Appendices

Date	City	Title	Catalog	Format	Rating	Quality	Notes
7.6.81	Helsinki	'European Night Helsinki '81'	PG-810706-1/2	2CD	3	Good	hence title. Limited edition of 300. Complete set. Echoey sound. Sound goes in drum solo and 'MNT'. Solid band effort, nothing inspiring, except maybe 'CTR'.
10.6.81	Essen	'Love's Night'	?	2CD	3	?	CD-Rs Possibly taken from footage shot of gig for short-lived fan club.
13.6.81	Rotterdam	'Lost in Hollywood'	Avon 198	2LP	4	Superb	'Love's No Friend' perf'd. but left off. 'LIH' fades after Airey solo. 'MNT' part of encore. RB occasionally really lets rip. 'CTR' excellent. Really top notch show!
13.6.81	Rotterdam	'Lost in Hollywood'	Black Suede BON124/5	2CD	4	Superb	From vinyl boot - crackles and all!
13.6.81	Rotterdam	'Down to Rotterdam'		2CD	4	Superb	Another copied from vinyl boot!
18.6.81	Cologne	'European Night Koln '81'	PG-810618-1/2	2CD	4	Excellent	Complete set. Inspiring show. Ace 'IS', 'CTR' and 'DTC'. JLT proves himself, and so inspires RB. 'LIH' fades at end CD1, continues CD2.
23.6.81	Sindlefingen	'Lost in Stuttgart'	?	?	2	?	
3.7.81	Barcelona	'Bullfighter'	?	?	?	?	
8.7.81	London	'Live at the Rainbow'	RR81	3LP	3	Average	Entire set. Performance workmanlike, few extd. solos, etc.
8.7.81	London	'London Rainbow Theatre July 8, 1981'	Black Suede	2CD	3	Average	Copied from vinyl bootleg. Full set.
20.7.81	St Austell	'Bright Night'	?	?	2	Average	
22.7.81	Manchester	'Condition Critical'	Concrete God CGR0007/8	2CD	3	Very Good	Good mix, another high standard show Great 'LNF', 'IS'. 'LIH' shorter than prev. Extra 7 tracks from Newcastle 24.7.81 incl. 'Fire' but poorer sound and cut in 'DTC'. RB Radio 1 interview included.

Rainbow RISING

Date	City	Title	Label/Cat. No.	Format	Rating	Quality	Notes
22.7.81	Manchester	'Made in England'	?	2CD	3	Very Good	Good mix, another high standard show. Great 'LNF', 'IS'. 'LIH' shorter than previously.
26.7.81	London	'Rainbow a Paris 1981'	Spotlight XL1508	3LP	4	Very Good	Sleeve lists tracks from Paris and Lille but is incorrect; first Hammersmith Odeon show and Japan '81. Little RB improv. Hendrix's 'Fire' is included, though a promising extended 'Blues' is edited right at end of Side 6!
26.7.81	London	'Difficult to Reappear'	?	?	3	Very Good	Complete. Good performance from JLT, 'IS' and 'MNT' brings best from RB. Airey plays all the solos in 'DTC'. One or two little improvs.
27.7.81	London	'Can't Happen Here'	POSP251	3LP	4	Good	
27.7.81	London	'Can't Happen Here'	Black Suede	2CD	4	Good	Lifted from the vinyl boot.
27.7.81	London	'Black Destroyer'	?	2CD	4	Good	Good performance from JLT, 'IS' and 'MNT' brings best from RB. Airey plays all the solos in 'DTC'. One or two little improvs as well.
18.8.81	Fukuoka	'Demon '81'	Wyvern WLG-121 R7/8	2CD	3	Good	Incomplete - 'CHH' fades out, encore missing. Good guitar in 'IS', 'CTR', 'DTC'.
18.8.81	Fukuoka	'What Happen Here'	Pandora 005/6	2CD	2	Good	Complete show but sound varies in speed and distorts. Includes a full 'CHH' and 'Fire'. Extra tracks 'IS' and 'CHH' from 27.8.81 in Tokyo.
20.8.81	Osaka	'Missing Point'	RHEA88R3-1/2	2CD	2	Average	Complete. Sound spoilt by noisy audience, though clear in quiet bits. No messing, few improvs, solid enough.
20.8.81	Osaka	'Missing Link'	RHEA88R1-1/2	2CD	3	Average	Complete. Less noisy. Few more improvs especially 'CTR', solid all-round effort.
21.8.81	Osaka	'Craze!'	?	?	4	?	

Date	City	Title	Catalog	Format	Discs	Quality	Notes
22.8.81	Fukouka	'Shades of Whitchy'	?	?	3	?	Complete sets including 28.8.81 as well. Lots of audience noise totally spoils two very good shows. JLT and RB especially inspired. Second show has Joe singing ad-lib in 'Blues'. Frustrating listening!
23.8.81	Nagoya	'Silver Night'	?	?	4	?	
24.8.81	Kyoto	'Kyoto N Yoru'	?	?	3	?	
27.8.81	Tokyo	'Missing Gate'	RHEA90R2-1/2	3CD	1	Very Good	
13.5.82	Michigan	'Machine Guns Of Michigan'	?	?	?	?	
15.5.82	Kalamazoo	'Super Sonic Sound Machine'	Pandora 007	CD	2	Average	Complete (73 mins). Rare take of 'DAD' and 'Rock Fever'. Average.
15.5.82	Kalamazoo	'Satisfaction Guaranteed'	Bondage BON 091	CD	2	Average	Different source to above. Complete set (73 mins).
12.6.82	Montreal	'Death Alley Driver'	Gryphon 017-18	2CD	2	Average	Complete set (85 mins). Noisy audience in quiet parts. Last take of 'DAD' on this tour. 'Stone Cold' plays fast, 'Power' is edited.
19.6.82	New York	'Stone Cold'	XL1519	3LP	3	Okay	Madison Square Gardens. 80 mins audience recording. Solid if unspectacular performance.
19.6.82	New York	'Stone Cold'	Black Suede	2CD	3	Okay	Madison Square Garden, lifted from vinyl. Part of 'Ritchie's Box'.
21.6.82	Harrisburg	'Harrisburg '82'	Wyvern WLG-136R5/6	2CD	3	Good	Part of 6 CD set - rare (unique?) version of 'Jealous Lover' featured.
21.6.82	Harrisburg	'Stone Cold'	Phoned 820216	Vinyl	2	Good	Another short (75 mins) set. Limited edition of 333.
23.6.82	Harrisburg	'Killer Night'	?	?	4	?	Only first half of show: 'SK', 'MM', 'CHH', 'TOMH', 'ANL' and 'SC'.
20.7.82	Largo	'Capitol Night'	?	?	?	?	

Date	Location	Title	Label/Cat#	Format	Rating	Quality	Notes
18.8.82	San Antonio	'Mixed Emotions'	Baby Capone 012/2	2CD	4	Good	Complete set taken from video. Additional tracks from Tokyo '84, Donington '80, Atlanta '78 and Boston '81. 'Bad Girl' b-side incl. probably from 'Finyl Vinyl'.
18.8.82	San Antonio	'Rainbow's Edge'	Main Event CDLP015	CD	3	Good	Boot of video soundtrack, with crude edits, runs fast. Just 47 mins!
18.8.82	San Antonio	'Snow White and the Seven Dwarves'	RB1 A/B	2LP	4	Good	Copy of Video soundtrack.
18.8.82	San Antonio	'Stone Cold'	Three Cool Cats TCC1012	CD	4	Good	Incomplete set not copied off video but radio broadcast.
18.8.82 16.10.82	San Antonio Kyoto	'The Cure For Herpes' 'Sorceress '82'	KEF Records A8268 Wyvern WLG-121R9/10	2LP 2CD	4 2	Good Fair	Copy of video soundtrack. Complete set though very noisy at times. Great 'TOMH' and 'DTC' by RB. 'Fire' included. Limited to 777.
17.10.82	Fukuoka	'Inspired Kneel Down'	Neptune NT-82601/2	2CD	3	Very Good	Complete set. Great all-round effort, especially DA and JLT. 'DTC' cooking but fades at end of CD1 to carry on to CD2. 'MOSM' unusually done as encore. Lots of fun RB improvs.
19.10.82	Nagoya	'Call Me Cab'	CMC-01/2	2CD	5	Average	Sounds like a desk recording. Short solos, no real improvs. Mundane. Unique 'Call Me Cab' medley.
21.10.82	Tokyo	'Child in Time'	Dirty 13-03A/B	2CD	4	Good	Short 'Blues' edit. Full show. Slow start by RB but last third of show excellent! Nice solos 'IS', and 'SK'. 'CHH' ultra fast version, JLT can't keep up. Good 'Power', 'TOMH'.
21.10.82	Tokyo	'Live at Budo-Kan'	Sacem 98BF	2LP	2	Fair	Audience noise in quiet bits. Sound breaks slightly in 'DTC'. Some with gatefold sleeve.
22.10.82	Tokyo	'Catch The Rainbow'	Dirty 13-004A/B	2CD	3	Good	Complete show, as good a perf. as prev. night, especially 'SK', 'TOMH'

Date	Location	Title	Catalogue	Format	Rating	Sound	Notes
22.10.82	Tokyo	'Tokyo 2 Nights'	Dirty 13-003/4 SP	4CD	3	Good	and 'DTC'. Sound a shade inferior. Two complete nights in a row, good performances. Released as separate 2CD sets 'Child in Time' and 'Catch The Rainbow' (above).
30.10.82	Aarhus	'Clear Night'	?	?	4	?	Clear sound, especially keyboards and drums. Superb 'TOMH'. JLT sounds rough in places.
6.11.82	Stockholm	'Brainstorm'	Stock Records 821106	2LP	4	Good	
6.11.82	Stockholm	'Stockholm Salute'	Trade Mark of Quality XL 1546/7/8	2CD	4	Good	Complete, prob. from 'Brainstorm'. Date in title incorrect - 'SBTE' tour but source unknown - probably Japan 10.82. Sound well balanced, good example of 'SBTE' tour.
?	?	'Dortmund Jan.1983'		3LP	3	Okay	
24.11.82	Stuttgart	'Powerful Night'	?	?	4	?	
28.11.82	Paris	'Long Live Paris'	?	?	?	?	
30.1.83	Long Beach	'Stranded'	?	2LP	?	?	
6.9.83	Liverpool	'Fade to the Mersey'	Demon's Eye 003-4	2CD	2	Fair	Date is wrong. Source not verified. Complete. Plays slightly fast. Edit in 'CTR' and 'Power'/'Blues'. Nice (i.e. short) drum and keys solos. Only short flashes of RB brilliance, good 'CTR'. Limited edition of 300.
7.9.83	Liverpool	'Liverpool '83'	?	?	2	?	
11.9.83	Bristol	'England Night'	?	?	4	?	
11.9.83	Cardiff	'Cardiff 1984'	LSCD-51541	CD	5	Good	Part show (47 mins). Wrong date - could be copy of 'Ritchie Blackmore's Rainbow'. Nice guitar touches but no long improvs. St David's Hall FM broadcast.
14.9.83	Cardiff	'Cardiff 1983'	R1/2	2LP	4	Good	Shouts for Dio during 'Stranded'! 'IS' and 'MM' highlights.
14.9.83	Cardiff	'Captured Live'	RBW 3412/3	2CD	5	Good	Complete. Best of the Cardiff releases by far.
14.9.83	Cardiff	'HM Holocaust'	LP844	LP	4	Good	Part. St David's Hall broadcast.

Rainbow RISING

Date	City	Title	Label/Cat	Format	Discs	Quality	Notes
14.9.83	Cardiff	'Ritchie Blackmore's Rainbow'	Time Records 541	CD	5	Good	Part show (47 mins). Some inlays state '14.9.84'. Probably copy of 'Cardiff 1984.'
15.9.83	Cardiff	'Cardiff Second Night'	?	?	4	?	Sobell Centre (sleeve wrongly says 'USA Feb 1984'). Thin sound. Full 105 mins show, drum solo edited.
17.9.83	London	'Stargazer'	?	2LP	3	Good	
17.9.83	London	'Freshness Night'	?	?	3	Good	Audience recording Sobell Centre. Distant sound/bad breaks in 'Stranded'. Includes 'tracks' (short reprises) from Gothenborg, Fairfax and New York.
18.9.83	London	'Sweet Silence'	XL1556/7/8	3LP	4	Good	
19.9.83	St Austell	'Stargazer'	Metal Mania SR1238	3LP	2	Average	
19.9.83	St Austell	'Stargazer'	Black Suede RHEA91R4-1/2	CD	2	Average	Incomplete set. Vinyl boot copy.
19.9.83	St Austell	'Stranded Death Alley'		2CD	3	Average	Complete set. High bass/low vocals mix. Audience sometimes noisy. Nice 'IS', 'LLR&R' starts few secs. into song and includes 'Hey Joe'.
23.9.83	Edinburgh	'Scotland Night'	?	?	4	?	
30.9.83	Gothenborg	'Live in Gothenborg'	Heavy Rec. LP115 A/B	LP	3	Good	Edited show. Limited edition 200. Features 'FFTN', 'DWTD', 'DTC', 'Stargazer, 'DAD', 'MNT', 'SOTW'.
30.9.83	Gothenborg	'Stranded in Sweden'	BS-58/9	2CD	3	Good	Complete set. 'FFTN' good version, as is 'CTR' (for 1983!) 'DTC' fades in. 'Power edited.
30.9.83	Gothenborg	'Monsters Night'	?	2CD	4	?	
5.10.83	Copenhagen	'Bent Out of Falconer'	?	?	3	?	
2.11.83	Philadelphia	'Street Of Dreams'	?	?	?	?	
11.3.84	Osaka	'Satan 84'	Wyvern WLG121R11/12	2CD	1	Good	Complete. Very noisy recording. Good versions of 'IS' and 'FFTN'. Limited edition of 777.
11.3.84	Osaka	'World Tour 84'	Black Suede	2CD	2	Good	Complete. Another noisy recording. Tracks out of set order. Part of the 'Ritchie's Box' set.

238

Date	City	Title	Label/Cat#	Format	Tracks	Quality	Notes
13.3.84	Tokyo	'The Day Before the Final Gig'	Shelter 001/2	2CD	2	Average	Complete set. Sound level varies, noisy in parts. Workmanlike band effort. JLT sings intro to 'CHH', drum intro to 'Power' different than usual takes. 'DTC' also sounds like it has strings backing.
14.3.84	Tokyo	'On Stage '84'	11-16/7	2CD	5	Very Good	Complete show recorded off TV transmission. Everyone up for last show, good 'IS', highlight is RB's intro to 'DTC'. Rare 'SOD' outing.
14.3.84 30.9.95	Tokyo Helsinki	'Last Stand' 'Rebirth of a Legend'	GAEA845-1/2 Magnum 001/2	2CD 2CD	5 2	Very Good Nervous	Complete show recorded off TV. Complete set. Nervous but promising start to tour. 'S&F' performed, thereafter dropped. 'HOTMK' suffers from PA problems, as does 'Burn'. CD2 includes Stockholm 2.10.95.
2.10.95	Stockholm	'Second Night in Sweden 1995'	Magnum 9/10	2CD	4	Nervous	Complete set - audience recording. Band overly cautious.
2.10.95	Stockholm	'Circus Night'	Kobra KKHM05	CD	5	Nervous	Recorded for radio - part show. Band overly cautious. Includes tracks from Tokyo 12.5.80.
2.10.95	Stockholm	'Strangers in Stockholm'	Bondage BON057	CD	5	Nervous	Recorded for radio - part show. Band overly cautious. Brilliant 'TOTK' not included. Includes 2 tracks Osaka from 16.11.95.
8.10.95	Hanover	'Ritchie Bows to Germany'	BS01/02	2CD	4	Excellent	RB and DW bang on form! Particularly fluid solo in 'TLFT'. 'MOSM' and 'Burn' great! 'Black Night' encore. Part of 10 CD set.
9.10.95	Dusseldorf	'At the Rainbow's End'	DIYE 59	CD	4	Good	Part set, taken from TV show. Tight and controlled performance,

Date	City	Title	Label/Ref	Format	Rating	Quality	Notes
9.10.95	Dusseldorf	'Black Shadows'	Oxygen OXY 026	CD	5	Good	not much improvisation. Very good 'BM' and 'Ariel'. Limited edition of 486.
9.10.95	Dusseldorf	'The Prince of Darkness'	Sideshow URICI 916	1CD	4	Good	Sourced from TV - part show only. 'SK' omitted due to interference, no 'TOTK'.
9.10.95	Dusseldorf	'Rising Again'	RBR 10/95/A/B	2CD	5	Good	Sourced from TV broadcast - part show only. Omits keys solo. Best of Dusseldorf (recorded for TV), incl. Munich 20.10.77 tracks.
9.10.95	Dusseldorf	'Temple Of The King'	Babylon 01/02	2CD	2	Good	Lifted from 3rd TV showing. Full show but worst of Dusseldorf CDs.
10.10.95	Berlin	'Ritchie Bows to Germany'	BS03/04	2CD	4	Average	Solid performance. Vocals low in mix. Good 'SK', 'TOTK' and 'Burn'. Part of 10 CD set.
12.10.95	Appenweir	'Germany Rising Again'	Eclipse EC-012-13	CD	4	Good	Full show. Good 'HH' solo, 'TOTK', nice 'Blues' too.
13.10.95	Ludwigshafen	'Ritchie Bows to Germany'	BS05/06	2CD	3	Good	Complete set. Blistering 'SK', 'MOSM' incl. verse of 'Rainbow Eyes'. Few DW intros. No extended improvs. Hard, fast and heavy! Also part of 10 CD set.
14.10.95	Stuttgart	'Rainbow in Germany'	Rain One/Two	2CD	3	Average	Complete set. Another good if straight-ahead heavier show with little improv. Extended encore.
16.10.95	Osnabruck	'Lost in a Distant Dream'	?	CD	4	Good	Full show. A short 'Rainbow Eyes' and 'Black Night' featured.
17.10.95	Rotterdam	'European Days'	R1/2	2CD	3	Very Good	Full show. Great 'SK', 'HH', and 'TOTK'. Includes Brussels 1.11.95 - 'MOSM' brilliant at 8 mins long.
21.10.95	Munich	'Ritchie Bows to Germany'	BS07/08	2CD	5	Superb	Brilliant 2 hour-plus show (best of the Euro tour?) Some good improv

Appendices

Date	City	Title	Source	Format	Rating	Quality	Notes
22.10.95	Leipzig	'Ritchie Bows to Germany'	BS09/10	2CD	5	Okay	- DW now fits in well. Again short verse of 'R.Eyes' and also 'CTR'. A heavy 'BN' then 'Mistreated' in place of 'SOTW'. Part of 10 CD set.
26.10.95	Zurich	'The Lord of Darkness Returns'	Moonlight Music	2CD	3	Good	Great 'BM' and intro to 'Ariel'. Interesting DW-led blues intro into 'WTTM'. 'HH' has keys solo only. Brief snatch of 'Steamroller Blues'. Slight cut 'LLR&R'. Part of 10CD set.
30.10.95	Lyon	'Long Live France'	Eclipse EC008/09	2CD	4	Below Average	Bad break in 'Perfect Strangers', otherwise full show. Doogie does his drinking song.
31.10.95	Paris	'Long Live France'	Eclipse 010/011	2CD	4	Very Good	Part of 4CD set. One of those gigs where RB is uninterested until encores.
31.10.95	Paris	'Parisien Masquerade'	Disc 1/2	2CD	3	Very Good	Part of 4CD box set. Again, show gradually improves. Highlights 'TOTK', 'PS' and 'Ariel'.
1.11.95	Brussels	?	?	2CD	3	Poor	Complete show, if bass-heavy. 'BM' faded out at end. Includes 4 tracks from Rotterdam 17.10.95. 105 mins, great 'LLR&R' and 'HH'. 'Ariel' suddenly dropped. No encore! Disappointing!
3.11.95	London	'Extra Long'	AMS1996-02-3-1/2/3	3 CD	4	Excellent	Hammersmith Odeon 1st show, complete 156 mins. Excellent and relaxed, great interplay between RB/DW. 'LLR&R', extended intro to 'DTC', 'HOTMK', 'TOTK' highlights.
4.11.95	London	'Rainbow Moon'	AMS9607-2-1/2	2CD	3	Okay	Complete. Anticlimax after 1st night. Little fooling around, straight-ahead and workmanlike. Occasionally frantic. 107 mins.

11.11.95	Tokyo	'1st Day'	Stranger Days, East Box WV181T1/2	10CD	5	Excellent	Guitar biased mix - vocals and keys lost sometimes. One of best '90's concerts - great 'LLR&R', 'TLFT' and best 'DTC' of 1995. Long blues into 'MOSM', long 'Ariel' intro, superb 'TOTK' too. Part of 10 CD box set.
12.11.95	Tokyo	'Perfect Strangers in Tokyo'	PTS007/8	2CD	4	Okay	Complete set. Anti-climax after 11.11. A bit of 'Rainbow Eyes' (DW/keys only). Reprise of 'Love Hurts' and 'SOD' and 'Stone Cold', albeit both with no solo.
11.11.95 12.11.95	Tokyo	'The First And Second Day'	DA&T005/6/7/8	4CD	3	Good/ Excellent	First two nights of tour. Complete shows. Sound not as good.
12.11.95	Tokyo	'2nd Day'	Stranger Days, East Box FR1117/1&2	10CD	4	Good	Anti-climax after 11.11. A snatch of 'Rainbow Eyes' (DW/keys only). Bit of 'Love Hurts' and 'SOD' and 'Stone Cold', albeit both with no solo. Part of 10 CD box set.
12.11.95	Tokyo	'Tears of Emperor'	11121/2	2CD	3	Good	Anti-climax after 11.11. A snatch of 'Rainbow Eyes' (DW/keys only). Bit of 'Love Hurts' and 'SOD' and 'Stone Cold', albeit both with no solo. Part of 10 CD box set.
14.11.95	Kyoto	'3rd Day'	Stranger Days, West Box WV181 K5/6	8CD	4	Excellent	Powerful 'SK'; highlights 'HH' and 'Ariel'. Better go at 'Stone Cold'. Brilliant show especially RB and DW! Vocals sometimes a bit lost in mix. Part of 8CD box set.
14.11.95	Kyoto	'The Ultimate Guitar Bible'	Jailbait CD 014/15	2CD	5	Excellent	Complete show. Guitar up in the

Appendices

Date	City	Title	Source	Format	Rating	Quality	Notes
16.11.95	Osaka		Stranger Days, West Box WV181 K5/6	8CD	4	Average	mix, vocals 'lost' for first 3 songs. Powerful 'SK', highlights 'HH' and 'Ariel'. Better 'Stone Cold'. Brilliant show especially RB and DW!
17.11.95	Nagoya	'4th Day'	FR1117/1 &2	2CD	5	Very Good	Guitar less clear. Long 'DTC' intro'. One of RB's more introverted nights. Keys solo in 'HH'. Includes 'SOD'. Part of 8CD box set.
17.11.95	Nagoya	'Stand Back'	Stranger Days, East Box WV181T1/2	10CD	4	Good	Full Show. A lot of bass in the mix. Solid, tight and occasionally inspired perfomance. 'SIS', 'TLFT', 'MOSM' and 'BM' real highlights.
17.11.95	Nagoya	'5th Day'	DA&T09/10	2CD	5	Very Good	Full Show.
19.11.95	Osaka	'The Fifth Show in Nagoya' '6th Day'	Stranger Days, West Box WV181 K5/6	8CD	5	Okay	Full Show.
20.11.95	Fukuoka	'Real Front'	Magnum 003/4	2CD	4	Good	Solid show with a little less improv than previous. 'BM', 'TLFT' and 'Burn' the best efforts. 'TOTK' solo by PM not RB. Part of 8 CD box.
20.11.95	Fukuoka	'7th Day'	Stranger Days, West Box WV181 K5/6	8CD	4	Good	Another good show, though shorter versions. Highlights 'SK', 'HH', 'DTC' and rare encores 'SOD', 'MNT'. Part of 8CD box set. Incl. tracks from Stockholm 2.10.95.
22.11.95	Yokohama	'8th Day'	Stranger Days, East Box FR1117/1 &2	10CD	5	Okay	Another good show, though shorter versions. Part of 8CD box.
							Fast, heavy and furious short versions with no frills. 'HH' great, 'TLFT' the opener. Shortened encores. Part of 10CD box set.

243

Date	Location	Title	Reference	Format	Rating	Quality	Notes
22.11.95	Yokohama/Tokyo	'The 8th and Last Show'	DA&T011/2/3/4	4CD	5	Okay	Last two shows.
23.11.95	Tokyo	'Last Emperor'	RB01,02	2CD	4	Good	Open with 'TLFT', 'SOTW' is 5th song in. Encores includes 'SOD', 'MNT', a bit of 'Love Hurts' and a few bars of 'Woman From Tokyo'.
23.11.95	Tokyo	'Rainbow Bridge'	PTS014/5 Stranger Days, East Box WV181T1/2	2CD	2	Good	Complete set, but worse sound.
23.11.95	Tokyo	'9th Day'		?	5	Good	Clearer sound picks up little nuances. Part of 10 CD box.
5.7.96	Sao Paulo	'Black Masquerade'	R96071	2CD	3	Very Good	Complete, another great gig. Opens with 'TLFT'. Superb 'MOSM' (esp. GM) and 'HOTMK'.
6.7.96	Sao Paulo	'Ritchie Goes South'	BIO33/34	2CD	1	Good	Complete. From video of concert but poor sound. Edits in 'TLFT', 'LLR&R' and 'MNT'. Another great gig, opens with 'TLFT'. Superb 'MOSM' (esp.PM), 'HOTMK'.
24.7.96	Vienna	'Made in Austria'	?	CD	4	?	Complete sets from Passau and Nuremburg 30.7.96. Nuremburg is better quality. Passau shorter set. Both open with 'LLR&R'.
26.7.96	Passau	'Bavarian Masquerade'	RSG01/2/3/4	4CD	4	?	
26.7.96	Passau	'Ritchie Serenades Germany'	RSG01-10	10CD	4	Good	4CD sets 'Bavarian Masquerade' and 'Waltzing with Ritchie' with 2CD set 'Ritchie Falls Down'.
26.7.96	Passau	'Come Back to Deutschland'	?	?	4	?	
28.7.96	Vosselar	'Bit of a Wet Dream'	?	2CD	3	Average	Full gig. Sound loses bass and vocals are low in mix. Edit at end of 'Burn'. No real highlights.
30.7.96	Nurnberg	'Waltzing with Ritchie'	PR96001/2	2CD	5	Very Good	Full show. 8 extras from Vosselaar 28.7.96. DW straining at times, but RB in a playful mood, lots of extra

Date	Location	Title	Ref	Format	Rating	Quality	Notes
1.8.96	Schmallenberg	'Waltzing with Ritchie'	RSG05/6/7/8	4CD	4	Average	bits and extended encores. Complete sets from 1.8.96 and Bad Worishofen 3.8.96. Standard perf. 1.8.96 features good 'SOD', 'BM'. Also snatch of 'SIUA' outtake?
2.8.96	Bremen	'Ritchie Falls Down'	RSG09/10	2CD	2	Okay	Complete set. RB falls off back of the stage prior to 'BM' (hence the title!). Standard performance, though 'SIS' good. 'SOTW' edited.
3.8.96	Bad Worishofen	'Back Again'	Heritage H002/3	2CD	3	Average	Edit between main set and encore. PA failure at end of both 'LLR&R' and 'Mistreated' spoils songs. RB apologises over the mike! Thereafter show bit throwaway, though brilliant 'TOTK'.
3.8.96	Bad Worishofen	'Waltzing with Ritchie'	RSG05/6/7/8	4CD	4	Average	Complete sets from 1.8.96 and Bad Worishofen 3.8.96.
7.8.96	Gothenburg	'Wolf in the Stone'	Moon 96871/2	2CD	4	Good	Full show. Audience/vocals high in mix. Lots of keys in 'DTC', DW sings in 'Blues'.
9.8.96	Lidkoping	'Raymond's Parade'	?	CD	3	Excellent	Great all-round band performance. Great 'HOTMK' and 'DTC'. Nice RB touches throughout.
11.8.96	Copenhagen	'Made in Denmark'	BIO07/08	2CD	4	Good	Complete set. Great 'Mistreated' from Doogie, as is 'PS'. Doogie sacked/reinstated after antics at this gig! Extra tracks from Skanderborg 10.8.96.
11.8.96	Copenhagen	'Made in Denmark'	R-Duck 9703	2CD	3	Good	Re-release especially for Denmark. Complete set. Very untogether at times. Extra tracks are soundcheck from Old Bridge 20.2.97 (below).
21.2.97	Providence	'Moon Walker'	R22197-1/2	2CD	3	Below Average	
22.2.97	Springfield	'Over Jaxx'	Jimmy Cat Recs. 9/10	2CD	3	Good	Complete set. Mix varies at times.

Rainbow RISING

Date	City	Title	Label/No.	Format	Rating	Quality	Notes
22.2.97	Springfield	'The Jaxx'	R22297-1/2	2CD	3	Good	Good 'TOTK'. Good improvs from RB and DW.
26.2.97	Toronto	'The Next Generation I'	?	?	4	?	Complete set. Treble varies at times. Good 'TOTK'. Some good improvs from RB and DW. See Schaumberg 2.3.97.
26.2.97	Toronto	'Twenties Century Rainbow'	?	?	4	?	
27.2.97	Canton, Ohio	'Ohio First Night'	H009/10	2CD	4	Very Good	Concert gets better as it goes on. 'Mistreated' has keys solo instead of guitar. Great 'Burn'. Includes 4 tracks from 20.2.97 New Jersey soundcheck. Edit at start of encore.
28.2.97	Columbus	'Ritchie Ad-libs Blues'	Heritage 007/8	2CD	3	Good	Complete set, keys low in the mix. Solid show. CD2 features fascinating 16 mins before-show soundcheck; brilliant guitar doodling, blues and heavy runs.
28.2.97	Columbus	'Alrosa Villa'	BIO 47/8	2CD	3	Good	Complete set. Solid show.
2.3.97	Schaumberg	'The Next Generation I'	R3297-1/2	2CD	3	Good	Superb 'TOTK', and 'Burn' is great too. First half Toronto 26.2.97 incl.
7.3.97	Minneapolis	'Doogie's Birthday Party'	Bondage BON119/120	2CD	4	Okay	Generally good but workmanlike performance. 'MOSM' is highlight. Great work on 'LLR&R', 'MOSM' from RB. Different 'Mistreated' solo than usual.
13.3.97	Tempe	'Tempe of the King'	Bondage 106/107	2CD	5	Average	
16.3.97	Los Angeles	'3 Nights in L.A.'	Bio 52/3/4/5/6/7	6CD	4	Good	Set features complete shows from 16.3.97, 17.3.97 and 18.3.97. First gig has RB in good form, keys low in mix. Second night sounds a little worse, DW in top form, good 'Mistreated'. Third night great 'BM', and RB again on form.

246

Appendices

19.3.97	Palo Alto	'The Edge'	?	2CD	4	Average	Incomplete. Solid, no highlights. 'SIS' has bass and drum solos. Encores missing.
31.5.97	Esjberg	'Mistreated in Denmark'	R-Duck 9701	2CD	5	Very Good	Full festival show. Good perf; great 'SIS' and 'TOTK'. 8 extra tracks from Skanderborg 10.8.96.
31.5.97	Esjberg	'Maybe Next Time'	?	2CD	4	Very Good	Last gig by the 'SIUA' line-up.

BOOTLEG VIDEOS

1977	'Rainbow - Young Music Show 1977'	?	?	3	Very Good	Japanese origin. 4 tracks from Munich 'Rockpalast' show. 'KTK'/ 'Long Live...'/'Still'/'Do You...' with Japanese subtitles.
Various	'Munich 20.10.77'	?	?	5	Very Good	Broadcast on 'Rockpalast'. Repeat on satellite/cable, easily available.
Various	'Dusseldorf 9.10.95'	?	?	5	Good	Broadcast on 'Rockpalast'. Repeat on satellite/cable, easily available.
28.10.95	'Milan'	?	?	2	Average	Recorded with 2 cameras. Full show. Acoustic start to 'SIS'. Quality poor.
1996	'Hammersmith '95'	?	?	3	Excellent	Audience shot. Picture and sound fair-good, great show. Ritchie's guitar was stolen and returned before the encore! Cuts during encore.

RAINBOW AND ASSOCIATED SOCIETIES, WEBSITES AND PUBLICATIONS

Many of those in the listing below have been unstinting in their support and assistance during the writing of this book. Many thanks to all concerned.

There are many other web-sites loosely associated with those central to the Rainbow story, but lack of space means we can only list a few here. Most of the other very good sources can be found via site links below.

Should the reader wish to investigate aspects of this biography further the following sites, clubs and societies come fully recommended.

Don Airey
Official site covering the multitude of work for other bands done by the versatile keyboardist, plus solo projects.
www.1212.co/a/airey/don

Ritchie Blackmore
Ritchie's official site, detailing his renaissance acoustic project. Not updated too often, though.
www.blackmoresnight.com

Ritchie Blackmore
An unofficial German site with lots of interesting bits and pieces, particularly on the recent Blackmore's Night tours and albums.
http://www.ritchieblackmore.de

Ritchie Blackmore Fan Club
Regular newsletters c/o Kris & Cathy, PO Box 1538, Miller Place, NY 11764, USA.

More Black Than Purple
The Ritchie Blackmore Appreciation Society magazine. Established in 1996 by current editor Jerry Bloom and Mark Welch, this is an excellent glossy magazine published several times a year, concentrating on Ritchie's current work but also features regular retrospectives on Rainbow and Deep Purple.
PO Box 155, Bedford, MK40 2YX.
Subscription details: Contact CeeDee Mail Ltd, PO Box 14, Stowmarket, Suffolk, IP14 1EN, England
Tel: 01449 770138/Credit card hotline 01449 770139/Fax 01449 770133
Email:113115.115@compuserve.com
http://www.mbtp.freeserve.co.uk

Sanctuary of Ritchie Blackmore
Portuguese/English site, fairly standard stuff but with interesting items of information.
http://intermega.globo.com/remystar

Sensitive to Light
This site is run by Matteo Filippini with Italian text.
Zanibelli 24, 26023 Grumello (Cremona), Italy.
http://lasvegas.pointest.com/ritchieblackmorefans

Graham Bonnet
The official site. Lacking in much detail, but useful for current news.
http://www.bonnet-rocks.com

Tony Carey
An official site. Little on his stint in Rainbow but plenty on his extensive solo career.
http://www.traquilitybase.com

The Deep Purple Appreciation Society
Headed by Simon Robinson since 1975, the DPAS is the longest running Deep Purple-related organisation. The excellent (if irregularly published!) glossy tome Darker Than Blue deals with Purple and its spin-offs (including Blackmore) from all eras in detail and

includes info on archive releases co-ordinated by Purple Records (of which Simon is an integral part).
Aizlewood Mill, Nursery Street, Sheffield, S3 8GG, UK
24 hour Fax line: 0114 2823116
http://www.purplepeople.co.uk

Ronnie James Dio
The official site.
http://www.ronniejamesdio.com

Ronnie James Dio/
Man On A Silver Mountain
Another well-detailed site, run by Ken and Marie and updated monthly, covering Ronnie James Dio's career to date. With downloads, news and an extensive archive.
http://www.dio.net

Tapio's Dio Site
Run from Finland by Tapio Keihanen. Rather dated, though lots of info on tour dates, albums, band members, etc.
http://www.diozine.com

The Highway Star
Purple's official website with extensive information, both current and historical. Regularly updated, a vast archive of facts, interviews, etc. An essential starting point for further investigation of Ritchie's career.
http://www.deep-purple.com

Roger Glover
A new and interesting unofficial site, with gig dates, lyrics, production credits, solo information and current news on the bassist's activities.
http://home.swipnet.se/rogerglover

Roger Glover
Official website. Contains solo information, basic biography and downloads.
http://w1.911.telia.com/~u91109277

The Music of Cozy Powell
A recently developed but increasingly detailed site covering the drummer's extensive 30-year career.
http://www.geocities.com/cp_hammer

Cozy Powell
The official Cozy site is maintained by Black Sabbath aficionado Joe Siegler. Little to report update-wise, though a good starting point for new Cozy fans.
http://www.cozypowell.com

The Rainbow Fan Clan
An excellent and informative site based around the Dutch fan club magazines Over The Rainbow previously published through 1980-84. Lots of interviews, reviews, etc in both Dutch and now (thankfully!) English.
http://www.rainbowfanclan.com

Rainbow
General Rainbow site, good factual content. Includes bass and guitar tabs.
http://www.rainbow.i8.com

Rockforever.com
Founded in 1999, rockforever/'voices of rock' is a comprehensive artist-owned digital record label, Internet music channel and live performance group dedicated to classic US rock, and includes Joe Lynn Turner (and Glenn Hughes) in its artist roster. This impressive site boasts a whole host of Turner-related downloadable tracks, interviews, biographies and discographies, tour information, memorabilia and merchandise. Highly recommended.
http://www.rockforever.com

David Rosenthal
Official site, detailing solo work, sessions, photos and other aspects of his extensive music career.
http://www.davidrosenthal.com

Slash Rock
Recently launched by Highway Star's Dave Hodgkinson, the site covers news and comment on all aspects of the Purple family, spin-offs and associated musicians, including Rainbow.
http://www.slashrock.com

Greg Smith
Official site, covering Greg's work with Alice Cooper, Rainbow and other projects. Irregularly updated.
http://www.gsmith.com

Temple Of The King
Another good basic site with emphasis on Blackmore rather than just Rainbow.
http://templeoftheking.hypermart.net

Joe Lynn Turner
Joe's official site, with nice graphics and plenty of information.
http://www.joelynnturner.com

Friends of Joe Lynn Turner FC
Run by Jacqui & Lisa who publish the Voice of Reason A5-sized fanzine.
Address: PO Box 14, Waterlooville, Hampshire PO8 0US UK
E-mail: mailto:jltfcmgnt@aol.com

Doogie White
Official site with lots of information on his tenure with Rainbow, Cornerstone, Malmsteen and other projects currently underway. Updated fairly regularly.
http://www.doogiewhite.co.uk

OTHER TITLES AVAILABLE FROM HELTER SKELTER

COMING SOON...

Steve Marriott: The Definitive Biography
by Paolo Hewitt and John Hellier **£18.99**
Marriott was the prime mover behind '60s chart-toppers The Small Faces. Longing to be treated as a serious musician, he formed Humble Pie with Peter Frampton where his blistering rock 'n' blues guitar playing soon saw him take centre stage in the US live favourites. After years in seclusion, Marriott's plans for a comeback in 1991 were tragically cut short when he died in a house fire. He continues to be a key influence for generations of musicians from Paul Weller to Oasis and Blur.

Pink Floyd: A Saucerful of Secrets
by Nicholas Schaffner **£12.99**
Long overdue reissue of the authoritative and detailed account of one of the most important and popular bands in rock history. From the psychedelic explorations of the Syd Barrett-era to '70s superstardom with 'Dark Side of The Moon', and on to triumph of 'The Wall', before internecine strife tore the group apart. Schaffner's definitive history also covers the improbable return of Pink Floyd without Roger Waters and the hugely successful 'Momentary Lapse Of Reason' album and tour.

The Dark Reign of Gothic Rock: In The Reptile House with The Sisters Of Mercy, Bauhaus and The Cure
by Dave Thompson **£12.99**
From Joy Division to Nine Inch Nails and from Siouxsie and the Banshees to Marilyn Manson, gothic rock has endured as the cult of choice for the disaffected and the alienated. The author traces the rise of '80s and '90s goth from influences such as Hammer House of Horror movies and schlock novels, through post-punk into the full blown drama of Bauhaus, The Cure and the Sisters of Mercy axis.

Marillion: Separated Out
by Jon Collins **£14.99**
From the chart hit days of Fish and 'Kayleigh' to the Steve Hogarth incarnation, Marillion have continued to make groundbreaking rock music. Collins tells the full story, drawing on interviews with band members, associates, and the experiences of some of the band's most dedicated fans.

Psychedelic Furs: Beautiful Chaos
by Dave Thompson **£12.99**
Psychedelic Furs were the ultimate post-punk band - combining the chaos and vocal rasp of the Sex Pistols with a Bowie-esque glamour. The Furs hit the big time when John Hughes wrote a movie based on their early single 'Pretty In Pink'. Poised to join U2 and Simple Minds in the premier league they withdrew behind their shades, remaining a cult act, but one with a hugely devoted following.

Bob Dylan: Like The Night (Revisited)
by C.P. Lee **£9.99**
Fully revised and updated B-format edition of the hugely acclaimed document of Dylan's pivotal 1966 show at the Manchester Free Trade Hall where fans called him Judas for turning his back on folk music in favour of rock 'n' roll.

The Nice: Hang On To A Dream
by Martyn Hanson **£12.99**
The Nice were Keith Emerson's band prior to superstardom with Emerson, Lake & Palmer. Formed as a backing band for soul singer P.P. Arnold, The Nice went on to lay the foundations for what would become progressive rock. Their debut LP mixed rock with jazz and classical music, but it was their hard rock reinvention of Leonard Bernstein's 'America' that took them into the US and UK charts, and influenced their biggest fan Jimi Hendrix to reinterpret 'The Star Spangled Banner'.

Marc Bolan and T Rex: A Chronology
by Cliff McLenahan **£13.99**
Bolan was the ultimate glam-rock icon; beautiful, elfin, outrageously dressed and capable of hammering out impossibly catchy teen rock hits such as 'Telegram Sam' and 'Get It On'. With their pounding guitars and three chord anthems, T Rex paved the way for hard rock and punk rock.

Back To The Beach: A Brian Wilson and The Beach Boys Reader
Edited by Kingsley Abbott **£12.99**
Revised and expanded edition of the Beach Boys compendium Mojo magazine deemed an 'essential purchase'. This collection includes all of the best articles, interviews and reviews from the Beach Boys' four decades of music, including definitive pieces by Timothy White, Nick Kent and David Leaf. New material reflects on the tragic death of Carl Wilson and documents the rejuvenated Brian's return to the boards.
"Rivetting!" **** Q
"An essential purchase." Mojo

Harmony In My Head: The Original Buzzcock Steve Diggle's Rock 'n' Roll Odyssey
by Steve Diggle and Terry Rawlings £12.99
First-hand account of the punk wars from guitarist and one half of the songwriting duo that gave the world three chord punk-pop classics like 'Ever Fallen In Love' and 'Promises'. Diggle dishes the dirt on punk contemporaries like The Sex Pistols, The Clash and The Jam, as well as sharing poignant memories of his friendship with Kurt Cobain, on whose last ever tour, The Buzzcocks were support act.

Serge Gainsbourg: A Fistful Of Gitanes
by Sylvie Simmons £9.99
Rock press legend Simmons' hugely acclaimed biography of the French genius.
"I would recommend 'A Fistful Of Gitanes' [as summer reading] which is a highly entertaining biography of the French singer-songwriter and all-round scallywag." JG Ballard
"A wonderful introduction to one of the most overlooked songwriters of the 20th century." The Times (No.3, Top Music Books of 2001)
"The most intriguing music-biz biography of the year." The Independent
"Wonderful. Serge would have been so happy." Jane Birkin

Blues: The British Connection
by Bob Brunning £12.99
Former Fleetwood Mac member Bob Brunning's classic account of the impact of Blues in Britain, from its beginnings as the underground music of '50s teenagers like Mick Jagger, Keith Richards and Eric Clapton, to the explosion in the '60s, right through to the vibrant scene of the present day.
"An invaluable reference book and an engaging personal memoir." Charles Shaar Murray

On The Road With Bob Dylan
by Larry Sloman £12.99
In 1975, as Bob Dylan emerged from 8 years of seclusion, he dreamed of putting together a travelling music show that would trek across the country like a psychedelic carnival. The dream became a reality, and 'On The Road With Bob Dylan' is the ultimate behind-the-scenes look at what happened. When Dylan and the Rolling Thunder Revue took to the streets of America, Larry 'Ratso' Sloman was with them every step of the way.
"The War and Peace of Rock 'n' Roll." Bob Dylan

CURRENTLY AVAILABLE FROM HELTER SKELTER...

Gram Parsons: God's Own Singer
by Jason Walker £12.99
Brand new biography of the man who pushed The Byrds into country-rock territory on Sweethearts Of The Rodeo, and quit to form the Flying Burrito Brothers. Gram lived hard, drank hard, took every drug going and somehow invented country rock, paving the way for Crosby, Stills & Nash, The Eagles and Neil Young. Parsons' second solo LP, Grievous Angel, is a haunting masterpiece of country soul. By the time it was released, he had been dead for 4 months. He was 26 years old.
"Walker has done an admirable job in taking us as close to the heart and soul of Gram Parsons as any author could." **** Uncut, Book Of The Month

Ashley Hutchings: The Guvnor and The Rise of Folk Rock - Fairport Convention, Steeleye Span and The Albion Band
by Geoff Wall and Brian Hinton £14.99
As founder of Fairport Convention and Steeleye Span, Ashley Hutchings is the pivotal figure in the history of folk rock. This book draws on hundreds of hours of interviews with Hutchings and other folk-rock artists and paints a vivid picture of the scene that also produced Sandy Denny, Richard Thompson, Nick Drake, John Martyn and Al Stewart.

Al Stewart: True Life Adventures of A Folk Troubadour
by Neville Judd £25.00
Authorised biography of the Scottish folk hero behind US Top Ten hit 'Year of The Cat'. This is a vivid insider's account of the pivotal '60s London coffee house scene that kickstarted the careers of a host of folkies including Paul Simon - with whom Al shared a flat in 1965 - as well as the wry memoir of a '60s folk star's tribulations as he becomes a chart-topping star in the US in the '70s. Highly limited hardcover edition!

Rainbow Rising: The Story of Ritchie Blackmore's Rainbow
by Roy Davies £14.99
Blackmore led rock behemoths Deep Purple to international, multi-platinum, mega-stardom. He quite in '75, to form Rainbow, one of the great live bands, with Ronnie James Dio and enjoyed a string of acclaimed albums and hit singles, including 'All Night Long' and 'Since You Been Gone' before the egos of the key players caused the whole thing to implode. A great rock 'n' roll tale.

ISIS: A Bob Dylan Anthology
Edited by Derek Barker £14.99
Expertly compiled selection of rare articles which trace the evolution of rock's greatest

talent. From Bob's earliest days in New York City to the more recent legs of the Never Ending Tour, and his new highly acclaimed album, Love and Theft, the ISIS archive has exclusive interview material - often rare or previously unpublished - with many of the key players in Dylan's career: his parents, friends, musicians and other collaborators.

The Beach Boys' Pet Sounds: The Greatest Album of The 20th Century
by Kingsley Abbott £11.95
Pet Sounds is the 1966 album that saw The Beach Boys graduate from lightweight pop like 'Surfin' USA et al into a vehicle for the mature compositional genius of Brian Wilson. The album was hugely influential, not least on The Beatles. This the full story of the album's background, its composition and recording, its contemporary reception and its enduring legacy.

King Crimson: In The Court of... Crimson
by Sid Smith £14.99
King Crimson's 1969 masterpiece In The Court Of The Crimson King, was a huge U.S. chart hit. The band followed it with 40 further albums of consistently challenging, distinctive and innovative music. Drawing on hours of new interviews, and encouraged by Crimson supremo Robert Fripp, the author traces the band's turbulent history year by year, track by track.

A Journey Through America With The Rolling Stones
by Robert Greenfield UK Price £9.99
Featuring a new foreword by Ian Rankin, this is the definitive account of their legendary 1972 tour.
"Filled with finely-rendered detail... a fascinating tale of times we shall never see again." Mojo

Razor Edge: Bob Dylan and The Never Ending Tour
by Andrew Muir £12.99
Respected Dylan expert Andrew Muir documents the ups and downs of this unprecedented trek, and finds time to tell the story of his own curious meeting with Dylan.
Muir also tries to get to grips with what exactly it all means - both for Dylan and for the Bobcats: dedicated Dylan followers, like himself, who trade tapes of every show and regularly cross the globe to catch up with the latest leg of The Never Ending Tour.

Calling Out Around The World: A Motown Reader
Edited by Kingsley Abbott £13.99
With a foreword by Martha Reeves, this is a unique collection of articles which tell the story of the rise of a black company in a white industry, and its talented stable of artists, musicians, writers and producers. Included are rare interviews with key figures such as Berry Gordy, Marvin Gaye, Smokey Robinson and Florence Ballard as well as reference sources for collectors and several specially commissioned pieces.

I've Been Everywhere: A Johnny Cash Chronicle
by Peter Lewry £14.99
A complete chronological illustrated diary of Johnny Cash's concerts, TV appearances, record releases, recording sessions and other milestones. From his early days with Sam Phillips in Memphis to international stardom, the wilderness years of the mid-sixties, and on to his legendary prison concerts and his recent creative resurgence with the hugely successful 2000 release, American Recording III: Solitary Man.

Sandy Denny: No More Sad Refrains
by Clinton Heylin £13.99
Paperback edition of the highly acclaimed biography of the greatest female singer-songwriter this country has ever produced.

Emerson Lake & Palmer: The Show That Never Ends
by George Forrester, Martin Hanson and Frank Askew £14.00
Drawing on years of research, the authors have produced a gripping and fascinating document of the prog-rock supergroup who remain one of the great rock bands of the seventies.

Animal Tracks: The Story of The Animals
by Sean Egan £12.99
Sean Egan has enjoyed full access to surviving Animals and associates and has produced a compelling portrait of a truly distinctive band of survivors.

Like A Bullet of Light: The Films of Bob Dylan
by C.P. Lee £12.99
In studying in-depth an often overlooked part of Dylan's *oeuvre*.

Rock's Wild Things: The Troggs Files
by Alan Clayson and Jacqueline Ryan £12.99
Respected rock writer Alan Clayson has had full access to the band and traces their history from '60s Andover rock roots to '90s covers, collaborations and corn circles. Also features the full transcript of the legendary 'Troggs Tapes'.

Waiting for the Man: The Story of Drugs and Popular Music
by Harry Shapiro UK Price £12.99
Fully revised edition of the classic story of two intertwining billion dollar industries.
'Wise and witty.' The Guardian

Dylan's Daemon Lover: The Tangled Tale of a 450-Year Old Pop Ballad by Clinton Heylin UK price £12.00
Written as a detective story, Heylin unearths the mystery of why Dylan knew enough to return 'The House Carpenter' to its 16th century source.

Get Back: The Beatles' Let It Be Disaster by Doug Sulpy & Ray Schweighardt UK price £12.99
No-holds barred account of the power struggles, the bickering, and the bitterness that led to the break-up of the greatest band in the history of rock 'n' roll.
"One of the most poignant Beatles books ever." Mojo

XTC: Song Stories - The Exclusive & Authorised Story by XTC and Neville Farmer £12.99
"A cheerful celebration of the minutiae surrounding XTC's music with the band's musical passion intact... high in setting the record straight anecdotes. Super bright, funny and commanding." Mojo

Born In The USA: Bruce Springsteen and The American Tradition by Jim Cullen £9.99
"Cullen has written an excellent treatise expressing exactly how and why Springsteen translated his uneducated hicktown American-ness into music and stories that touched hearts and souls around the world." Q****

Bob Dylan by Anthony Scaduto £10.99
The first and best biography of Dylan. "The best book ever written on Dylan" Record Collector
"Now in a welcome reprint it's a real treat to read the still-classic Bobography." Q*****

COMING SOON FROM FIREFLY PUBLISHING...
(AN ASSOCIATION OF HELTER SKELTER AND SAF)

The Nirvana Recording Sessions by Rob Jovanovic £14.99
Drawing on years of research and interviews with many who worked with the band, the author has documented details of every Nirvana recording, from early rehearsals to 'In Utero'. A fascinating account of the creative process of one of the great bands.

Marty Balin: Full Flight - A Tale of Airplanes and Starships by Marty Balin & Bob Yehling £20.00
Marty Balin founded Jefferson Airplane - which he fronted as the male half of American rock's greatest vocalist duo - Marty Balin & Grace Slick. A key figure at Woodstock, Monterey and famously beaten up onstage by Hell's Angels at Altamont, Balin wrote many of the band's key songs. He also took Airplane's successor, Jefferson Starship, to the top of the '70s singles and albums charts with self-penned hits like 'Miracles'. Balin left Airplane with 17 scrapbooks containing memorabilia and photos of the band's history, which form the basis for this heavily illustrated book.

The Music of George Harrison: While My Guitar Gently Weeps by Simon Leng £18.99
Often in Lennon and McCartney's shadow, Harrison's music can stand on its own merits. Santana biographer Leng takes a studied, track by track look at both Harrison's contribution to The Beatles and the solo work that started with the release in 1970 of his epic masterpiece 'All Things Must Pass'. 'Here Comes The Sun', 'Something' (covered by Sinatra who considered it the perfect love song) and 'While My Guitar Gently Weeps' are just a few of Harrison's classic songs. Originally planned as a celebration of Harrison's music, this is now sadly a commemoration.

CURRENTLY AVAILABLE FROM FIREFLY...

The Pretty Things: Growing Old Disgracefully by Alan Lakey £20
First biography of one of rock's most influential and enduring combos. Trashed hotel rooms, infighting, rip-offs, sex, drugs and some of the most remarkable rock 'n' roll, including land mark albums like the first rock opera, SF Sorrow, and Rolling Stone's album of the year, 1970's 'Parachute'.
"They invented everything, and were credited with nothing." Arthur Brown, 'God of Hellfire'

The Sensational Alex Harvey by John Neil Murno £20
Part rock band, part vaudeville, 100% commitment, the SAHB were one of the greatest live bands of the era. But behind his showman exterior, Harvey was increasingly beset by alcoholism and tragedy. He succumbed to a heart attack on the way home from a gig in 1982, but he is fondly remembered as a unique entertainer by friends, musicians and legions of fans.

U2: The Complete Encyclopedia by Mark Chatterton £14.99

Poison Heart: Surviving The Ramones by Dee Dee Ramone and Veronica Kofman £9.99

Minstrels In The Gallery: A History of Jethro Tull
by David Rees £12.99

DANCEMUSICSEXROMANCE: Prince - The First Decade
by Per Nilsen £12.99

To Hell And Back with Catatonia
by Brian Wright £12.99

Soul Sacrifice: The Santana Story
by Simon Leng UK Price £12.99

Opening The Musical Box: A Genesis Chronicle
by Alan Hewitt UK Price £12.99

Blowin' Free: 30 Years of Wishbone Ash
by Gary Carter and Mark Chatterton
UK Price £12.99

CURRENTLY AVAILABLE FROM
SAF PUBLISHING...

The Zombies: Hung Up On A Dream
by Claes Johansen (limited edition hardback) £16.99

Gentle Giant - Acquiring The Taste
by Paul Stump (limited edition hardback) £16.99

Free At Last: The Story of Free and Bad Company
by Steven Rosen £14.99

Necessity Is... The Early Years of Frank Zappa and The Mothers Of Invention
by Billy James £12.95

Procol Harum: Beyond The Pale
by Claes Johansen £12.99

No More Mr Nice Guy: The Inside Story of The Alice Cooper Group
by Michael Bruce and Billy James £11.99

An American Band: The Story of Grand Funk Railroad
by Billy James £12.99

Wish The World Away: Mark Eitzel and American Music Club
by Sean Body £12.99

Go Ahead John! The Music of John McLaughlin
by Paul Stump £12.99

Lunar Notes: Zoot Horn Rollo's Captain Beefheart Experience
by Bill Harkleroad and Billy James £11.95

Meet The Residents: America's Most Eccentric Band
by Ian Shirley £11.95

Digital Gothic: A Critical Discography of Tangerine Dream
by Paul Stump £9.95

The One and Only - Homme Fatale: Peter Perrett & The Only Ones
by Nina Antonia £11.95

Plunderphonics, Pataphysics and Pop Mechanics: The Leading Exponents of Musique Actuelle
by Andrew Jones £12.95

Kraftwerk: Man, Machine and Music
by Pascal Bussy £12.95

Wire: Everybody Loves A History
by Kevin Eden £9.95

Dark Entries: Bauhaus and Beyond
by Ian Shirley £11.95

HELTER SKELTER MUSIC BOOK MAIL ORDER

All Helter Skelter, Firefly and SAF titles are available by
mail order from the world famous **Helter Skelter Bookshop**.

You can either phone or fax your order to Helter Skelter
on the following numbers:

Telephone: +44 (0)20 7836 1151
Fax: +44 (0)20 7240 9880

Email: helter@skelter.demon.co.uk
Website: http://www.skelter.demon.co.uk

Office hours: Monday-Friday 10.00am - 7.00pm,
Saturday: 10.00am - 6.00pm, Sunday: Closed.

Postage prices per book worldwide are as follows:
UK & Channel Islands £1.50,
Europe & Eire (Air Mail) £2.95, USA, Canada (Air Mail) £7.50,
Australasia, Far East (Air Mail) £9.00,
Overseas (Surface Mail) £2.50

You can also write enclosing a cheque, International Money Order
or cash by Registered Post. Please include postage.
Please DO NOT send cash. Please DO NOT send foreign currency
or cheques drawn on an overseas bank.
Send to: Helter Skelter Bookshop, 4 Denmark Street, London,
WC2H 8LL, United Kingdom.

If you are in London, why not come and visit us and
browse the titles in person!